About the author

David Roberts is a lecturer in the School of History and International Affairs at the University of Ulster. He has previously published *Power, Elitism and Democracy: Political Transition in Cambodia, 1991–1999* (2000) and over thirty articles on human security, state building, democratisation and Cambodia.

David Roberts

Human insecurity: global
structures of violence

Zed Books
LONDON | NEW YORK

Human insecurity: global structures of violence was first published in 2008 by Zed Books Ltd, 7 Cynthia Street, London N1 9JF, UK and Room 400, 175 Fifth Avenue, New York, NY 10010, USA

www.zedbooks.co.uk

Cover designed by Andrew Corbett
Set in OurType Arnhem and Futura Bold by Ewan Smith, London
Index: ed.emery@thefreeuniversity.net
Printed and bound in the EU by Biddles Ltd, King's Lynn
www.biddles.co.uk

Distributed in the USA exclusively by Palgrave Macmillan, a division of St Martin's Press, LLC, 175 Fifth Avenue, New York, NY 10010.

ISBN 978 1 84277 824 1 hb
ISBN 978 1 84277 825 8 pb

Contents

Tables and figures

For my mother, who started it;
for Anne Riley/Lloyd and her family,
who twice saved my life;
and in memory of Sonia Khatun,
whose short life and unnecessary death
foreshadow our possible futures

Acknowledgements

I am indebted to Lisa Brown, Ellie Ffeiffer and Hanna Nilsson Sahlin, three of my then-undergraduate students, who willingly contributed to the collation of statistics used in this work. When the going got too tough, Chris Gilligan's thoughtful and patient moderation of the extremes of my thinking kept my focus clear.

I would also like to thank the two reviewers for their thoughtful, constructive and positive comments. My editor, Ellen McKinlay, patiently persisted with advice that made this book so much better. Their contributions were invaluable, and this work is all the better for their support and their encouragement. Finally, and in the first instance also, it was David Munro who urged a group of my undergraduates that the most dangerous word in the English language is 'why'. Asking this of Sonia Khatun's death set this work in motion.

Abbreviations

DCR	direct control violence
FGM	female genital mutilation
G8	group of 8 leading industrialized nations
GATT	General Agreement on Tariffs and Trade
HDR	Human Development Report
HSR	Human Security Report
ICFTU	International Confederation of Free Trade Unions
IFI	international financial institution
IMF	International Monetary Fund
IR	international relations
MTP	Medical Termination of Pregnancy
NGO	non-governmental organization
SAPs	structural adjustment programmes
U5MR	under five infant mortality rate
UN	United Nations
UNDP	United Nations Development Programme
UNFPA	United Nations Fund for Population Activities
UNICEF	United Nations International Children's Fund
UNIFEM	United Nations Development Fund for Women
UNRISD	United Nations Research Institute for Social Development
WB	World Bank
WHO	World Health Organization

ONE | Introduction

Watching the disastrous and unequal impact of the Asian tsunami and Hurricane Katrina brought back to mind the origins of this book. The earliest inspiration had come from the slow-to-dawn but impossible-to-deny realization that people drowning in typhoons on the flood plains of South Asia rarely choose to live in such life-threatening environments if other accessible options are available. It became ever clearer that people who are routinely vulnerable are so because other people with greater power control safer land, and governments and political institutions determine where poor and vulnerable people live by denying access to better land through a range of means and justifications. Caroline Thomas suggested that such vulnerability and insecurity result 'directly from existing power structures that determine who enjoys the entitlement to security and who does not' (2000: 4). In other words, it became harder and harder to understand why such views as Thomas's and my own were not more commonplace. Thereafter, specific incidents served to move my intellect and heart, and reinforced my desire to understand why such social travesties remained so far off the political agenda when notions of power so clearly defined their cause.

One such travesty moved me particularly, in part because of the very human, very personal and very sad dimension; but also because of the enormous range of causative factors that it shared with so many other situations of human insecurity *that could be changed*. The *Observer* reported on 25 September 2005 that a twelve-year-old Indian girl killed herself because she could not face the 'shame' of not being able to afford the one-penny cost of her school lunch (see also Reuters India, 25 September 2005; *Mazzadri*, 2 May 2007). She lived with her mother 'under a tarpaulin' in West Bengal. Her name was Sonia Khatun. She lost the will to live as a consequence of structural forces ranged against her existence which were responsible for her precarious living conditions in the first instance, and which simultaneously maintained her violent oppression and led to her fatal and final despair.

Sonia Khatun died for many reasons; her passing is instructive because it demonstrates how the crushing deprivation faced by her and her mother is human made. Nearly two years later, in a decade of globalization and prosperity for many, including in India, human-made conditions led to the suicides of 25,000 Indian farmers, 'trapped by debt and falling prices ... since 1997' (Mishra 2006). Again, their avoidable deaths demonstrate the human components of the political and economic contradictions that force ever increasing exports, which increase competition and consequently lower income, in order to service misdirected external debts. Global society is human engineered and human directed. Its component parts and their precise roles are not invisible, if we care to look closely.

A year into my research, I was again reminded of the brutality of another of our self-made human structures in another small and barely reported death, equally sad, but also equally preventable in the future. Navjeet Sidhu threw herself and her two children under an express train near London as a result of a terrible depression (*The Times*, 27 September 2006). The depression was brought on because her first baby was a girl, and her Sikh husband left her because he and his society demanded a boy child. Navjeet Sidhu felt she had failed her family, herself and the wider expectations of a brutally patriarchal order. She died because of value systems that have been learned and which find ultimate expression in the concept of female infanticide. Six months later, her mother returned to the site at which her daughter died and killed herself. Everyone lost, from the children whose lives were wrenched from them, through Mrs Sidhu and the Sikh family she was part of, through the grieving grandmother, to the male-dominated capitalist economy that loses a worker. None of this violence needs to be sustained.

Thousands of miles away, another South Asian woman died but in quite different circumstances. A female Pakistani minister, Zilla Huma Usman, was murdered by a male stranger because she refused to wear a full veil (*The Times*, 21 February 2007: 7). There are many Pakistani women who do not wear the veil; the killer could have attacked elsewhere. What brought about the rage of the murderer, a Mr Sarwar, was that his victim was a politician and that she promoted women's rights in a society known for its alienation and deeply repressive treatment of women. Mr Sarwar was threatened, as many men feel they are, by female emancipation. 'I have no regrets,' he told the press. 'I will kill all those women who do not follow the right path.' 'His' path was laid down by social rulings that differentiate men from women on the grounds of sex, and which are in turn determined by global ideational structures. What they have in common is that they are constructed actions and consequences and thus malleable and subject to transformation. That these women need not have died is obvious; but perhaps less apparently, their lives and deaths offer an opportunity, if we have the courage and wit to confront the complexities of their man-made causes.

This skewed distribution of power and resources pervades the global system. In 2006 a 'tycoon' spent £85,000 ($170,000) on a truffle at an auction in Italy (*Guardian*, 15 November 2006). Just after Christmas that year, it was reported that a US chairman had been awarded £108 million ($210 million) 'on exit' from his employer (*Washington Post*, 16 January 2007: D02). A Long Island businessman 'spent $10 million on his 13-year-old daughter's [birthday] party, which included performances by the rock group Aerosmith and the rapper 50 Cent together with $10,000 party bags for the teenage guests' (*Forbes*, 31 January 2007). In India, the wedding of two film stars, Miss Aishwarya Rai and Mr Abhishek Bachchan, was projected as likely to cost more than £30 million ($60 million) in *The Times* (18 March 2007).

Nor is it solely private individuals who expose the inequity of the market. Public politicians like the North Korean dictator Kim Jong Il exemplify the disparity between exorbitantly rich and crushingly poor: he was reported as spending £350,000 ($700,000) on Hennessey cognac while millions of his country folk starved in famines (*Guardian*, 30 November 2006: 16). During the cold war, such excesses in 'Third World dictator chic' were routine and justified by their support for capitalist states against the Soviet Union (Hancock 1989; Blum 1998). Such excesses are no less evident in the 'New World Order'. In 2006, it was noted that 'Europeans spend more on perfume each year than the £7 billion needed to provide 2.6 billion people with access to clean water' (Massey 2006: 65).

The skewed distribution of resources and the systems that underpin it kill millions of humans per year, in both the developed and developing worlds. The wealth gap between people in these two worlds has widened continuously (Greig et al. 2007). Rapley writes that 'although absolute prosperity [has risen], relative prosperity [has] declined for a growing part of the world's population ... Immiseration has declined, but marginalization has increased' (2004: 7). Galeano filtered through a maze of statistics and recorded the following consequences of distribution and access issues: 'ten people, the ten richest men on the planet, own wealth equivalent to the value of the total production of fifty countries, and 447 multimillionaires own a greater fortune than the annual income of half of humanity' (2005: 391). This situation, he continues, 'shows no sign of becoming any less ugly' (ibid.: 88–9) For Greig et al., the 'gap between "unprecedented opulence" and "remarkable deprivation"' confirms a 'sharpening of inequality' which 'represents one of the distinguishing features of contemporary life' (2007: 5). In French, this process is known as '*capitalisme sauvage*'.

While we are all aware of such ranges of reward and deprivation, we are also aware that such extremes have long been a part of the experience of humans throughout history; the argument has been that they are as rare as they are disparate. But such distortions are no longer rare. They have become commonplace, raising profound questions regarding the efficacy of neoliberalism as an 'efficient' distributor of scarce goods, and concerning the reasons why it remains so effectively entrenched in the face of such incontrovertible opprobrium. These enormous ranges of wealth distribution and the inequalities that lead to millions of deaths when there are more than enough essential resources to go round is more than a simple, scientific question of economics. It involves asymmetries of power that are routinely fixed against weaker groupings by powerful states that prioritize electoral self-preservation and inefficient and often corrupt arms industries. It involves fundamental questions of humanism and enforced ignorance through selective education. But it is not immutable.

As I watched with increasing concern reports of the millions dying because of human decision-making, so my intellectual inquiry expanded too. It became clear that most security studies were at once preoccupied with 'global terrorism' and nuclear proliferation and simultaneously blind to or uncaring of a global catastrophe of human suffering that, most felt, had no context for 'security'. Their research and policy agendas largely missed the scale of avoidable human misery and avoidable death; what Thomas (2000: 4) referred to as 'the ancient and enduring concerns of humanity'. I became increasingly perplexed by the absence of serious mainstream debate on the part of research bodies and government representatives about this clearly avoidable suffering with its roots in human choice and actions, or human agency. This prompted me to critically examine the 'alternative' security literature, and the result, this book, is a contribution born from intellectual inquiry but originating from private concern.

Belatedly reading the work of scholar Johan Galtung also expanded my intellectual inquiry. It became clear that realism, the field of studies concerned mainly with the state, weapons and a largely unchangeable international system, and related liberal schools of thought persistently missed a key area that had already been enunciated by the UNDP and by a range of independent researchers, scholars and activists who were concerned by the same phenomena I had observed myself. As realism underwent a series of attacks from the Critical Security Studies approach, so too emerged from the literature a growing consensus relating to a relationship between development and security, especially when security was defined in terms of the environment, natural resources and poverty. Few connections were made initially between human agency and human security outcomes, but an alternative field began to develop and refined an approach that became known as human security studies. The central difference that crystallized from this school, if it should be so called, is a conceptual one. It urges focus not on the conventional icons of security, such as the state, the economy and armaments, but on human beings who are not engaged in conventional security issues, but whose deaths far exceed anything experienced and recorded in the more traditional approaches. Thus, the new research 'referent', or 'object', was to be the human being itself, and how to render that vulnerable object less exposed to conditions that threatened its security.

The problem had become how to define human security, a challenge discussed in greater detail in Chapter 2 of this work. The debate had become stalled between a very wide-ranging and indefinable conceptualization, at one end, and one that failed to capture the gravity of the human condition at the other. One of the key contributions I hope this book makes is to direct the debate by differentiating between what constitutes human security (which no one could agree on), on the one hand, and what might comprise human *insecurity*, on the other. Refocusing the debate allowed me to respond to one of realism's most touted complaints about the human security school. What vexed both realists and human security proponents was that if 'human security' as a concept couldn't be defined, then it couldn't be identified and it couldn't be counted or analysed. There was no case to answer. Defining the concept in terms of human insecurity allowed me to propose that there were conditions of insecurity that allowed conventional methodologies to be applied that might satisfy, or at least arouse the curiosity of, some realists who might be convinced that it should be taken more seriously and debated in a wider and more influential literature.

Defining human insecurity in terms of avoidable civilian deaths enables a quantitative assessment of the extent of the issue, but it would be meaningless if the deaths were naturally occurring, or if they were already the subject matter of security research. For this reason, I chose to focus on deaths that could have been avoided and which were not caused by guns, bombs or machetes. Such deaths are both unintentional and intentional and, crucially, avoidable for the most part. By the former, I refer to the problem of good intentions having lethal unintended consequences which are then ignored or denied. It is not the same as omission of action; it is recognizing ignorance and denial in the causative chain connecting a perceived good intention to a destructive outcome that is not reversed or halted. What remained then was to identify the extent and scale of these deaths in order that they might be compared with deaths from conventional causes already identified and addressed by the 'regular' security research agendas and bodies. If, as I suspected, human insecurity as I had defined it exceeded by a significant order of magnitude the mortality caused as a result of the security phenomena addressed by the majority of security schools, then there was a case to answer. The figures suggest there is a strong case indeed.

These statistics, gathered from sources like the World Health Organization (WHO) and various agencies of the United Nations (UN), are mostly not new. They are compiled in order to demonstrate the enormous discrepancy in human mortality in what is studied and supported with millions of dollars of research grants in well-funded international institutions and disseminated through literally thousands of journals and books (conventional security studies), on the one hand; and that which is the subject matter of the human security debate, still struggling with its own language, concepts and methodologies. Demonstrating this discrepancy is the first element of this work's approach to human insecurity. It is the evidential foundation stone on which the second rationale rests. That second stage is to offer a more sophisticated, meaningful and comprehensive explanation for why this should be the case; why it should persist; and why it doesn't have to.

The arguments that this book presents differ significantly from realist wisdom, which prefers the state and the international state of anarchy as its main subject matter. Rather than considering global human insecurity in terms of states whose behaviour reflects a fixed and disruptive human nature which in turn creates the anarchy of international disorder, severing human acts from consequences, this work is concerned with cause and effect. The second rationale of this work, then, is the identification of mainly benign and ignorant or misunderstood human activities that lead to the human insecurity catastrophe that impacts upon millions of women, children and men unnecessarily and, for the most part, as we shall see, quite avoidably. In other words, it is the contention of this work that the global scale of terminal insecurity is, for the most part, caused by humans, in our many private, institutional and structural guises. It is not necessarily an intentional series of acts for the most part; although it is in some. But, nonetheless, the actions or omissions of responses to lethal outcomes by people in government policy-making, or through greed and corruption, in international financial policy or dogmatic foreign policy, all contribute to human insecurity. Furthermore, international institutions derive from larger global structures of human organization and beliefs that determine the lives and deaths of millions upon millions of people around the world, without a shot being fired or a machete being drawn.

This work has a yet broader purpose. Demonstrating the role of human built and operated global financial institutions and the ideological structures that project and command them speaks to a deeper debate on the wider global system. How much is it fluidly structured and dynamic, rather than randomly fixed in a static conception of irreducible power? Critical feminist theories demonstrate and explain the masculine domination of both the disciplinary field and the policy process world. Social constructivist approaches, in turn, show how these processes of power and domination operate in international relations theory and practice. This body of understanding of the world, or ontology, claims international and national behaviour is not, and cannot be, permanent or fixed because it has been designed and constructed by human beings over lengthy periods of time. It is this, rather than an impersonal, anonymous 'international system', which has led to the evolution of the ideational constructions that define, direct and order the power that shapes a persistently unequal world. Payne suggests that this type of approach and the challenge it represents to established orthodoxies of the realisms in international relations shows that 'people are not just bearers of structures, they create them ... Historical structures mean no more but no less than persistent social practices, made by collective human activity and transformed through collective human activity' (2005: 17). If this can be shown to bear on human insecurity, it has substantial critical ramifications for the broader security and realism debates.

This book then:

- Outlines the evolution of post-realist human security studies.
- Identifies the evolution of the *human* as security referent point as distinct from the state.
- Proposes a new approach to render the concept workable, meaningful and usable.
- Demonstrates the scale and extent to which human insecurity exists, and how in some cases this can lead to direct violence.

- Identifies international institutional determinism in avoidable civilian death.
- Identifies and discusses two socially constructed transglobal structures from which derive the institutions that communicate, through human agency, intentional and unintentional violence to millions of people unnecessarily.
- Draws on critical feminist arguments to assess the notion that the masculine composition and assumptions of international relations blind the discipline to its role in creating and defending violent structures and institutions and priorities which directly and indirectly energize direct and indirect terminal human agency.
- Argues that these structures, institutions and agency are changeable social constructivism, rather than intransigent reflections of fixed values, and comments on the implications of this for the discipline of international relations.

Before we begin, however, I would like to address some concerns that confront such an endeavour. A confrontation with established and dominant belief ordinarily meets resistance because the range of vested interests implicit in such a challenge is great. Like many people, I have long been interested in how ordinary people stand up to the state and its monopoly of 'legitimate' power and the way in which past confrontations have led to the demonization of opposition. This provided an early introduction to language as power. Without realizing why at the time, certain statements and experiences attached themselves to my memory. Above all, I became aware of the impact of labelling, a sensation that crystallized when the writer Rebecca West declared that people called her a feminist 'whenever I express sentiments that differentiate me from a doormat or a prostitute ...' (1913: 18). For this reason, I have tried to neutralize terminology, especially that attached to disciplines. Fierke expressed this concern well when she wrote that 'labels all too often become weapons in disciplinary mud-slinging matches, which can close down discussion and inquiry' (2007: 3). The earliest and, for me, the most powerful example of this came from a postcard sold in a Student Union office. It read: 'when I give food to the poor, they call me a saint. When I ask why the poor have no food, they call me a communist'.

The quote is normally attributed to Dom Helda Camara, a South American Catholic bishop, but could have come from anyone with enough critical consciousness to recognize when incontestable evidence is being denied by elite power interests that manipulate public 'fears'. Dom Helda

Camara's oft-quoted comment is instructive because it reflects how the sustained assault on vulnerable children globally is deprioritized by omission; and it implies how his legitimacy was challenged by the appellation 'communist'. Contemporaneously, and in similar fashion to Dom Helda Camara's experience, aid agencies are lauded when they bring relief to starving infants, but when the nostrums of the global liberal economy are identified as causing in part such hunger, this rarely finds its way into security studies agendas or revised government security policy. Most people know malaria is a killer of children (and older people); most people know there are cheap and easy preventive steps that can be taken to prevent infection. But if government and international institutional inaction is associated with mass avoidable deaths of infants from malnutrition and malaria, critical challenges to their perspectives are likely to be the subject of denial, rebuttal, propaganda or, more normally, all three.

'Securitizing' the millions of children, boys and girls, who die from avoidable illnesses and the millions of female infanticide victims has already invoked the ire and concern of many traditionalists. In such views, this reinterpretation will render the field of security incoherent. Perhaps this is because they themselves are secure from such threats. Asked of a young child in Africa, Latin America or South Asia whether they considered infanticide and starvation as security threats, no doubt the two groups would differ markedly. Furthermore, security is normally easier to understand when there are mechanistic 'vehicles' and agents to observe and count, rather than when our own inaction is associated with the deaths and marginalization of the most vulnerable of our species. The reluctance to consider that vulnerable children are deserving of being 'securitized', and in many cases outright rebuttal, reflects a disinclination to engage with the complex and less obvious explanations for what are clearly social phenomena, and a denial of adult responsibilities for their actions and the consequences of those actions on infants and other vulnerable people. Defending the narrow interpretation of human security is easy and perhaps for some necessary to minimize the impact on their own consciences of ignoring the obvious fact that most of those children do not have to die. Their deaths are not accidents, but are instead end points in a causal chain created by human beings. In a sense, challenging the legitimacy of a wide interpretation of human security facilitates the 'forgetting' of what this book takes as its reference points and referent objects: the most vulnerable people in the world.

In a very real sense, a core aspect of this book is power relationships and the capacity of dominant structures and institutions to ensure aims and outcomes that suit the interests of what Pasha and Murphy call an 'insolent' minority, against the human security of the poorest (2002: 1–2). It is not a coincidence that giant pharmaceutical corporations and other transglobal proprietors of financial power have aims that align with and are often supported by the elites they empower and who empower them. Neither is it a coincidence that they also influence the life destinies of millions of people who too often suffer deadly consequences without reasonable retribution. The tens of thousands of people who continue to suffer in Bhopal, India, from the devastating accident at a Union Carbide plant there in 1984 have not forgotten the origins of their condition, but the US operators, owners and courts have long dismissed claims against them. Likewise, the thousands of Vietnamese people who suffer hideous illnesses from the deadly dioxins dropped on them by the United States government in the 1960s, and whose children are to this day born with terrible physical and mental deformities, have little effective recourse against the perpetrators.

The challenge of mainstreaming human security as a global human concern at least on a par with the more traditional notions of security that preoccupy government thinking is also a power struggle. It is a struggle for critical feminists not to have rigorous scholarship and analysis delegitimized by sexist states, institutions and individuals who consider such insights 'sentimental, feminine, Utopian' (McSweeney 1999: 15). It is a struggle to separate perceptions of human insecurity from assumptions of gender. It is the struggle to render visible rather than denying or forgetting the massive global loss of priceless human lives which violates our humanity and demeans the powerful who, by omission or act, so easily sanction such avoidable mortality. It is a contest of who determines security for whom; elites' perceptions of security are almost always tied to conventional conceptions while those worst affected are almost always marginalized peoples. It is not, however, a new struggle. Milan Kundera wrote that 'the struggle of man against power is the struggle of memory against forgetting' (1996: 4). It is the ceaseless struggle of power and denial that accompanies hierarchies of entrenched privilege. It is these power structures and the manner in which elements of global society mirror that composition which underpin the lethal global structures of violence this book is concerned with.

In 2000, the UN made a profound announcement. It declared that: 'No shift in the way we think can be more critical than this: we must put people at the centre of everything we do. No calling is more noble, and no responsibility greater, than that enabling men women and children ... to make their lives better' (UN 2000: 7). If this is to be achieved, our analysis must be fully conscious of what Eade (1997: 5) referred to as the 'mind-forg'd manacles' that are the human-built structural chokes that prevent those millions of lives from being lived when they could be. This book seeks to demonstrate and explain the global structures and institutions of violence that create and perpetuate this crisis and, in rendering them visible, identify elemental opportunities for transformation.

TWO | Thinking about security and violence

This chapter examines some of the ways in which academic approaches to security and violence have changed since the end of the cold war. It does not claim to be a comprehensive survey of all the literature; but it does attempt to demonstrate shifts in ideas regarding security referents. It also takes account of some of the earlier literature that pointed towards the post-cold-war debate. This is sometimes ignored or forgotten, but it remains important all the same.

The dominant security tradition is that of realism, which for the most part remains focused on the state and various measures of power. These include the economy and military might. Where it has been criticized for systemic weakness, neo-realism has emerged to fill the theoretical vacuum regarding the role of international systems as contributory to security (Clemens 1998: 14). Numerous schools have challenged realism's claim to be the most comprehensive and satisfactory explicator of a violent world order, and new subjects of study have been added to the repertoire of security issues. These include environmental destruction and resource shortages, among many others. Interstate warfare has largely given way to civil war and intercommunal violence; it is these types of insecurity which now draw much realist and neo-realist attention.

More recently, however, a trend has emerged which proposes that rather than the state being the central object of research into global violence, consideration should be focused on the human being. Furthermore, reflecting increasing awareness that the state is no longer necessarily the main inflictor of violence towards the human being, the causes of human security problems have also come to be addressed anew. Mass human vulnerability to non-state forces globally has pushed the security debate outside its traditional ambit and into the global problem of non-military violence against civilians. Where once violence was crudely defined to encompass primarily armed attack by states, it now incorporates many other forms of assault on many other subjects and objects. This gradual evolution of thinking has resulted in the conceptualization of the human as security referent and the parallel fomentation of the field of human security studies. How we got to this point has been fairly arduous.

The beginning of the academic debate in the West

The discipline of international relations (IR), established in the liberal tradition of idealism in 1919 as a response to the industrial destruction of the First World War, has since been dominated by the school of realism. This was in large part a response to the crushing of the idealist paradigm, which followed the creation of the League of Nations to prevent the 'scourge of war', by the outbreak of the Second World War. Realism and its sub-fields have been mainly concerned with the state and its external relations with other states (Pettman 1996: 87). Throughout the cold war, thinking on the state of nature remained Hobbesian; weapons of mass destruction (WMD) set the agenda for security studies and brutal, kleptocratic and murderous Third World dictators were cynically manipulated by the Permanent Five members of the United Nations to maintain balance or perpetuate imbalances between the superpower rivals of the cold war. This period was largely dominated by the search for a means to manage or end armed confrontation with nuclear missiles and large land-based military scenarios (Smith 2000). Rightly so, perhaps, the cold war threat was treated as the most serious to humankind, requiring, in the minds of realists and others, that security analysis be directed towards a misperceived impending nuclear disaster. It is sometimes not hard to understand why Grant and Newland characterize both realism and statecraft as 'excessively focussed on competition and fear' (1991: 5).

Early alternative thinking

From within realist security studies, however, two scholars gained early prominence in reconstituting the security debate. In 1983, Richard Ullman published, in the journal *International Security*, an article entitled 'Redefining Security'. In the same year, Barry Buzan published his seminal work on *People, States and Fear* in which he concludes that: 'Narrow views of national security ... are increasingly inappropriate and counterproductive ... The first reason for adopting a broad conception of security is ... simply that the realities of the policy environment call for it' (Buzan 1991: 368–9).

Both authors marked a departure from realist argument, but along with the state retaining its centrality to study, neither stands alone as an entirely independent breakthrough. Alternative thinking on security was in fact already being conducted in the field of development studies as far back as the early 1970s, as scholars in the discipline observed first hand in the field the implications of human insecurity from environmental degradation, civil wars and impoverishment (Feit 1973; Walton and Seddon 1994; George 1976).

Buzan and Ullman, however, did make an incision into the dominant literature on security. Sheehan was later to remark that

> [T]he contributions of Buzan and Ullman, and those that followed, would suggest that the concept of security needed to be opened in two directions. First, the notion of security should no longer be limited to the military domain. Rather, it should have a more general meaning that could be applied not just to the military realm, but also to the economic, the societal, the environmental, and the political fields. Second, the referent object of 'security', the thing that needed to be secured, should not be conceptualised solely in terms of the state, but should embrace the individual below the state, and the international system above it. (2005: 45)

Sheehan continued that their contribution was to 'break the intellectual stranglehold of the "national security" concept' (ibid.: 48). This is perhaps to heap too much praise on Ullman and Buzan's work. Little changed in the mainstream literature, and the state and national security remained the main objects of focus in the security debate, with alternatives overshadowed by the continuing hostilities and instability of the second cold war. Indeed, Buzan reminds us that as late as 1988 arguments were still being made to identify security as 'anything that concerns the prevention of superpower nuclear war' (Buzan et al. 1998: 2).

Human security

The end of the cold war left the door open for a new security agenda. While traditional schools remained concerned with states and weapons, and while variations on these schools addressed ecological, environment and economic security matters as discrete issues, another movement emerged that marks an important departure from traditional foci. Human security studies define the human being as the new security referent. For example, Thomas asserts that 'people, rather than states, are the subject of evidence-based analysis' (2004: 353). This is significant because it refocuses the concept of security to concern people's everyday existences and, while this may be of less import for those in the developed world (the Minority World), for the billions who live in far less luxury and with far greater insecurity, its implications may be profound. Attention is turned by the human security debate away from a smaller population and high-technology issues to the most vulnerable people whose lives can be radically improved with low-technology interventions determined by political will.

Sheehan sees government and the state as key influences in the human security process. He posits that 'if government is a means to ... protection and improvement of the well-being of its citizens – then the central issue concerns how this should be done, how people can be made secure' (2005: 57). In this view, the solution lies in the state. For others, however, the state is part of the problem, as much as it may be part of the solution. The state may be domestically oppressive by marginalizing minorities or by being gender blind or exclusive (Tickner 1992). It may also be internationally destructive through participation in international institutions believed by some to be harmful to human security, such as the World Bank (Buzan 1991: 44–5). To some extent, then, the state can be the actor in the wider international system that perpetuates processes of unintentional or deliberate violence.

Where the human security proposition has met its greatest problem, however, is in defining its remit. In short, two schools have emerged. Those closest to realist conventions have tended to favour a minimalist conceptualization, characterized by narrow definitions and associated ambits and agendas. This would permit more pragmatic and 'realistic' policy formulation. Others, however, favour a broader, more imaginative and maximalist approach (Booth 2005). This latter approach inspires great comment but has been much harder to pin down in definitional terms. Minimalists have identified methodological impossibility and an inability to produce effective and reliable policy responses, in contrast to the maximalist definitions. Buzan et al., surveying hostility towards the maximalist perspective, noted that 'progressive widening endangered the intellectual coherence of security, putting so much into it that its essential meaning became void' (1998: 2). That is, if too many issues were 'securitized', then solutions would be impossible. Commenting similarly, Sheehan expressed concern that 'if expanded too far, the concept would cease to have any clear meaning at all' (2005: 58). In short, it appeared that 'although a case could be made for including such things as pollution, disease and economic failure as security threats, this would represent an excessive expansion of the definition' (ibid.: 58).

Thus, 'defining the field [too broadly] would destroy its intellectual coherence and make it more difficult to devise solutions to any of these important problems' (Buzan et al. 1998: 3–4). Stoett also expressed concern regarding an excessive reconfiguration of the concept, and urged 'more specificity, lest potentially progressive terms such as human security end up suffering from the affliction of conceptual promiscuity and thereby become devalued' (1999: xii). Or, in Freedman's words, 'once anything that generates anxiety or threatens the quality of life in some respect becomes labelled a "security problem" the field risks losing all focus' (1998: 53). This suggests an experiential dimension to interpreting the problem; a broad conceptualization of human security is more easily understood by those directly affected by broad-spectrum human insecurity. None of the scholars cited here defending narrow human security is routinely close to the human security extremes that many millions of people in the Majority World experience. In this sense, it may be a 'standpoint' issue, in the sense that only those experiencing such conditions will be able to see or fully comprehend them.

The problem of human security, if we consider all the millions that face gross insecurities of food or water deprivation, malaria and TB in their infants and the murder of newborn babies for economic reasons, cannot by its very constitution be approached in a narrow manner. Human security is vastly complex, multifaceted and heavily nuanced with global interconnectivities and global structures connected through institutional causality. Reflecting this concern and intellectual distinction, Booth discusses the dangers of the traditional orthodoxy in terms of what security means. He fears 'the consequences of perpetuating old orthodoxies in a fast-moving political landscape'. For Booth, 'the price for old thinking about world security is paid, daily, in the death, disease, poverty and oppression of millions' (2005: 260). He argues that security is derived: 'from ways in which different political theories conceive the structures and processes of human society, the entities that make up social and political realities, the major threats to privileged values and groups, the agents who can change things, and so on' (ibid.: 13). In other words, our view of the world, be it 'realist' or 'social constructivist', will determine what we view as being 'secure' or 'insecure'. Thakur enunciated this well when he made the point that 'security is an essentially contested concept because it is an intellectual and cognitive construct, not an objective fact' (2005: 8). From this perspective, it is a changing and necessarily subjective concept that involves many realities depending on one's ontology and, of course, one's power in the world.

The methodological stumbling blocks in the broad-spectrum, maximalist model of human security shifted significantly when Booth and a number of others attached causation to the definition. When explanatory notions were connected to wider human insecurity concerns, the concept firmed up further. Developing the notion of *structures* as influencing human security, in much the same way that guns and missiles influence traditional security concerns, rendered visible connections that had been much less apparent for many of those studying security in the 1990s and after. Booth elaborates:

> Human society in global perspective is shaped by ideas that are dangerous to its collective health ... It is revealed in the extent of structural oppression ... it is apparent in the threats to the very environment that sustains all life; it is seen in the risks arising out of unintended consequences from developments in technology; and, as ever, it is experienced in the regular recourse to violence to settle political differences. (2005: 263)

This implies notions of human-built structures with a capacity for undermining human security. It seems that, while not obviously or immediately visible in much of the literature, Galtung's notions of human-built structures that cause violence unintentionally (as well as intentionally) persist in the development of the concept of human security. It is interesting to note that those who take the view that security needs both broadening and deepening (in line with Galtung's concept) are also subject to the same criticisms of it, while their critics neither recognize nor take seriously the extensive role of human agency in creating and perpetuating global structures of violence. For example, when urging a 'broad research programme' on human security, Bajpai suggests that we 'focus on threats that can be traced back to identifiable human agents ... not to structural ... causes' (2004: 360). The argument seems to deny the role of human agency and activity in both *creating* structures and institutions and in *populating* them with action and beliefs. We shall come to this later.

What is violence?

As has been noted above, what constitutes security has been affected by what defines violence. Violence takes many forms and its definitions range in breadth. At one end of the spectrum, it may be the consequences of the action or actions of an actor; at the other, it may be the result of the activities of an institution or a structure, either of which might be construed as a perpetrator. *Direct* violence normally results in visible victims and survivors. But there is also a debate regarding whether recipients of violence are able to perceive what is happening to them as 'violent', or whether violence can occur to recipients without it being perceived as such. For some, it is this perception and interpretation which link indirect violence to structures.

Most traditional definitions of violence are not particularly helpful because they limit themselves to rather narrow considerations of direct, physical force, in the same way that narrow definitions of security have been accused of being constricted and one-dimensional (Roberts 2005, 2006). We often tend to understand violence as a premeditated act by an individual against perhaps another individual, in a physical 'fist-fight', or as gangsters using guns in turf wars, or as large-scale terrorism. Or we might think in terms of violence as directed international warfare, such as the trench fighting of the First World War, the aerial dog-fights of the Second World War, or the conflict against Saddam Hussein's Iraq between 2003 and 2007. This is how many people imagine violence when the term is proposed to them.

The emphasis on such conventional forms of violence, however, re-inforces Anglin's notion that we generally level our observations at 'overt forms of coercion such as warfare, suppression of dissent by government forces, or physical assault' (1998: 145). For a growing body of writers, these conventions are too narrow. Different approaches to understand-ing peace and conflict have led some to consider that violence can take psychological and economic form, and the definition and comprehension of violence have expanded to take these concerns into consideration. Furthermore, to the various conventions noted here can be added the problematic but insightful concept of structural violence. It is this con-cept which benefits from some degree of qualification to remove it from the abstract and place it in the visible and definable.

Structural violence and structures of violence

This work is partly concerned with further qualifying, developing and refining, in the context of human security studies, a particular form of violence first enunciated in the academic press by Johan Galtung in 1969. Galtung attempted to guide people away from the limitations of direct, intentional, armed physical warfare towards a more *structural* analysis that might be in part characterized as unintentional violence caused by systems. Galtung argued that violence could be expanded to include situations when 'human beings are being influenced so that their actual somatic and mental realizations are below their potential realizations'. He made reference to situations 'where there is an actor that commits ... violence as personal or direct, and to violence where there is no such actor as structural or indirect' (1969: 167–8).

Galtung was one of the earliest to publish in the Western academic press an expanded definition of violence which identified and distinguished between direct and indirect actions, and also identified 'invisible' actors such as institutions, systems and structures rather than simply human beings acting directly. Violence, then, could be committed directly and deliberately, but could also be conducted indirectly and largely unintentionally, by structures populated by humans. Furthermore, the analysis started to probe new criteria that were considered by some at the time quite radical. Violence was to be understood as a force that unintentionally prevented humans from realizing their actual potential. Limits placed on human personal development represented for Galtung another form of violence that affected far more people than conventional warfare. Thus, something that resulted unintentionally in someone not being able to achieve what they otherwise could was a form of violence to be called structural.

This had clear implications for the expansion of the field of peace and conflict research and studies, because it implied that, for example, people who died as a result of lack of access to drinking water caused by poor government policies had been prevented from achieving their Galtungian potential through acts of a human-structural nature. It also suggested that people impoverished as a result of their governments selling their land, for example, were victims of structural, indirect violence with the capacity to lead to impoverishment, illness and death – direct violence. In 1985, Galtung summarized his views and synthesized analysis that had taken place between then and his 1969 publication. He noted that the structural forms of 'normal' existence that he had identified, and which had been analysed over the previous decade, were often:

> Settings within which individuals may do enormous amounts of harm to other human beings without ever intending to do so, just performing their regular duties as a job defined in the structure ... Structural violence [is] unintended harm done to human beings ... as a process, working slowly as the way misery in general, and hunger in particular, erode and finally kill human beings. (1985: 145–6)

It was Galtung's conviction that 'if people are starving when this is objectively avoidable, then violence is committed', and he extended his view to the notion that 'when one husband beats his wife there is a clear case of personal violence, but when one million husbands keep one million wives in ignorance there is structural violence' (ibid.: 145–6). Structural violence, then, undermined the simplistic notion of peace as the absence of war. His view was that the absence of structural violence and war would yield the presence of 'positive peace' (1969). This is in contrast to the more traditional approach which conceptualized peace as merely the absence of war. In the Galtungian, structural sense, the absence of war does not imply that other forms of mass violence, more broadly defined, are also absent.

Weigert (1999: 433) refers us to empirical research undertaken by Alcock and Kohler, who looked to test Galtung's hypothesis. Their work concluded, in Weigert's words, that 'there were unnecessary (i.e., theoretically preventable or "premature") deaths, differentially distributed, and these deaths could be attributed to the structures of power and resource allocation in the particular arena' (domestic or international) – in short, to structural violence. These are fairly complex definitions and discussions that move far beyond some people's initial considerations of violence; Farmer more succinctly defines structural violence as 'the social machinery of oppression' (2002: 1).

These structures are rarely easy to imagine. Nor do they readily take concrete form. Many of the structures surrounding our lives may appear benign when in fact they can be unintentionally (or intentionally) malignant. This malignancy can be ignored or indeed invisible if the subsequent marginalization of somatic realizations is, as Webb wrote, 'legitimised by the prevailing political or social norms, or sanctified by religious belief' (1986: 431). Despite this legitimization through accepted culture or norms, supporters of Galtung's arguments would view a system of allocation determined through the credo of capitalism, deregulation and privatization as the key cause of some childbearing mothers' marginalization and death (among many others). The debate in this sense is about perception. There are those who argue that one has to perceive that one is being abused to be abused. On the other hand, there are those who maintain that one can be abused without being aware of an unintentional act that results in one's marginalization. Weigert summarises:

> [T]he subjectivist model maintains that there must be at least some perception of incompatible values or goals by the actors involved to justify calling something a conflict. The objectivist model, on the other hand, argues that conflict can exist without the awareness of the social actors since conflict, in this view, has to do with 'interests' and interests are not a matter of the subjective definition of the actors but are instead 'determined' by the social structure. (1999: 432)

Galtung may have been the earliest enunciator in the Western academic press of this concept, but he is far from the only one concerned with structures in shaping violence. For example, Prontzos declares that structural violence could be thought of as 'deleterious conditions that derive from economic and political structures of power, created and maintained by human actions and institutions' (2004: 300). Picciotto and Weaving (2006: 73) illustrated the issue of perception when they claimed that social structures and institutions are phenomena 'that are required to shield people from threats'. The converse of this, however, is that it is often such human-engineered institutions which indirectly are the cause of much human insecurity. Thus, rather than seeing institutions, processes and structures as part of the solution, they can also be part of the problem. The usual examples of this dichotomy are the IMF and the World Bank, but they are far from the only dual offenders/benefactors. In - many countries around the world, the state may be imagined as fulfilling the social contract of protecting citizens in return for their loyalty. But in many other states, the rights of individuals and groups are routinely abused and the state can act in its own interests at the expense of wide-scale human security. Such misdemeanour is not restricted to pariah states; significant miscarriages of justice directly impacting on human rights happen in every advanced democracy in the world.

Other writers identify structural violence in the formation of gender-based violence as one of the key causes of women's general position in relation to men around the world. Anglin, for example, identifies violence as 'the expropriation of vital economic and non-material resources and the operation of systems of social stratification or categorization that subvert people's chances for survival'. She moves on to argue that '... gender relations ... can be understood as the imposition of categories of difference that legitimate hierarchy and inequality' (1998: 145). She explains the stratification of women below men as a consequence of 'normalised' social rules and instituted hierarchies permitting male domination of females as a key cause of women's marginalization, in much the same way as Galtung identifies structures of violence as inhibiting general human realizations. For Anglin, recognition of the presence of structural violence allows us to:

> Better understand that social and government policies ... engender a kind of structural violence that is normalized and accepted as part of the 'status quo', but that is experienced as injustice and brutality at particular intersections of race, ethnicity, class, nationality, gender and age. (ibid.: 145–6)

Summarizing her thoughts and synthesizing them with the research of others, Anglin argues against biological determinism and maintains that human beings are not 'inherently violent ... rather ... certain contexts and social formations seem to produce violence' (ibid.: 146). But this is to neglect the wide range of literature that suggests strongly that human genetic composition should not be ignored. A more nuanced notion might consider that our biological background developed as a response to extremely violent and hostile surroundings many millennia ago, but current and recent social conditions have undermined the necessity for our original genetic predisposition. It would appear that social conditions have evolved far more rapidly than our genes, which may explain in part the tension between the 'nature and nurture' protagonists.

Such structures require identification, along with the human agency involved in their construction and activity. The more that research 'denormalizes' the 'normal' structural precepts, the more the extent of structural violence will move from the 'invisible' to the 'visible' domain. This is especially important, since the dominant and most influential school of security does not consider that any organizing international structure, insofar as they see one existing, might be of human and transformable origin, as opposed to something rather vaguely related to biological determinism. The 'normalcy' and immutability of realist-conceived international systems exclude them from critical reconsideration as deterministic of avoidable humanitarian disasters that are otherwise represented as unavoidable. Directing intellectual energy towards identifiable, mutating and transformable international structures has the obvious potential to challenge violence-creating structures to the benefit of human security. As Galtung put it more than two decades ago, 'a focus on structural violence will lead to a critical analysis of structures and possibly to efforts to transform structures pregnant with violence into less violent ones' (1985: 146). More recently and more lyrically, Galeano referred to the problem as deriving from 'power, which ... sweats violence through every pore' (2005: 393).

Galtung's work was criticized at the time as largely untenable because of its enormous breadth, not unlike the challenges facing maximalist human security. But it retains utility as a generic conceptualization, from which a more specific, and workable, approach to understanding security can be developed. If the generic is too broad and deep to be analytically sustainable and policy oriented, specific *structures* and *institutions* of violence are more readily apparent and offer the opportunity for analysis and policy prescription.

The UN Development Programme (UNDP) and human security

The range of differences identified in the emerging literature noted above, between minimalist and maximalist, found pointed expression in two major security and development documents that were published not far apart in the same year. These were the UN *Human Development Report* of 2005 and the *Human Security Report* of the same year. Their differences reflect the same agenda and divide as ever, and are broadly illustrative of where the debate went.

The 2005 *Human Security Report* defined human security as 'the complex of interrelated threats associated with civil war, genocide and the displacement of populations' (Mack 2005: viii). But as the report writers concede, their conceptualization of human security is narrow and focuses mainly on political violence. Furthermore, the data sets they identify draw mainly on 'battle-deaths ... between 1946 and 2002 in conflicts where a government was one of the warring factions' (ibid.: 5). Some of the report's claims, while recognizing the broader impact of what Schwab (2001: 3) called civil wars' 'apprentices[:] famine, hunger and disease', do not factor-in sufficiently the statistics associated with these menaces (which they do discuss in Part IV of the document). In this respect the report, while offering some evidence to suggest that conflicts defined in certain ways are in decline globally, is a primarily descriptive foray into a limited interpretation of human security. Indeed, for a maximalist, the title of this document might be misleading.

In contrast to this, the wider human security school is an extension of at least two intellectual and analytical trends. In 1994, a UN Development Report argued for a shift 'from exclusive stress on territorial security to a much greater stress on people's security ... [and] from security through armaments to security through sustainable human development' (UNDP 1994: 2). This mirrors the human security notion of the human as the central point of protection. The debate has moved forward, and definitions of human security and the utility of the approach have been argued with some vigour. In beginning to define human security, the UNDP claimed that such 'security symbolized protection from the threat of disease, hunger, unemployment, crime, social conflict, political repression, and environmental hazards' (ibid.: 3). These threats can all be argued to have a structural origin, as long as the intellectual approach is sufficiently open to recognize the serious challenges this implies. The central concern in generalized terms became known as 'freedom from want and freedom from fear', two vast interlinked concepts that quickly fell prey to those who regarded such expansionist thinking as analytically self-destructive. Perhaps a more useful conceptualization would be concerned with freedom from need; freedom from want is conceptually impossible to subjectively define or provide.

Krause, in an attempt to properly 'delimit' the debate, suggests that 'freedom from want' should be dropped so we 'keep human security focussed on "freedom from fear" – from the threat or use of violence' (2004: 367). This seems a more practical agenda but it does not identify the type of violence that produces the fear and is thus not reflective of the debate on its changing conceptualizations over the last thirty and more years. Definitions designed to fit national strategies have not been much more helpful. For example, the Japanese definition of human security 'comprehensively covers all the measures that threaten human survival, daily life, and dignity'. For Paris, this was too vague to work, and it would not work without fundamental changes to global economic institutions and attitudes (2001: 90).

The developing debate was surveyed in a special edition of *Security Dialogue* published in September 2004. Some of the contributors, drawn from academia, field development and policy-making units, were convinced of an absolute centrality for human security in the broader security debate. For example, Thakur remarked that 'to insist on national security at the expense of human security would be to trivialize "security" in many real-world circumstances to the point of sterility, bereft of any practical meaning' (2004: 347). He was referring to identifying humans as the centre of analysis, from which new policy could be developed to enhance security. He notes also the presence of 'structural coercion so severe as to turn human beings into chattels ...' (ibid.: 347). The essence of Thakur's concern is far reaching. For him, 'the reformulation of national security into human security ... has profound consequences for how we see the world, how we organize our political affairs, and how we relate to fellow human beings ...' (ibid.: 348). Thakur's position enunciates the concern that structures that oppress are causing part of the human insecurity condition. It does not, however, delineate a tangible, researchable corpus of material from which change can be implemented.

The growing caucus of scholars concerned with structural determinism in the human security debate includes Fen Osler Hampson, who also perceives of human security as determined in part by human-inhabited structures (2004: 350). For Hampson, 'the problems of human security are often ... structurally dependent ... They are rooted in political and social structures and ecological conditions'. While human security itself is related directly to changeable social and political structures, there is a larger relationship, wherein 'human security is critical to international security and that international order cannot rest solely on the sovereignty and viability of states ...' (ibid.: 350).

The debate still turns on breadth and depth. If some scholars are beginning to accept the human as the central security referent, they remain divided on how to define the concept's rubric. Some still favour a narrow approach because this is more manageable for research methods that can then feed into policy. Others persist in maintaining that a certain futility afflicts this approach, because the range of threats to human security is so broad as to include tsunamis and other 'non-man-made' events. But there may be a middle road that takes into account structural breadth but delimits the security threat so as to make it identifiable and assessable, with the corollary that policy may be positively influenced towards change.

Making a good idea work?

In a sense, we appear to have come full circle: there are significant similarities between the idea of human security as expressed in the development studies/UN angle, on the one hand, and on the other Galtung's theory of structural violence and human psychosomatic potential. Indeed, Sabine Alkire defines the objective of human security as 'being to protect the vital core of all human lives in ways that advance human freedoms and human fulfilment', a definition that reflects Galtungian dimensions of human development (2004: 359). Both disciplines – development and security – present similar dilemmas in terms of definition and breadth. But there is no doubt that the direction of inquiry is drawing us towards social structures of violence. As Newman maintains, 'exploring the relationship between human agency and structure in solutions to human security challenges is a pressing next step in the human security discourse' (2004: 359).

But Newman's 'pressing next step' seems to have been halted by methodological constraints and conceptual disagreements. Owen, however, proposes a 'threshold-based definition' which addresses the 'paradox [whereby] the closer the concept [of human security] gets to its original conceptualization, focusing on all threats to the individual, the more difficult both human security theory and policy become' (2004: 381). Owen argues that we can use a threshold-based conceptualization 'that limits threats by their severity rather than their cause, allows all possible harms to be considered, but selectively limits those that at any time are prioritised with the "security" label'. He notes that the early UNDP philosophy was 'not to securitize everything, but to shift attention away from Cold War threats to what was actually killing people ... If human security could cover the most basic threats, development would then address societal well-being' (ibid.: 381). Owen determines that the key to the definitional and conceptual problem lies in the following classification: 'human security is the protection of the vital core of all human lives from critical pervasive, economic, food, health, personal and political threats' (ibid.: 383).

Liotta challenges Owen's 'threshold' concept and identifies the issue of 'creeping vulnerability' in human security (2005: 51, 67). Liotta is concerned to again widen the debate to issues such as unsustainable urbanization in part of the developing world. But once more, no reference is made to the roles of human agency in increasing vulnerability/insecurity. Liotta, rather than challenging institutionalized human influences in the creation of human vulnerability or insecurity, seeks greater input of already extant forces. These include 'sustainable development' and 'long-term investment strategies'. No suggestion is made that the very forces of contemporary, extant strategic thinking and emphasis on the present development approach may aggravate, rather than offset and reduce, human insecurity. Liotta is far from wrong to be concerned with his sectoral classifications of vulnerability, but his proposals differ significantly from the argument I shall make, identifying the extent of human causation in the creation of insecurity and vulnerability.

King and Murray also sought definitional clarity. They proposed a 'simple, rigorous, and measurable definition of human security'. This was to be 'the number of years of future life spent outside a state of "generalized poverty" [which] occurs when an individual falls below the threshold of any key domain of human well-being' (2001: 585). Their approach concerns life expectancy undermined by poverty, where poverty is expressed in terms of particular aspects of ill health. This approach, however, identifies only poverty as a determinant of human security; and it does not appear to invite debate on the human, institutional and structural forces that lay behind the creation of poverty and health vulnerability. Further, it does not seem to consider lethality. Finally, the methodology is firmly quantitative in assessing numbers of years of life outside poverty, resulting in complex mathematical formulae that may not consider the qualitative influence of social structures of violence. Thus, in line with other approaches, King and Murray have identified only one sector of human security, and there is no attempt to isolate and capture human agency, institutional power and ideational determinism to explain poverty creation or wealth destruction.

King and Murray influenced a quite different departure in this debate, however. Duffield and Wadell noted the limits identified in these authors' work and applied a Foucauldian conception of biopolitics to the human security dilemma that might be linked to global governance, a particular theme of Duffield's research. Duffield and Wadell defined biopolitics as 'those varied economic, educational, health and political interventions aimed at improving the resilience and well-being of people whose existence is defined by the contingencies of "underdevelopment"' (2006: 43). Given that underdevelopment is a political condition and that 'underdevelopment' is a key determinant of much human insecurity, biopolitics is a reasonable framework for considering human security. In many respects, this reinforces the notion that human security could be broadly conceived. Duffield and Wadell propose realignments of existing Northern international institutions such as NGOs and states, whose focus would be on populations in the global South whose broad human security needs were not being met by the state systems in which they lived (based in part on the 'responsibility to protect' concept).

'A biopolitics of life' includes 'educational measures aimed at enabling the poor to understand the contingencies of their existence and to manage better, and compensate for, the risks involved' (ibid.: 43). In this statement lies a conceptual pitfall. One problem lies in the proposed use and maintenance of key elements of the international framework that are responsible for undermining human insecurity in the first instance. In other words, the tools for biopolitical life and security are in some instances the same as the causes of human insecurity. This is because both biopolitics and human security are dependent on power relationships, North to South, and the priorities determined by international institutions dominated by particular ideologies of wealth provision and priorities. Biopolitical human security attends to the sustainable development needs of vulnerable populations, but the reasons why states are ineffective in providing such services for their populations remain at large. States are often ineffective owing to their own spending priorities, sometimes influenced by Western arms sales initiatives, for example, or because they are corrupt or at war.

State priorities, however, are increasingly subject to interstate forces over which they have limited control. Constructive national policies of sustainable development are frequently undermined by the international financial policies of global Western institutions like the IMF and the World Bank, which very clearly dictate debt repayment and domestic social policies that are crippling to Southern populations. Thus, while

Duffield and Wadell quite reasonably reformulate human security as a biopolitical issue related to states and provision, their approach suggests that a realignment of international institutions with a refocusing on vulnerable populations in ineffective states is the way forward. But this is akin to giving with one hand while taking with the other. It becomes a Sisyphean struggle, and it does not address the ideational and structural forces that cause damage in the first instance. Ultimately, it maintains the legitimacy of the patronage model of international development without addressing the role of power patronage in determining human security problems in the first instance.

Duffield and Wadell's contribution is perhaps the most conceptually diverse and definitionally aware, but it remains incomplete. The debate continues to be shifting and mired. It is shifting because scholars are recognizing that the debate can be expanded if we accept the notion that human agency can influence human security outcomes. This marks a departure from the rigidity with which some realists (and others) viewed Galtung's concerns about structures. But it is mired because progress on defining human security has stalled. There is no firm agreement on what constitutes human security; indeed, the breadth and depth of current definitions have provoked almost endless criticism and controversy. To overcome this difficulty, I propose to approach the subject from the other side, to look at what constitutes human insecurity; what it is that humans do to make the world a more dangerous and dysfunctional place. Considered in this way, human insecurity can be defined as follows: avoidable civilian deaths, occurring globally, caused by social, political and economic institutions and structures, built and operated by humans and which could feasibly be changed. This interpretation of human insecurity means it can be transformed because it is conspicuously caused by demonstrably dysfunctional global structures, international institutions and civil human agency.

Structures in this sense are overarching global beliefs expressed through institutions. They are the dominant ideas which direct institutional and human agency and priorities. They are constructed of beliefs and assumptions that claim a monopoly of righteousness and authenticity by virtue of the absence or failure of alternatives and/or by virtue of the capacity to reject internal and external criticism and so retain their discursive hegemony. They are thus, in this interpretation, hegemonic, but misfounded, ideals. Institutions transmit the beliefs of the dominant structures. They may take formal or informal shape; and they may be social, political or economic; or they may combine aspects of some or all of these organizing systems. They are, in this interpretation, collective belief vessels that communicate values determined by structures to create human agency and outcomes according to a given ideational agenda contained within the structure. Furthermore, they may preserve or transform a status quo, but, where their origins may suggest impartiality, they are rarely neutral in outcome.

Rather than considering human insecurity as inevitable in many instances, the approach of this work discusses the role of global structures, international institutions and human agency in the creation and perpetuation of human insecurity. It reflects Galtung's conceptualization of structural violence but it is not extended into the realization of full human psychosomatic potential, and is concerned with identifiable structures of violence. Identifying the scale and role of unintentional and intentional human action as causes of global civilian deaths on a colossal and preventable scale is central to this work. The implication is that if human insecurity is a consequence of human behaviour, that behaviour can be re-evaluated and influenced to enhance policy-making and improvement for human security. Thus, while narrowing the definition to revolve around avoidable civilian deaths, the understanding of human security is simultaneously expanded to include human agency and indirect (as well as direct) violence communicated through institutions at the behest of global structures. Thus, while the approach may be criticized for narrowness in defining human insecurity as avoidable death, it offers breadth (and a long-awaited starting point) by examining human, institutional and structural agency as causative factors in such unnecessary lethality. This reflects in part Paris's proposal that human security can:

> Serve as a label for a broad category of research in the field of security studies that is primarily concerned with non-military threats to the safety of societies, groups and individuals, in contrast to more traditional approaches to security studies that focus on protecting states from external threats. (2001: 96)

The approach here draws on clear empirical data to build on the new focus in the human security literature, but goes farther to identify the institutional and structural sources of violence, rather than merely offering a sustained critique of realism. It also extends the general conceptualization of human security and insecurity beyond what Fierke called its 'strategic objective' of alleviating poverty, shifting wealth and developing democracy (2007: 146), which does not thoroughly address gross avoidable mortality levels in practice or construction.

Conclusion

A reminder of the question we seek to address. If humans are dying unnecessarily in their millions by virtue of non-state, non-military, non-traditional security threats, *what* is doing this, and *how* and *why* is it happening? Here, I have surveyed the origins and elements of the human security debate, and the reconceptualization of violence, security and development through subsequent critical feminist reformulations. Finally, this chapter has offered an operating framework – the number of avoidable civilian deaths connected to institutional and structural determinism – for overcoming the main challenges to the human security debate to date.

THREE | Global human insecurity

This chapter examines avoidable civilian deaths in two areas. These are preventable female deaths, subcategorized as infanticide, maternal mortality, intimate ('domestic', 'honour' and 'dowry') killings and lethal female genital mutilation; and avoidable deaths in children under five, measured by the Under-Five Mortality Rate (U5MR).

Many of the examples that follow occur in very poor places found mostly south of the equator, so terminology should be briefly considered in the hope of reducing confusion over what is meant by the terms Third World, the Global South, the Majority World and the developing world (see Williams 1994: 2–5). I use the terms interchangeably throughout this work, because all of them can be understood in terms of expressing a power relationship, which is how the concept has arisen.

Currently, these terms are mainly associated with geographical regions within which there are so many differences as to render each term alone largely ineffectual. The Third World title is the subject of different perspectives. While there is general agreement that it is the earliest of these terms, there is disagreement over whether it came from a French term reflecting poor and marginalized people in 1952, or from high US political office at the beginning of the cold war. Thereafter, alternative terms were mostly introduced as the weaknesses of each new term became clearer. The introduction of a 'Fourth World' demonstrated relative impoverishment as well as absolute; the 'Global South' includes New Zealand, Australia, Brunei and other quite wealthy places; the 'Majority World' is only a majority depending on what measurement point is used; and the 'developing world' contains states that are not developing, either at all or relatively.

Furthermore, the terminology assumes that a certain level of development has been achieved by some states against which that of others might be measured, and can be criticized as Eurocentric. Other terms such as the 'colonial' and 'post-colonial' world were weakened by the problem that states such as Thailand were never colonized. Such efforts at identifying geo-historical commonalities have foundered, mainly because what unites the states in question is their location on a fluid, not static, *power* continuum. The most politically powerful states are very rich, while the weakest states are very poor. This is not coincidence but, as we shall see in the following chapters, a function of advantage and disadvantage that have been maintained over time through a changing but asymmetrical power relationship. I now turn to the phenomena I have classified as subjects of human insecurity. They are arranged in descending order of deaths.

Infanticide

Watts and Zimmerman describe infanticide as the 'deliberate killing of children after birth' (2002: 1236). The phenomenon also includes sex-selective abortions where the child is aborted because of her sex and the low value associated with being female. It happens currently on the widest scale in India and China, but has also been practised in Ireland, the UK and other parts of Europe historically. It is sometimes euphemistically referred to as 'son preference' (Seager 2003: 13), in much the same way as large-scale civilian deaths from aerial bombardment in Vietnam and Iraq have been euphemized as 'collateral damage'. This linguistic distortion is a method of anonymizing and disguising the severity and lethality of the practice. It is a process whereby children are disposed of at, before or soon after birth because of their sex, and affects almost exclusively females. Warren surveyed the phenomenon throughout history and across geographical boundaries and concluded that:

> There are very few cultures in which males are more apt to be killed than females ... [in the Arab world] the birth of a daughter was regarded ... as a humiliating calamity – and often still is ... [In India they] killed virtually all female infants at birth ... [In] nineteenth and early twentieth-century Western Europe it was publicly condemned but practiced covertly, in ways that made it appear accidental or inadvertent. (Warren 1985: 32–41)

Watts and Zimmerman summarize research from various regions showing abnormal ratios of males to females caused by 'sex-selective abortion, female infanticide ... and systemic and often fatal neglect of the health and nutritional needs of girls' (2002: 1236). They estimate that worldwide there are 'between 60 and 100 million women and girls' who are 'missing' from normal population counts, and refer specifically to the case of India. There, 'after adjustment for expected differences in fertility and life-expectancy ... census figures suggest that between 22 and 37 million Indian girls are "missing", with the greatest excess mortality rate in girls younger than 4 years' (ibid.: 1236; Sen 2003). Two UN reports, in 2000 and 2005, noted similar findings (UNFPA 2000: 25; UNFPA 2005: 2). It is claimed that up to 500,000 girls go missing in this manner each year and, according to Seager, the issue is so serious that 'the Punjab-Haryana-Himachal Pradesh belt in northwest India is sometimes dubbed "India's Bermuda Triangle"' (2003: 20).

Infanticide is a global phenomenon. As well as in the Asian subcontinent, the practice occurs in Libya, Turkey and other parts of the world characterized by gender stratification, impoverishment and machismo, as well as noticeably traditional male and female role stereotypes. Perceptions of relative sex and gender value are not, however, restricted to the very poor world. A case of a British woman attempting to procure a baby boy in Bulgaria revealed that prices attached to baby boys were almost 20 times higher than for baby girls (*The Times*, 18 December 2006: 3).

Furthermore, the practice of preferring a male child to a female child extends after birth and throughout early years. In other words, even when a girl is not killed at birth because of the onerous 'burden' she represents, her brothers will be fed, clothed and favoured before her as she grows up in their shadows. Penn and Nardos note the importance of this process, and suggest that there is evidence not only of preferring sons but of the long-term 'neglect of female children' (2003: 26). They maintain that female life expectancy has declined in parts of Africa and Asia and attribute that diminution to 'son preference'. Even when infanticide does not kill girls at birth, boys will be fed and dressed before and better than their sisters to the extent that female lives are shortened; there is, in Sen's words, a 'sex bias in relative care' (2003: 1297). It can only send a very clear signal to males that their worth is greater than that of females, a conscious and subconscious sensation around the globe, and not restricted to poor economies.

A variety of methods are employed, ranging from medical abortions through backstreet operations to illegal post-natal fetus disposal. Sudha and Irudaya Rajan argue that 'practices regulating the number of female children in a family traditionally included ... female infanticide, abandonment or out-adoption of girls, under-reporting of female births and selective neglect of girls leading to higher death rates' (1999: 585). It should be noted that in many societies and countries, health professionals and legislators identify reasonable grounds for prenatal terminations, or abortions. These might be on health grounds, or when the child is the product of peacetime or war rape (Koo 2007). But in other countries, often characterized by large populations, excess demand for scarce resources, decentralized polities and male social domination, those children are killed because their sex is identified with low utility. Allahbadia declares that in India 'women who discover that their fetus is female often opt for legal abortions referred to as MTPs (Medical Termination of Pregnancy)'. Confirming the practice, Indira reported that 'a study of amniocentesis in a large Bombay hospital found that 95.5 per cent of female fetuses were aborted compared to only a small number of boys'. Furthermore, she added, 'another study conducted in Maharashtra (West India) indicated that of 8,000 fetuses aborted, 7,999 were girls' (1995: 51).

In terms of illegal post-natal infant disposal – the murder of just-born infants – various practices are common. These include:

Feeding [the infants] poisonous milk of irukkam and kalli plants ... dropping crude husks into just-born's throats ... asphyxiation ... tobacco juice ... feeding hot, spicy chicken soup to the babies [who] writhe and scream in pain for a few hours, and then die. [Parents also] over-feed babies and tightly wrap them in a wet cloth. After an hour of breathless agony, they die. In yet another chilling infanticide, the umbilical cord is let loose, leading to excessive bleeding and eventual death. (*The Hindu*, 24 June 2001)

Penn and Nardos further elaborate:

If the delivery is at home, the child is often born, killed and buried the same day ... At ... hospital, a mock illness is frequently declared ... after which the child is killed ... [for example] by force-feeding the infant excessive cow's milk and hanging the bottle upside down from the cradle so that the child chokes; feeding the infant a mixture of soapy water and dissolved salt until she chokes; using a cloth with dripping water to cover the face of the infant to suffocate her; giving the poisonous milk of the Calatropis plant to the infant; feeding the child with husks of paddy grains until she chokes; administering pesticides; and so on. (2003: 26–7)

This unnerving description reveals the extent of the human participation in infanticide. But more than being mere testimony to the depths of human desperation involved in the social, political and economic subjugation of women's independence, capacities and desires, it forces us to confront the question of why so many probably otherwise good people would undertake such a grim and macabre, medievalesque practice.

Mothers often undertake such gruesome killings themselves and defend their actions on the grounds that lives for females are far worse than those for men. This reveals the structural nature of the problem. It is not simply male domination or preference; it is also female acquiescence and economic prioritization, wherein so many women both participate in this tragic practice but also accept the structures that lead to infanticide. Furthermore, the relative impoverishment of women and men is also structurally determined within the capitalist system.

Women often cite their own experiences without realizing that those very circumstances are a product of oppression and the social systems it deploys, endorses and perpetuates. Venkatramani records another tragic passing: tragic not merely for the child who never had a chance, but tragic for the indictment it makes upon a section of humanity dominated by 'cultural' patriarchy and the women who are ruled by it. It is worth quoting at length because of the range of control and domination issues contained within the short record of a tiny child's birth, and her almost immediate and violent disposal:

> The new-born cried lustily as it came into this world ... when the mother laid eyes on her baby, tears welled up in her eyes. They were not tears of joy ... What crossed [the mother's] mind was not the anticipation of the joys of motherhood but the trials that lay ahead. How could a family of day-wage agricultural workers ... afford to bring up and marry off two daughters? How could they, when the dowry demanded by bridegrooms was always astronomical? The couple had decided to have a second child only in the desperate hope that it would be a boy. But on this sunny day, the dream lay shattered. (1992: 127)

The author goes on to describe the 'solution'; the child was poisoned with berries:

> Within an hour the baby began to twitch and tremble fitfully. Slowly she started spouting blood through her nose and mouth ... A few more min utes, and all was quiet. The mother explained thus: I killed my child to save it from the life-long ignominy of being the daughter of a poor family that cannot afford to pay a decent dowry ... My husband and I concluded that it was better to let our child suffer an hour or two and die than suffer through life. (ibid.: 127).

That child, and the others who perish alongside her, is a microcosm of fatal violence against and control of females. It is an avoidable tragedy. But is it only one element of 'disposal' due to 'traditions' and prefer-ences for males.

Adoption and abandonment are rife; the two combine in China in what have become notorious as the 'dying rooms', where almost exclusively female babies die owing to state-facilitated and culturally condoned neglect. Despite Chinese government denial, a British documentary captured the conditions that prevail. One baby's death was described thus:

> Mei-ming [the child] has lain this way for 10 days now: tied up in urine-soaked blankets, scabs of dried mucus growing across her eyes, her face shrinking to a skull, malnutrition slowly shriveling her two-year old body ... When Mei-ming dies four days later, it will be of sheer neglect. Afterwards, the orphanage will deny she ever existed. (Hilditch 1995: 39)

Looking at and dissembling the circumstances of Mei-ming's death allows us to understand complex and interrelated social, economic and gender concerns. Mei-ming's non-value – her superfluousness and irrelevance as a female human being – was a result of economic activity dominated by men and the placement of women in the home to undertake population continuity once men have completed the sex act. Invoking women's inherent and natural 'nurturing' vocation keeps them in unpaid home labour and susceptible and vulnerable to male dominance, and undermines women's independence. It replicates this lower status in girl children and ensures that the rules that lock mothers into homes and vulnerability continue to relegate girl children as they become wives and mothers.

Infanticide is routinely denied by governments accused of condoning such practices. Furthermore, the figures cited above have been challenged substantially. Johansson and Nygren accept that studies in the 1980s suggested that there were approximately 500,000 missing girls per year in China. They claim, however, that of those missing girls:

> Adoptions are estimated to account for about half ... Some girls whose births went unreported are presumably living with their parents, but the inability to estimate the size of this phenomenon hampers estimates of female infanticide. Excess female infant mortality is postulated at about 39,000 per year, or about 4 infant deaths per thousand live-born girls. (1991: 35)

This implies that the figures postulated by Watts and Zimmerman (2002) and Arnold et al. (2002) may be artificially high. The divergence reflects a wider debate. We encounter once more when dealing with violence against women, mainly through or by men and male-dominated institutions and structures, the problem of establishing verifiable, reliable figures concerning female mortalities. Multi-tiered barriers to reliable reporting, which include the acceptance and preaching of anti-female violence, the absence of sanctions and punishment and the resistance of the constabulary to apprehending for domestic private-sphere activities that are socio-culturally considered less an offence and more as acceptable conventions, converge to perpetuate such gendered violence.

The result is that, as with domestic violence as recently as the 1980s in western Europe, the social conventions that perpetuate infanticide in Asia and ensure that reporting is made humiliating and painful for women and is scorned by males and male-dominated institutions, such as families, villages, courts and legislatures, persist. Rummel comments that 'governments and other actors can be just as guilty of mass killing by neglect or tacit encouragement, as by direct murder' (1994: 65). Such acts and the beliefs that underpin them are linked by many human-built conventions, but they all share patriarchal roots, in that they reflect negative values attached to women as well as control processes to manage female 'deviations' from male codifications of behaviour. It is no surprise that reliable figures are hard to obtain or estimate. Mei-ming and the millions of other girl-children do not die solely because of their sex; they die because of the socially constructed roles placed around them as a consequence of an impoverishing male-ordained and prioritized economic model enshrined in male-dominated determinism of the gender division of labour. Such beliefs and attitudes are learned and enforced with criticism of the dominant ideology normally ignored, ridiculed or punished in a variety of ways for challenging and transgressing 'reality', 'the way it is' and 'the natural order'.

In a sense, however, the variation in estimates is not important. Even if the figures were inaccurate by a factor of 50 per cent, the scale of the problem is still evident to those prepared to confront it. There is ample reason to believe that the trend of denial facilitated by barriers to reporting and familial privacy will continue. This is because some of the motivating elements for infanticide lie along the same continuum that creates and permits many other types of violence against women. As reporting improves owing to greater challenges to systemic limitations, the trend is that initial figures based on projected absences will prove to be only the tip of the iceberg. Already, official Chinese estimates on what are referred to as 'halted births' show how high real figures will be. In early 2007, the Chinese head of the Population and Family Planning Commission, Zhang Weiqing, openly discussed numbers and causes. As well as the general problem of overpopulation and 'unbalanced economic and social development', he added that there has existed 'for thousands of years ... a deep rooted view that men are worth more than women' (*Guardian*, 24 January 2007: 22). Such roots predate both organized religion and large-scale economic organization, but they have been reinforced through various belief-systems like Confucianism, Islam or Christianity and replicated and maintained by capitalist divisions of labour and gender.

The net result, according to Zhang, was that Chinese population planning had 'halted 400 million births in 30 years' (ibid.: 22). This amounts to 13.3 million 'halted' births per year. This figure, and the horribly euphemistic meaning of 'halted', remains unexplained in sufficient detail. Men's 'greater value' and social, economic and political domination, all taught and learned notions, lead to the slaughter of girl infants. But as we shall see in later chapters, they contribute also to rape, domestic violence, relative pay, sexual commodification and trafficking, and many more ills that females face from birth.

Avoidable deaths in children under five (U5MR)

In response to the limitations of standard economic measurements of 'growth' or 'progress' in developing countries, the UNDP introduced a more emphatic range of variables with which to understand development. The study of the Under-Five Mortality Rate (U5MR) is one of these variables; it is important because it acts as a diagnostic indicator of the state of necessary health provision for the most vulnerable of the human species. Its use in the UN Human Development Index (HDI) indicates levels of national socio-economic development quite broadly. Child health is especially vulnerable to unclean water and the prevalence of water-borne diseases that can easily kill children when untreated, especially since the human immune system is not normally adequately developed until around the age of eight. Child survival is, for the UNDP, 'one of the most sensitive indicators of human welfare, the comparative health of nations and the effectiveness of public policy' (2005: 27). It indicates cohesiveness of government policy health strategies, and it also responds to changes in subsidized supplies of health materials. High or low levels of U5MR are broadly indicative of development levels generally within a state.

Despite the obvious importance of children to our species' survival and to the esteem we as humans may hold ourselves in, the status of child mortality is problematic. According to the United Nations, it is so serious that it is 'fast approaching the point that merits declaration of an international emergency ... roughly one child died every three seconds' in 2002, with 'an estimated 4 million in the first month of life' (ibid.:

27). The UNDP's 'law of inverse care' applies: health spending is generally higher where it is less needed, and 'almost all child deaths' are in
poorer countries where lower health spending occurs against a backdrop
of much greater need (ibid.: 26; Kim et al. 2000: 4).

Despite these phenomena, however, there is little real reason why
they should be occurring as they are. Most of the illnesses from which
children suffer and die are either preventable, treatable or both. The
UNDP notes that:

> Almost all child deaths are preventable. It is evident that, of the types
> of intervention required to diminish this avoidable moral cataclysm,
> most are low-cost and [are] highly cost-effective. Two in every three child
> deaths could be averted through provision of the most basic health serv-
> ices. Yet a health catastrophe that inflicts a human toll more deadly than
> the HIV/AIDS pandemic is allowed to continue. (2005: 24–33)

Pilisuk (2001: 151) adds that 12 million children under the age of five
die each year, or '33,000 per day' despite the 'six-fold' growth of the
global economy since 1950. The UN's vast global resources are normally
and historically deployed in a development context. But their collation
offers an opportunity for the field of security studies, because, with the
definition and reconceptualizations arrived at in the preceding chapter,
they can be used as indicators of human insecurity.

First, as noted above, they allow for quantification of a key human
insecurity indicator. Second, applying this methodology allows us better
to evaluate the forces at work in maintaining child mortality. That is, as
well as providing us with essential and useful empirical information for
human security studies, it also tells us why those deaths are occurring at
the rates they are. As the *Human Development Report* succinctly puts it,
'nothing more powerfully underlines the gap between what we are able
to do to overcome avoidable suffering and what we chose to do with
the wealth and technologies at our disposal' (UNDP 2005: 27). Thus, if
causation is contaminated water, then we may ask what is required to
make water supplies potable, and we may then explore the causal chains
involved in not rendering water drinkable and safe for children. The
continuing insecurity situation highlights the failure of culpable humans
in all parts of the world to create relevant interventions. It also reveals,
however, the roles of institutions and ideologies, or belief-systems, at
the structural level.

Returning to child mortality, the UN estimates that 'communicable
diseases and systemic infections, such as pneumonia, septicaemia,

diarrhoea and tetanus cause two in every three child deaths – nearly all of them preventable' (ibid.: 33). Baylis and Smith declare that 'more than 5 million die per annum from diarrhoeal diseases (caused by water contamination)' (2001: 566). In 2003, roughly 10.6 million children died in their first five years (UNDP 2005: 24; WHO 2005: 190). Of these, pneumonia accounted for 19 per cent, diarrhoea 17 per cent, malaria 8 per cent, newborn blood infection 10 per cent, preterm delivery 10 per cent and asphyxia at birth 8 per cent. This amounts to 'over 27,000 per day, more than nine times the number of victims of September 11 ...'. Prontzos added that regarding the scale of deaths, 'the word "holocaust" ... is appropriate for many reasons' (2004: 299–300).

In particular, malaria, an illness that can be prevented, 'kills one child every 30 seconds. In absolute numbers, malaria kills 3,000 children per day under five years of age. Fatally afflicted children often die less than 72 hours after developing symptoms' (Nobelprize.org 2006). Despite this, between 1991 and 2001, 'less that 2% of children from endemic malaria areas slept under insecticide-treated nets every night' (WHO 2005: 25). Recent research suggests that malaria may kill more people than HIV/AIDS, and certainly more than those civilians killed in military conflicts (*Guardian*, 10 March 2005: 22).

Throughout 2005, in all, 2.7 million people of all ages died from malaria, and the vast majority of these deaths were preventable by low-level, low-cost multi-dimensional interventions (*Cambodia Daily*, 20 July 2006: 20). The UN adds that 'vaccine-preventable illnesses – like measles, diphtheria and tetanus – account for another 2–3 million childhood deaths'. Furthermore, it is no coincidence that of all those relatively easily avoidable deaths, '98%' occur in the developing worlds (UNDP 2005: 24; WHO 2005: 9). In addition, the UN records that, after breathing illnesses, 'diseases transmitted through water or human waste are the second leading cause of death among children worldwide ... an estimated 3,900 ... every day' (UNDP 2005: 24).

There are multiple influences on children who become infected through water and excrement (they are often found together in river effluence, which can provide the sole source of drinking water), as there are regarding malaria. Education is central: many people know to cover their water containers in the mosquito season to avert malaria and dengue crises. But many more are not aware of the ease with which human faeces can be transmitted into children's mouths, or that another group of people upstream may be using a shared water supply for defecation or other poisonous waste disposal. Infection happens in myriad ways, but education and awareness are central to prevention. Simple instructions in hygiene that were common in northern Europe forty years ago and considered essential for the health and productivity of nations, as well as to minimize pressure on state provision of public health, are often absent.

The illnesses are mostly preventable and therefore avoidable. The *Cambodia Daily* questioned why so many died 'when there are medicines that cure for $0.55 a dose, mosquito nets that shield a child for $1 a year and indoor insecticide spraying that costs about $10 annually for a household' (20 July 2006: 20). A UN report identified 'the indefensible underuse of effective, low-cost, low-technology interventions – and ... a failure to address the structural causes of poverty and inequality' (UNDP 2005: 33). What appears most potent, then, is perhaps not so much the scale of the deaths but the possibilities for intervention. *The Lancet* identified in 2003 twenty-three different methods of tackling this phenomenon that would save 6 million of those lives if humans chose to act. No one intervention was particularly challenging and the medical journal estimated the cost of such an attempt at $5 billion (ibid.: 33).

But such interventions are infrequent and not strategically oriented. A medical researcher declared that 'it is unquestionably a shameful indictment of our global society that, when known effective interventions have been developed and could be financed ... millions of children are denied them' (*Guardian*, 24 June 2005: 18). Public sector choices that negate or ignore such interventions derive from human agency in policy-making, curricula formation and state resource allocation. If education is insufficient, and spending on healthcare is undermined, the social, political and economic actors and institutions that are responsible for such allocations are indirectly responsible for avoidable child deaths, among much other mortality. Recognizing this role in the cause and effect chain is central to changing the current lethal outcomes, and this causal relationship is explored in greater detail in later chapters.

Avoidable child mortality is affected in other, interdependent, ways. Many healthy children around the world are exposed to a variety of life-threatening diseases but do not necessarily succumb to them. Key to minimizing the impact of such diseases and illnesses is nutritional health. Food supply is critical for children. Food production globally has increased hugely since the end of the Second World War, but the question is not one of supply (Global Health Watch 2005: 226, 228; Sen 1999). Earlier thinking in relation to starvation during and after the numerous African famines of the 1970s and 1980s concluded that food supply was determined by availability and the problem was characterized as 'Food Availability Decline' (FAD). There are numerous situations, however, in which food is available but people still starve and children still do not get the nutrition they need to fuel their immune systems to ward off disease. This happens when people cannot afford to buy food (Sen 1999, 1982).

People are also deleteriously affected by hunger or hunger-related illness when they cannot *access* food that is available. In some instances, food denial can be a product of government policy, either benign through ignorance or malicious through intent (Sen 1999, 1981; Pierce 1991). In other instances, markets may well supply food, but the market mechanism may fix prices beyond the reach of poor people. It can be less a question of food availability and more a question of the conditions and structures that permit access at affordable prices; and when demand goes up, as during famines, so too will prices, according to the logic of the market. During Niger's 2005 hunger crisis, food availability was not the main issue, because it was available in the markets. Similarly, market stalls were packed with provisions just outside a variety of make-shift refugee camps in Cambodia in 1993, but few could afford to take advantage. Every element of these crises reveals, under close scrutiny, changeable behaviour, barring rainfall (Sen 1999).

Food supply and nutritional development are vital for a child's healthy development, and are central to their ability to fight water-borne diseases, among other illnesses. Global Health Watch reported in 2005, however, that 'undernutrition is by far the most important single cause of illness and death globally, accounting for 12% of all deaths ...' (Global Health Watch 2005: 225; Sen 1999). Thomas notes that 15 million people die of hunger-related causes each year, roughly the equivalent to the number killed in eleven years of world war (2000: 9). Baylis and Smith argue that while:

> The production of food to meet the demands of a burgeoning population has been one of the outstanding global achievements of the post-war period, there are nevertheless around 800 million people in forty-six countries who are malnourished, and forty thousand die every day from hunger-related causes. (2001: 574)

Bellamy and McDonald identify a similar range of deaths from mal-nutrition (2002: 374). Global Health Watch further note that 'low weight for age is associated with more than half of all deaths in young children, accounting for more than six million children a year' (2005: 225). Gold-stein spares no punches when he declares that:

Every six seconds, somewhere in the world, a child dies as a result of malnutrition. That is more than 600 every hour, 14,000 every day, and 5 million every year. The world produces enough food to nourish these children and enough income to afford to nourish them, but their own families or States do not have enough income. They die, ultimately, from poverty. (2006: 457)

It is not a coincidence that the high percentage of deaths occurs in poor countries, because poverty ensures many things, including underfunded education and healthcare, debt repayment, subjection to external economic intervention, and many other elements that indirectly lead to direct lethal consequences for the most vulnerable people. These are the indirect, institutional and structural determinants of direct killers of children.

The U5MR is a reflection of a range of factors determined by human decisions normally set in national and international institutions and governed by what are claimed to be objective truths. When human activity is openly recognized as the predominant cause of more than 10 million child deaths per year, it reveals priorities in political, social and economic interventions that can be changed. Careful accounting of the relationship between millions of children's deaths, on the one hand, and changeable human agency, on the other, leads to the inexorable conclusion that those children do not have to die; but resource accessibility issues determine who lives and dies. The market does not function in a vacuum, however; it is governed by human-made rules such as protectionism, as well as by public international financial institutions (IFIs).

Maternal mortality

It is an accepted fact that some women and children will die during their pregnancy or in the act of birthing. This happens in states that have fully functioning, accessible nationwide health protection, as well as those less advantaged. But in general, these figures are low because many of the conditions that lead to prenatal, perinatal and post-natal complications are treatable if access to qualified professionals with appropriate resources can be affected. Maternal mortality refers to:

The number of women who die from any cause related to or aggravated by pregnancy or its management (excluding accidental or incidental causes) during pregnancy and childbirth or within 42 days of termination of pregnancy, irrespective of the duration and site of the pregnancy. (WHO 2005: 10)

The World Health Organization (WHO) records that 'every minute of every day a woman dies in pregnancy or childbirth' (ibid.). They add that '529,000 [expectant mothers] die each year ... with few signs of global improvement in this situation' (ibid.: 10). The UNDP commented that most maternal mortality affects the developing world, 'where the maternal mortality ratio is 540 deaths per 100,000 live births' with most occurring in Africa and Asia (ibid.: 32). Typically, these figures will be unrepresentative of reality. The WHO 'estimates that maternal deaths are under-reported by as much as 50% because deaths are not classified correctly, or more often, not counted at all' and adds that in '62 countries ... there are no maternal mortality data whatsoever'. The WHO Assistant Director-General on Family and Community Health remarked that 'if dead women are not even counted, then it seems they do not count. We have an invisible epidemic' (www.news-media.org). Things are only invisible, however, if people do not look.

Of these deaths of pregnant women, the UNDP claims, 'most ... are avoidable: around three-quarters could be prevented through low-cost interventions' (UNDP 2005: 32). The absence of 'low-cost interventions' is the core of this concern. This diversion of resources – for they exist, but not in the right place at the right time for half a million women – leaves surviving children without their mothers, adding yet more to the burden upon young and vulnerable people globally, but especially in the developing world. It creates orphans, it can overburden those who are forced to adopt and ensures that the youngest do not have the protection and legitimacy of mother parents. It can also result in lifelong attachment disorders that prevent normal social development and result in emotionally unstable youths who may never recover from the absence of an early primary carer bond (Levy and Orlans 1998).

There are normally multiple reasons for women's deaths during pregnancy. The WHO argues that, regardless of the concept of healthcare, it is the context in which that model of healthcare is delivered which explains limited progress in reducing more widely the maternal mortality figures. WHO claims that 'when women die in childbirth, it is usually the result of a cascade of breakdowns in their interactions with the health system' (2005: 22). Women are rendered vulnerable to lethal outcomes because of poor state healthcare; limited communications infrastructure and transport between rural areas and health centre provision; poverty and ignorance causing susceptibility to poor childbearing practice; limited birth attendance by adequately trained medical staff of all levels; and waiting lists for abortions where pregnancy causes health problems.

One report identified 67,500 maternal deaths from severe anaemia alone, the majority of which cases could have been treated with relatively low-level medical intervention (UNICEF 2004: 36). Another report identified 19 million unsafe abortions per year leading to 70,000 deaths (Grimes et al. 2006; Shah 2004). Many of those deaths occur because pregnancy has not been planned or prevented, and this is aggravated by various conservative religious interventions that admonish and threaten punishment for the use of contraception. Glasier et al. are concerned that 'the increasing influence of conservative political, religious, and cultural forces around the world threatens to undermine progress ... and arguably provides the best example of the detrimental intrusion of politics into public health' (2006: 1598).

Just as significantly, but underscored by deeper structural causes, is the long-term denial of essentials to female children from birth. It is common in poor societies with inadequate state social provision set in a deeply patriarchal context for females to be discriminated against routinely. Maternal mortality is also strongly affected by this destructive phenomenon, because in such societies and circumstances 'women are denied adequate nutrition and health care right from their births [and] consequently they have poor physical growth' as a result of their second-class status in comparison with their male counterparts. Figures released in 1996 suggested that 'a smaller proportion of girls (three girls versus seven boys out of ten) showed normal growth' (Karkal 1996: 2).

Such obviously unequal treatment from birth has lethal ramifications as children become adults and active in the reproductive cycle. It is not just the failure of adequate healthcare provision and poverty which cause women to die in pregnancy, or the prioritization of boys above girls for scarce food and medical care. Partner violence during pregnancy also 'accounts for a substantial but largely unrecognised proportion of maternal mortality'. The WHO report added that 'being killed by a partner has ... been identified as an important cause of maternal deaths in Bangladesh and in the United States' (2002: 102). This violence is commonplace, in that it is not restricted to a particular era, class or geography. This is because it shares its origins with most other forms of violent male-to-female relations. These are habitually based on male perceptions of 'ownership' of a woman; challenges to 'masculinity' and associated notions of 'honour'; and religious and social endorsement of male superiority. These attitudes are here considered aspects of andrarchy: the common rule, domination and primacy of males all but globally.

Statistics are as yet unreliable owing to under-reporting and under-recording for the same systemic reasons that afflict the reporting of domestic violence and rape, which Watts and Zimmerman claim is 'almost universal' (2002: 1232). It is not a coincidence that other areas of female mortality and physical violence are under-reported. The inaccuracy of rape and domestic violence statistics in Europe and the USA occurs for the same reasons that maternal mortality is not properly investigated or recorded. A key issue in the context of this work is that, of those recorded with any degree of reliability, some 75 per cent of the women who die during pregnancy do not have to die and can be saved by human agency and intervention, according to the UNDP. Any response requires recognition of root cause to implement change. But it will also require that men and some other women place greater value on women's health. To do that, attitudes that view women as inferior at the conceptual sex and gender level will have to be considered. It is this structured relationship which explains much that happens to women when men dominate global, national and local power structures that determine the allocation of scarce resources.

Intimate murder

Radford and Russell (1992), Penn and Nardos (2003) and Russell and Harmes (2001) have developed accessible and comprehensive surveys of evidence and argument regarding a wide range of female deaths which are presented together as 'intimate murder'. Although a superficial examination of female killing around Europe, the USA, Asia, the Middle East, Latin America and Africa might not immediately suggest an association, closer scrutiny suggests that they share similar institutional and structural determinants relating to male control of women's behaviour.

'Intimate murder' is here used to refer to three classifications of killings of women which may initially appear discrete but which, it will be argued, are connected on a continuum of control. These are 'regular' domestic (partner or spouse) murder; dowry murders; and 'honour' killings. Motives may overlap in many cases. UNIFEM considers violence to include 'any act ... that results in, or is likely to result in, physical, sexual or psychological harm or suffering to women including threats of such acts, coercion or arbitrary deprivation of liberty, whether occurring in public or private life' (2003).

According to Amnesty International, of all women murdered globally, up to 70 per cent are murdered by male partners (2004: 26). In many places, it is accepted socially. Ahmed-Ghosh refers us to India, but her comments could as easily apply to most other places now and at different historical points. She notes that 'the socialization of girls and women has been so powerful that women feel they deserve ... abuse and [they] consent to subservient roles'. She adds that 'in a familial setting, [women] also "consent" to perpetrating violence against other women'. Often mothers-in-law, by virtue of their authority over a wife, will also use violence against their sons' wives and/or will be involved in their murders, cover-ups and disposals. More than 56 per cent of women surveyed on the matter in India:

> Thought they deserved ... beatings and considered a moderate amount of abuse as justifiable for disciplining the wife ... Neglecting the house or children was a valid reason for a beating [as was] food that was not cooked well or served on time, talking disrespectfully to the husband or to the in-laws, complaining about the in-laws, excessive socializing, infertility or the inability to bear sons, inadequate dowry, and essentially not making the husband the priority and centre of attention at all times. (Ahmed-Ghosh 2004: 109–10)

Surveys and experiences in Europe have revealed that similar attitudes persist, despite democratic and social 'enlightenment'. The World Bank records that 'in Europe, domestic violence against women is the major cause of death and incapacity for women aged 16–44 and accounts for more death and disability than cancer and traffic accidents' (UNFPA 2005: 1; Amnesty International 2004: 7). Amnesty International declares that 'in the USA, four women die each day as a result of violence in the family – about 1,400 women per year' (2004: 26) In Pakistan, 300 women are killed every year in domestic murder cases and 'husbands are known to kill their wives even for trivial offences' (Yoodee and Quezada-Zagada 2003: 48). In Russia, 14,000 women were killed by an intimate partner or ex-partner in 1998 (*The Times*, 9 January 2004: 27). Many more are murdered by other relatives, including from their own families. This unequal relationship occurs in every country on earth, and beatings convert easily into murders. Amnesty International estimates that violence will be used against one in every three women on average (2004: 7). That is, approximately every third female on the planet has been or will experience male abuse.

Because such a high proportion of these violent incidents derive from controlling behaviour, they share common origins with intimate partner murder. Reasons for most violent incidents include, but are not limited to, behaviour recollected and replicated from childhood experiences; male absorption of wider social conditioning regarding the propriety of violence in the home; perceptions of it being 'appropriate' punishment of women for perceived/actual infidelity; punishment for leaving; punishment for non-conformity with expectations of domestic role-play; non-payment of dowry; and insults to male and familial 'honour'. Considering intimate murders' structural and institutional causes therefore helps us also understand the structural and ideational roots of other incidents of violence against intimate partners. This sense of a structural, persistent aspect to intimate murder is considered by Radford and Russell (1992: 3–4). In common with many other writers and researchers who preceded them, they argue that:

> Rape, sexual harassment, pornography, and physical abuse of women and children are all different expressions of male sexual violence rather than discrete, disconnected issues ... The notion of a continuum ... facilitates the analysis of male sexual violence as a form of control central to the maintenance of patriarchy.

Noting various connections between attitudes towards women who may be involved in openly independent, norm-defying sexual and social behaviour, some scholars have concluded that the greater the deviation from the male control norm, the more severe the punishment meted out. Radford and Russell (1992) discuss these punishments in some detail, and it is well worth quoting at length. Punishment may consist of:

> A wide variety of verbal and physical abuse, such as rape, torture, sexual slavery (particularly in prostitution), incestuous and extrafamilial child sexual abuse, physical and emotional battery, sexual harassment ... genital mutilation ... forced heterosexuality, forced sterilization, forced motherhood, psychosurgery, denial of food to women in some cultures, cosmetic surgery and other mutilations in the name of beauty. (ibid.: 15)

Radford and Russell conclude that widespread deaths from such treatment deserve and require conceptualization as 'femicide' (ibid.: 15; Siyachitema 2003: 29). Distinguishing and deploying this term are important because it identifies the sex of the victims distinct from the homicide category, with which many people are familiar as a general term. The problem with homicide's generality is that it obscures the difference between male and female and, with it, the intent of the killing, while it is obscured itself by some official constabulary recording methodologies.

For an increasing literature, lethal intent is considered political, in the sense that much woman-killing has a power dimension, and the study of politics is for many the study of power. Russell argues that 'the killing

of females by males because they are female ... [will] reject
conception of woman killing as a private and/or a pathologi
She adds, crucially, that 'when men murder women or girls, ___
dynamics of misogyny and/or sexism are almost always involved' [Rus-
sell and Harmes 2001: 3). Hence, male-to-female killing in this context
is a product of learned/experienced hatreds, perceived and externally
reinforced fears and mistrust of females, and reactions to challenges to
traditional male-dominated assumptions. It is thus often conditioned by
very broad experiences accumulated over time and through institutional
purview. The stereotype of the 'loner' and 'outsider', suggesting that
such killings are anomalies, may be true in specific instances, but it is
not true with regard to the vast majority of deaths of intimate partners.
Such considerations lead Russell and Harmes (ibid.: 4) to define femicide
as 'lethal hate crime' against females. It is the product of accumulated
experiences reinforced by and within social, political and economic
institutions and 'cultures' resulting in the murder of girls and women
because they are female. Its extent is global.

Male murder of female partners occurs all over the world as a persistent, structural action. In some places, however, it is represented using
different language and definitions, with 'culture' also introduced to both
explain and legitimize partner murders. Two other examples of partner
murder are rarely considered in the same sentence as domestic violence
in the West, but they share the same outcome – the deliberate murder
of a female spouse or partner. They also share the same determinants
– failure to satisfy male expectations and social and institutional condemnation of the females' 'failures'. These are 'honour' killings and
dowry deaths.

'Honour' killings

As has been noted, proposing a connection between domestic murder in Europe and the USA, and 'honour' killings and 'dowry' murders,
primarily in Africa, Latin America, Asia and the Middle East, may seem
incongruous. Close inspection of the determinants of these categories of
femicide, however, reveals marked commonalities which link the world's
continents and countries in terms of female partner murder.

These variants of the killing of females (and sometimes men) by partners and relatives are normally sanitized and insulated by association with
'culture'. It is considered by many that the culture of other peoples is not
the subject of intervention from outside, partly because it is associated
with the arrogance and hubris of imperialism, or contemporary racial

superiority. The cultural legitimization that attends these acts, however, conceals their brutality and their learned nature. Once this veneer is removed for observation purposes, the killings have little or nothing to do with a specifically claimed culture, and much more to do with inherited misogyny, anticipated control 'rights' and male domination. They share, in fact, all their basic causes with partner killing in the West.

Where they differ slightly, however, is in the degree to which social and institutionalized legitimacy is conferred upon them. That is, the learning environments in which they occur most routinely rarely uphold sexual equality in any significant form. Furthermore, aberration from male rules is either punished lightly, not punished at all, concealed from constabulary, excluded from legislation, or broadly supported. Since all these social institutions share learned origins, and since perpetrators can be understood to have learned legitimately and believe in the propriety of their actions, 'honour' and dowry killings here are referred to as *belief* killings. This term will be applied throughout this book after the concept of 'honour' has been more thoroughly dissected.

The term 'honour killing' is a disturbing expression. First, the concept of 'honour' is rarely the subject of critical consideration. Second, while masculine in construction, its rules are applied to both sexes. A man's 'honour' in relation to the behaviour of an intimate female codifies the behaviour he must follow in certain circumstances and which she must display at all times. Males rarely ever consider how they themselves are bound to and disadvantaged by 'honour'. For example, a man may have to 'defend a woman's honour'. This reveals a complex web of behaviours that can readily result in fear, violence and death. That a man may also be stripped of 'honour' and ostracized for failing to participate in suicidal activities, such as trench warfare, when he is understandably terrified, already emotionally battered and often suffering from post-traumatic stress disorder, is still considered reasonable. Indeed, recent attempts to posthumously pardon British soldiers executed for 'cowardice' or deser-tion during the First World War meet with very mixed reactions.

But across the board, these behaviours and responses, and the values that drive them, are learned, subjective social and moral codes: they are not fixed, permanent written rules. Rather, they are fluid notions that change with the times. For example, conscientious objection was once considered cowardice and, in some quarters, it still qualifies a candidate as Lacking in Moral Fibre (LMF). But society broadly will not routinely condemn the man that refuses to go to war for his country, even when he is a serving officer.

Honour is also considered differently in different regions simultaneously. In the Second World War, Japanese suicide pilots who killed themselves deliberately by crashing their aircraft into American warships were perceived quite differently on the other side of the Pacific at the same time. Furthermore, within Japan across time, the practice of 'honourable' suicide has declined in virtue, while in parts of the Middle East its currency has increased. Suicide by Islamic fighters is considered 'honourable' and is claimed to result in martyrdom; few in the West accept this or attempt to understand how such an act may be considered 'honourable'.

In the West, 'honour' is constituted and acquired in a range of ways. Perhaps the most obvious and ultimate form comes from winning in institutional conflict. It is celebrated with medals, among other things. Outside of traditional conflict, honour can be achieved in sport, especially in a violent competition like rugby, among others. In Victorian England, a man retained his honour by fighting with other contenders for his choice of woman, and such honour was codified in rituals, such as slapping an offending male across the face with gloves and then casting them on the floor in front of the other male's feet (Kunzel 1993). Non-response to such a challenge was considered 'dishonourable', as were most forms of not 'bravely' facing confrontation and violence. The female played only a very limited role in these exchanges, but her acceptance of her place and meaning in such behaviours is evidence of structure, rather than mere gender domination.

Women also actively perpetuate this taught social construction. Women as mothers and sisters, aunts and grandmothers or friends participate in and pass on the oratory and rhetoric of 'honour' as 'appropriate' behavioural codes. They have regulated one another in a most remarkable form of self-censure, considering that it can so easily work against them as a demonizing agent. Women rebuke other women for their rejection of male mores and expectations and discipline their own sex in accordance with male-instigated rules that ensure that male expectations of female behaviour are met. Women that refuse to cooperate with this particular control regime are castigated and punished continually. In short, such has been the normalization of social rules designed by males and perpetuated through long-standing institutions that the majority of males and females uncritically accept a social order that unnecessarily in many cases facilitates male domination of females' choices and rights.

For women, 'honour' was also something that had to be preserved. In the past, it was codified in the retention of virginity before marriage; by adopting particular social graces in Victorian times; and more recently in the last century by taking only few (or no) sexual partners prior to early marriage. Contemporaneously, the notion of a woman's 'virtue' is still, to some degree, measured by her sexual abstinence. Women who take 'too many' sexual partners may be vilified in language, by both men and women conforming to 'honour' codes, as 'sluts', 'whores' or 'cheap'. Conjoining the two, it has been men's duty to 'protect' a woman's 'honour' from abuse by other men. In such a manner, a woman is deemed of sufficient 'virtue' to be married to particular males. If the honour is in some way judged to be absent, she is a 'fallen woman' and less suitable for the 'higher-end' male. This system of 'honour' before betrothal remains routine in many parts of South and South-East Asia.

Where the term 'honour' is most often applied to women, it refers to women's accession to and maintenance of male-determined sexual and other social codes of behaviour that differentiate the socially acceptable sexual behaviours of men and women throughout most of the world. In other words, a woman's 'honour' is upheld by her adherence to male rules and various males in this endeavour protect her, including those from her own family. 'Honour' killing is normally committed by males and supported by the females of the family of the males conducting the murder, for the notion of 'honour' extends from the patriarch through his sons and daughters. In many societies, because of male domination over social affairs, many women and men condone actively or through their enforced acquiescence this extreme form of female behaviour control. It is associated in its most obvious and condoned forms in 'macho' societies where masculinity is widely respected or condoned for its socially constructed content and its 'legitimate' domination of women.

Thus, associating woman partner-killing (and many more kinds of non-terminal violence) with 'honour' readily legitimizes the act and sets it in a particular and specifically constructed cultural context. Social and institutional legitimization function in unison and ensure that the practice is conducted with relative impunity. Murderers are rarely punished proportionately, if at all, for their acts, and 'honour' dignifies the murder of a woman where the practice is socially accepted. The longer such language is applied to what in other countries would be classified as a spousal murder, the longer women will be murdered for offending men. Because of this problem of legitimation, this book refers to 'honour' killing as belief murder; the men involved believe they have the right to murder women when the women do not conform to a variety of private and public 'rules' of social and private expression.

Having established some of the social rules and conventions governing this particular form of woman murder, and having established that 'culture' is only learned behaviour and thus neither inviolable nor immutable, we may turn to the conduct of belief killings. According to the UN Population Fund, such rituals occur in Bangladesh, Brazil, Ecuador, Egypt, India, Israel, Italy, Jordan, Morocco, Pakistan, Sweden, Turkey, Uganda and the United Kingdom (Penn and Nardos 2003: 87). Given the range of national identities that populate the United States, it will also occur there. It is pervasive and normally either unpunished or feebly sanctioned by formal institutions in many places, which equates to state condonement. According to Goldstein: 'In the late 1990's, "honour" killings accounted for more than two-thirds of all homicides reported among Palestinians in the West Bank and Gaza. In 1997, roughly 400 women were killed for "honour" in Yemen. In 1999, over a thousand Pakistani women were killed for this cause [sic]' (2002: 31). In Alexandria, Egypt, it was found that of female deaths '47 per cent of the women were killed by a relative after [because] they had been raped' (WHO 2002: 93). Reported incidents are 'on the rise worldwide', according to the UN special rapporteur on 'extrajudicial, summary and arbitrary executions' (UNFPA 2000: 29). The killings occur in most of the places dowry killings happen and their occurrences are normally denied to foreigners who investigate. Overall, the United Nations Population Fund 'estimates that over five thousand women die in honor killings every year' (ibid.: 35); while the WHO affirms that 'in many places, notions of male honour ... put women at risk' (2002: 93; Connell 2000: 218–19). A neglected aspect of this is that men are also put at risk; they may be the victim of attacks; they may be injured physically or mentally during the reprisal; and they may be jailed and removed from their sons and other family members.

Belief killings are responses to women's behaviour that challenges male dominance. Francis argues that:

> It is an important element in prevailing models of masculinity that men should be dominant. A man who is not in command of his wife [or other socially determined 'subject'] is seen as a figure of fun, comical because he is not a 'real man'. From a position of control he may properly behave 'gallantly', but that is a matter of ... the choice of the powerful to act with magnanimity. (2004: 66)

The punishment is not always lethal. One example that demonstrates the public shaming role as a means to end a woman's life was that of

Mukhtaran Mai. Mukhtaran was gang-raped, a common punishment in Pakistan (one of the worst offenders in extremes of violence against women), for 'wrong-doing'. Her 'crime' had been that her younger brother had consorted with, or raped, depending on the sources, a girl from a higher caste (*Sunday Times*, 26 November 2006: 21). Because the boy from the lower caste brought shame on the family of the girl from the higher caste, punishment was meted out to Mukhtaran Mai.

Mukhtaran Mai got the blame and punishment because of male conceptions of honour. The punishment physically was directed at Mukhtaran Mai, but the psychological intent was to recoup male honour. In rape, however, especially group rape and even more so public group rape, massive long-term psychological trauma attaches to the victim. The punishment was both direct and indirect. The direct attacks of gang rape in themselves would have been unbearable, almost certainly likely to cause severe tissue damage, haemorrhaging, bruising to the genitalia as well as to other parts of her body where restraint was applied by a group of males, before we even consider the emotional long-term damage done to the woman. But the 'shame' attached to having been violated by males other than a spouse in Pakistan besmirches a woman's 'honour' to the extent that her 'culture' directs her to commit suicide. In other words, as well as the males' direct, physical brutality, which is less likely to end in her death, an indirect sentence is also passed whereby her death is the expected outcome as a result of male-directed codes of honour.

Mukhtaran Mai survived, however, and, controversially, took her attackers to court and won in an internationally supported and reported trial. Critics in Pakistan claimed she was damaging Pakistan's reputation because rape happens everywhere. While rape does happen everywhere, in many parts of that country it is, however, socially institutionalized as just and appropriate, and has the long-term consequences of social disembowelment for any woman who survives it. It is therefore a life-long punishment that transcends one of the most basic of civilizational rights not to be arbitrarily violated on the grounds of sex and gender. Attempts to change the law and make rape more prosecutable have met with deeply entrenched resistance. This is because the institutions that preserve or transform these kinds of behaviour almost always comprise males locked into behaviours that damage them, as well as women. In other words, challenging 'tradition' and 'culture' would likely result in social ostracism and, sometimes, verbal and physical attacks from enraged men.

These are not straightforward issues. Belief murders are, according to Sev'er, 'the premeditated murder of preadolescent, adolescent, or adult women by one or more male members of the immediate or extended family' (Sev'er 2001: 964–5). This definition unfortunately neglects the evidence that shows that women are also participating in this act. Sev'er's work expands, however, to include the motivation of such acts. She argues that they occur when there is an 'allegation, suspicion or proof of sexual impropriety by the victim' who is not subject to any rule of law other than the family and community's belief and is presumed guilty on the basis of nothing more than an allegation (ibid.: 965; HRW 2004: 1). For Kordvani, it is the murder of 'a woman who has … breached a social norm of female sexuality or is merely under suspicion of acting as such' (2002: 8). These codes of conduct do not emanate from nowhere; they have been and are formulated and codified by men. Gendercide Watch claim that:

> A woman is killed for her actual or perceived immoral behavior … Such 'immoral behavior' may take the form of marital infidelity, refusing to submit to an arranged marriage, demanding a divorce, flirting with or receiving phone calls from men, failing to serve a meal on time, or – grotesquely – 'allowing herself' to be raped. In the Turkish province of Sanliurfa, one young woman's 'throat was slit in the town square because a love ballad was dedicated to her over the radio'. (2006)

Similarly, a Turkish wife who publicized her husband's violence was shot five times by her son, who told her she 'had disgraced the family' (*Guardian*, 21 May 2005: 17). Sev'er notes that 'disgraceful' and 'immoral' behaviour may include 'going to the movies without [male] approval or a [male] chaperone, to kissing, holding hands, dating or having intercourse with a man who is not one's culturally or legally sanctioned husband' (2001: 965). Rape is perceived as caused by female behaviour and thus the man cannot be blamed; this differs little from quite recent expressions of responsibility placed on female rape survivors for wearing particular types of dress in Europe. They are responsible for the male's behaviour and the law has quite often sanctioned such attitudes, in the West and elsewhere. Punishment can be harsh:

> In Jordan, one woman was knifed to death because she wanted to continue her education and refused to marry the man chosen for her by her family. Another woman was shot five times because she ran away from her husband who continually beat and raped her. Another had her throat

slit because her husband suspected her of adultery – he saw her speaking with a man from their village. In Pakistan, a young mother of two sons was shot dead by a family acquaintance because she had sought divorce from an abusive husband. Another woman was shot dead in front of a tribal gathering after she had been repeatedly raped by a local government official. (Feminist.com 2006)

This level of violence is commonplace and to be found in dowry killings also. Men and women, as well as children (more often male), participate in plotting, executing and concealing the murders. Sev'er maintains that punishment is severe because in various locations, 'The greatest dishonour of a man derives from the impurity of his wife ... Fathers and other male kin before marriage exercise full rights to sanction women who deviate. Husbands and their male kin assume this task during marriage and even after its dissolution' (2001: 973; Fadia 2001: 70–72). The attitude towards such instances of violence of the mainly male perpetrators and the absence of remorse, regret or self-doubt demonstrate the levels of social conviction and condonement involved. For example, two men who murdered their younger sister in Pakistan declared that they 'felt no shame ... [They] did it for honour ... In our society a man without honour is nothing'. Others present at the same killing added their verdict that 'it was a good job ... It was the correct thing to do' (*Guardian*, 7 February 2007: 23).

Adherence to 'honour' determines the social status of a woman before her betrothal to a man. Social nonconformity diminishes the opportunity for marriage with a 'respected' male because he must have a 'respectable' female or his 'honour' is contaminated. During marriage, the female must continue to conform to these expectations of public behaviour, but she must also adhere to additional private rules. Failure to do so implies that the man has married below his position and she thus humiliates him in his choice. But more than this, she demonstrates that he does not control her because she breaks the rules made by men. In turn, his status is questioned and the way to re-establish it is to kill the offender. In this way are women's lives controlled in many parts of the developing world. It is a product of specific institutions that communicate values attached to women's behaviour everywhere and is informed by the belief systems of andrarchy and the permissible roles of women in wealth creation, poverty avoidance and the varilocal family structure.

Thus, the onus on predetermined social behaviour falls very much on females. Yet men also are victims, in that their responses to such issues are formulated by rules which, if they do not follow them, will result in a loss of perceived 'honour' in front of other males. The social rules, then, are painfully deleterious for both men and women; but women are killed for them (as well as a relatively very small number of males). It should also be borne in mind that heterosexual males also kill homosexual males, for some of the same reasons: that is, homosexuality in many places remains a severe and unacceptable aberration from 'acceptable' normality.

Problematically, this 'culture' migrates from where it is practised in social environments that may condone it to other regions where it is not supported. This has led to debates regarding cultural relativism and multiculturalism across Europe and America. The reluctance with which legislatures involve themselves in sometimes murderous imported customs reveals the sensitivities attached to intervening in the cultures of others. Given, however, that such 'cultures' are little more than learned behaviours that deny mainly female human rights to lives free of violence, intervention is entirely appropriate and perpetrators can reasonably be punished in the setting of the law of the land without risk of accusations of racism. An example in Europe where this has occurred is Germany, where a variety of extreme instances of violence against Asian women are conducted by their husbands, whose behaviour was both condoned and legitimized with paltry sentences that would not have been applied to ethnic German husbands for the same crime. This itself was racist (Coomaraswamy and Fonseka 2004: 27).

Dowry murder

The third intimate murder category of dowry is a complex but nonetheless rule-governed social issue and the rules that lead to its execution are shared with many of the causes of female children dying before the age of five, and as victims of infanticide. These mortalities are connected by sex (female) and economic value (low) caused by the social relegation of females generally. That is, public life options, such as paid employment, may be restricted by social views of the place of females in the home. Capacity to take up higher-level employment is undermined by girls' relegation behind boys in education opportunities. This decreases female independence, which in turn is reflected in the social value and marriageability of females in terms of the 'honour' they achieve by staying in the home. These are all control issues. Furthermore, the cost of raising a female child undermines the social security of a family during the child's early life, and then adds greater financial toll to her family when it is time for her to marry – and she will have been less likely to have her own job to militate against the impoverishment she brings because this may decrease her chances of marriage. These are all socially connected problems.

At its most simple, dowry is a payment made by the family of a bride to the family of the groom. It is undertaken because, economically speaking, the woman will be 'unproductive' in her new family. She will be a wife and will tend to her husband's parents in their infirmity, as well as rear his children, which should be boys. She will buy food at the market, cook and clean, and ensure her husband's 'honour' is sustained and authenticated by her own social conduct. None of these responsibilities, however, generates cash for her sustenance: food, clothing, healthcare and so on. The dowry is designed to cover such economic 'shortfalls'. It reflects the 'exaltation of the married state as the only desirable or socially acceptable state for women ... Parents of girls ... offer a dowry, in cash and kind ... as enticements to prospective grooms' (Narasimhan 1994: 45). (It should be noted that a diminished element of 'dowry' persists in the West; the father of the bride often pays for the wedding.)

Dowry should not be confused with a sale. It is instead a more complex economic compensation programme which reflects the perceived and actual cost of 'maintaining' a woman whose patriarchally fixed household role excludes her from recovering her 'cost' through working outside the home for payment. The contradiction is immediate and obvious: she is marginalized economically from working and earning an income to pay her way, but simultaneously her family must bear the costs of this deficit. Male rules often normally exclude dowry wives' economic independence and in so doing reinforce their dependence on the bride's family's income, for which the bride's family may be penalized from the time of proposal onwards. This is a fairly strict interpretation of conditions that aggravate dowry; understanding the most elemental aspects, however, reveals the extent of social institutionalism involved.

In a sense, it is a debt transfer: the debt was owned by the family into which she was born, but the cost involved in 'maintaining' her after she is married remains the responsibility of her biological family. Her family must pay this cost; she is a financial burden while she cooks, cleans and cares for her new husband's parents and bears and raises the children of her new family. Her economic needs appear as a debit to the new family partly because her household input is discounted, in much the same way as a Western woman's contribution to the household is only recently attracting the financial recognition it deserves. Mies records that:

The bride's family is eager to marry off their daughter because an unmarried woman still has neither place nor status in patriarchal India. Therefore, brides' parents eventually give in to the dowry demands of the 'other side'. If they don't have the money to hand, they take out loans. In a survey of 105 families in Bangalore ... 66 per cent of the families had incurred debts in order to marry off their daughters. Or they promise to pay more after the marriage ... Often the harassment starts immediately ... She is often subjected to all kinds of humiliations and brutalities. (1998: 147)

In societies in which dowry remains common practice, failure to provide such transfers of cash and goods can result in punishment. Sometimes, social gossip can be enough to damage a poor family's community standing and reputation. Failure to pay dowry costs, however, can also result in the murder of the bride. Wives are commonly killed because their families are unable to subsidize the cost attached to transferring her to another family. The killings are also linked to 'honour'. The 'honour' of the bride's family has been besmirched by their son's marriage to a low-value family that embarrasses them by being unable to complete the socially contracted dowry payments.

For this reason, and many others shared with partner killing, murder figures are difficult to estimate because of their similarity to and crossover with belief killings. The two processes can overlap; failure of a wife's family to produce the appropriate dowry dishonours the bride and his family and the 'failed' wife is then subject to death for crimes of honour and dowry combined (WHO 2002: 93). Yoodee and Quezada-Zagada (2003: 49) and Amnesty International (2001: 12) put the figures at a little short of seven thousand in 1998. The Indian National Crime Records Bureau records that every day, one woman is burned because she has insufficient dowry value. It also records that other marriage killings happen approximately once per hour (*The Times*, 26 December 2006: 37). On the basis of the Indian National Crime Records Bureau figures, then, roughly 8,760 women are murdered as a result of marriage in India per year. Despite being banned, dowry abuse is 'on the increase' (Mies 1998: 147); and 'honour' killings in Pakistan are 'reported to have increased by 50%' in 2003 (Gaag 2004: 26). As has been noted before, these figures are bound to be on the low side because of reporting and recording acts and omissions.

Rising expectations, or 'relative deprivation', have aggravated this situation (Jeong 2000: 69–70). The 'cost' involved in a woman's family

transfer indicates the relative economic value of women in such situations, common in South Asia. This in turn reflects other social issues. In
the worst cases, she is of low value because her gendered role is restricted
to the home and she is expensive because she cannot be economically
productive and will be expensive to pass on to another family through
marriage. This is changing as women achieve greater independence in
some places, but conditions in many parts of Asia are still especially
severe. As long as wider social and institutional determinants of her
possible roles remain, she will always be an economic burden, a drag,
on either her own family if she remains single, or the one into which
she marries. If she stays single, she may look after her parents in their
old age, but she is unlikely to have sufficient income to sustain herself
and her parents because of her early years' educational marginalization
and her subsequent labour exclusion. She may also be mistrusted in her
community: unmarried women 'of a certain age' may be seen as threats
to the married women. Furthermore, she is less likely to have her own
children and therefore less likely to be able to sustain herself in older
age. Things are not well set up for girls and women in these types of
social orders.

Dowry killings draw attention to other social practices that sustain
and legitimize this process. Women are sometimes killed for dowry in
public places, quite openly. The nature of such punishment is violently
humiliating. As if poverty were not enough to mark out a family and their
lives, their daughter may be publicly burned, like rubbish. Some have
argued that this reflects a far deeper view of women by men as 'less than
human' (MacKinnon 2006). Others suggest that the social development
of males from an early age conditions them to expect quite profound
sacrifice by women, a process that may indeed lead to misogyny regarding 'failed' women. A public dowry burning is not far removed from the
voyeurism and hatred of a female 'snuff' killing.

Dowry killings follow the failure of the bride and her family to satisfy
the historically, socially informed (and thus learned, not innate) expectations of the groom and his family upon marriage, and to satisfy the
economic demands of the groom's family for assuming varilocal (household) responsibility for the expenses incurred by the bride. This occurs
in a social, learned environment that prohibits women's independence,
and thus undermines their ability to support themselves or otherwise
contribute to their cost of living. A working bride may reflect badly on
a groom, in that he fears being perceived as unable to sustain his own
family; this was also the case in parts of Europe just a few decades ago.

Similarly, a wife's social behaviour beyond the confines of the marital home (where she is allowed to go out; many women in South Asia and elsewhere are forbidden such freedoms) determines levels of respect for the man responsible for her future. Hence the brutal treatment of the women outlined above when they have had contact with males outside the groom's family. Killing the female restores the groom's 'honour', while not taking severe action damages his honour and lowers the status of his family in its locale. This is further underscored by institutional condonement through individuals' socialization. That is, the broad comprehension of women's relative cash worth, and the capacity to exploit for greed a girl's family in more recent times, is carried into the constabulary and judiciary, because these institutions are dominated by males and females who condone, or who reject but refuse to challenge, such violent practices which may be legislatively forbidden.

Fatal female genital mutilation (FGM)

FGM refers to the deliberate removal of a woman's sexual organs, healthy or otherwise. It is not comparable with male circumcision, which has negligible impact on male sexual enjoyment; it is normally explained in terms of hygiene. When performed on women, FGM includes removal of the clitoris, labia and other sexual organs (see below). The clitoris is the only part of the human anatomy whose function is solely to provide pleasure. The penis, for example, has a dual function; it gives pleasure but is also a vessel for waste passage. The clitoris has no other biological function than to give females pleasure. FGM also controls women's adult relationships; a woman who refuses it is stigmatized and considered suspect. She is less likely to marry in her own environment as her social sisters might and her perceived morals and mores render her socially excluded.

The practice is defended both by those who have been cut and those who cut on the grounds of 'custom' and 'culture'. Other dubious defences have included the need to avoid confusion of the clitoris with a penis, the former of which may overgrow, narrowing the distinction between the sexes (Banda 2005: 210). It is also argued that the practice 'makes women clean, promotes virginity and chastity and guards young girls from sexual frustration by deadening their sexual appetite' (Amnesty International 2004: 5). This casts a woman as 'dirty' and likely to enjoy an independent sex life and therefore be 'dishonourable'. That her 'sexual appetite' may remain 'deadened' throughout her life appears not to be a relevant concern.

The process is normally hideous. Amnesty International documents:

> Chronic infections, intermittent bleeding, abscesses and small benign tumours of the nerve associated with the most 'basic' cutting. Infibulation can result in chronic urinary tract infections, stones in the bladder and urethra, kidney damage, reproductive tract infections ... pelvic infections, infertility, excessive scar tissue ... and dermoid cysts. (ibid.: 3)

FGM varies in severity. Infibulation – where all external sexual organs are cut off – is the most extreme. UNICEF declared that 'apart from the immediate fear and pain, the consequences can include prolonged bleeding, infection, infertility and death' (1996: 1). Confusingly for some, many women both condone and perform the operation, sometimes with a qualified nurse using anaesthetic, but mainly using a non-sterile cutting tool in unhygienic circumstances without anaesthetic (Penn and Nardos 2003: 8, 90). Post-cutting sexual activity also carries significant health risks. Sometimes, the woman has to be cut open again – occasionally by her husband – before penetrative sex can occur. This can lead to the increased 'risk of HIV transmission during intercourse' as well as unbearable pain – but not for the man (ibid.: 92; Amnesty International 2004: 3). FGM may not take long, but the consequences are lifelong and, during pregnancy, may also cause the death of a fetus in the womb, as well as that of the pregnant mother.

FGM affects approximately two million women a year. Roughly 98 per cent of Somali women are 'cut' and the practice occurs in states with claims to democratic values such as Egypt, Nigeria, and the Gambia (UNICEF 1996: 1). A demographic survey in Egypt revealed that 97 per cent of post-pubescent women had been cut (UNICEF 2004). The UN records that FGM 'is practiced in about 28 countries in Africa and in the Arabian Peninsula and the Gulf region. It also occurs among some minority groups in Asia, and among immigrant women in Europe, Canada and the United States' (UNFPA 2000: 15–16). An unknown number of women are cut and killed because socially constructed masculine mores reject the propriety of female sexual independence, which might threaten the established hierarchy of male above female. Rowbotham argues that independent female behaviour strikes 'horror into the patriarchal soul' (1977: 124). One medical journal explained that FGM 'conveys a message of control over the sexuality and social position of women and girls. While women themselves appear to defend [FGM] and [perform] it on others, this has to do with women's perception of their role in the world' (El-Dawla 1999: 1). That women will perform this agonizing and sometimes lethal act on other women, when they themselves have often endured it, reflects the extent of male influence over women, and women's projection of male violence on to other women. Howland argues that it will continue with impunity if international legislation does not accept 'a woman's right to control her sexuality and her reproductive capacity'. She continues that 'until [it] is recognized as a universal right superior to cultural norms, this practice and many others will persist' (2001: 83). The commonalities of treatment and excuse – violence disguised by social normalization, and non-commitment on the part of the constabulary underscored by absent protective legislation – are hard to deny or ignore.

FGM is undertaken to wreck a women's sexuality such that her character and social behaviour are more controllable. It is specifically undertaken to reduce women's sexual experiences, sometimes to the extent of negating them altogether or, in other situations, leaving her sexual organs so badly damaged that sex causes indescribable pain and may result in death from blood loss, among other prognoses. Many in the developed world may be unaware that the subject of women's sexuality has long been mythologized and exaggerated to justify male control. History is replete with tales of women whose sexuality has caused the demise of men: Adam and Eve, Samson and Delilah, Antony and Cleopatra, Herod and Salome, Lady Macbeth, David and Bathsheba, Gilgamesh and Enkidu, Lucrece and Tarquin, the Whore of Babylon. For Sanday, 'th[is] association of women with sin and evil gives men the right to dominate' (1981: 11). She further notes that 'the spectacle of the female temptress in the Garden of Eden is by no means unique' (ibid.: 11). Reflecting the perceptions of woman in the Christian Garden of Eden, a respected legal tome was entitled *Eve Was Framed* (Kennedy 1993).

Such social mythologizing is commonplace and used to justify and visit upon women a range of control interventions initiated by men but condoned by many other women who do not wish to be ostracized, expurgated or excommunicated from their wider social environment. The UN notes that 'women's sexuality is often feared and is the subject of bizarre and ferocious myth; severe female genital mutilation is only the most extreme means taken to control it, short of murder' (UNFPA 2000: 37). In this way, women's independent social movements are more controlled in line with male demands and social diktats. Like 'honour' and dowry killings, FGM is routinely explained or defended in terms of culture but is a function of male domination and control. It is exclusive to no single religion or country, no one region or specific historical experience, and it is not the product of any one specific 'tradition' or 'culture'.

The commonality is control by males, often codified and sanctioned by organized and institutionalized religions that condone and enforce male domination of females.

In many cases, FGM does not result in immediate or recorded death, which places it at odds with the other material covered here. The remit of this chapter has been to identify various facets of human insecurity that result in death and, thus far, all the above have satisfied this categorization. FGM is included here because of the likely propensity for undiscovered deaths. Unsurprisingly, the likelihood of reliable, or even available, statistics on FGM deaths being made accessible to international organizations and individuals is low. FGM is a closed practice in the societies in which it is practised but, as we shall see, it affects not dozens but millions of women. Given the levels of male insecurity that attend its 'cultural' origins, the brutality with which it is practised, the lack of medical training in most cases, the institutional endorsement of the practice, and the fact that it is often performed by women on women, two things are apparent. There is likely to be death; and such death is unlikely to be reported and recorded.

These problems are connected by male control expectations, as we have seen, but they are further problematized by the social legitimization of the practice and the absence of Weberian-bureaucratic institutional norms and resources in the states in which they mostly occur. This problem is further underscored by reluctance to notify deaths outside the family. Amnesty International claims that 'the secrecy surrounding FGM, and the protection of those who carry it out, make collecting data about complications resulting from mutilation difficult' (2004: 4). Where no legislation exists to criminalize a culturally legitimized anti-female process conducted in the main by other females who are part of a broader 'family' that encourages and condones the demonization and social exclusion of uncut women, there is neither motive for accountability nor due process for civil or criminal punishment, since no 'crime' has been committed.

Such problems continue to surround domestic violence and the murders associated with this phenomenon, and have similar roots in female control in all spheres by men (see among many other Watts and Zimmerman 2002: 1232; Hanmer and Maynard 1987). It is included here because of its shared causation with other forms of lethal violence against women; because it is similarly hidden but condoned by 'culture'; because like the other forms of violence it is learned and therefore preventable; and because, as with 'honour' killing and domestic violence, its early exposure is associated with low levels of data which later prove to be gross underestimations. When the figures become available, the extent of the practice will likely be as shocking as the revelations surrounding the number of women who have been raped, beaten or killed by their partners and former partners all around the world.

Structural femicide?

What seems to be missing is an overarching term that conveys or categorizes the phenomenon defined as avoidable killing of females resulting from the social rules and economic determinism attached to females in a male-dominated system. Radford and Russell (1992) apply the term 'femicide', in parallel with other terms relating to mass death in relation to a specific identity (for example, 'genocide' or 'ethnocide'). This may not, however, communicate the systematization involved. Rummel (1994) proposes 'serial massacre', but this terminology falls short of a more comprehensive consideration linking single events to broader occurrences over time and geography.

I propose the term 'structural femicide'. Direct and indirect lethal and non-lethal violence against women on a global scale does not happen by chance. It is not independent action by crazed males between whom there are no connections. The violence is linked by socially constructed attitudes that originate in social belief systems that have been culturally codified and correspondingly normalized. Legal systems traditionally have strengthened this power and domination relationship, which in turn legitimizes such locally accepted behaviour as acceptable and normal. It is thence perpetuated over time until challenged, normally by the oppressed group (women), which then faces enormous challenges from entrenched social and legal structures that seek to perpetuate structured relationships that reinforce hierarchies of gender power and inequality.

It is no surprise that women have found it so difficult to adequately challenge and change those hierarchies. Most powerful social, legal, religious and political institutions that exercise power and control public policy are dominated by men whose positions therein are a result of the hierarchies they themselves have created over time. That institutional domination is reflected in an alliance between male perpetrators of crimes against women, on the one hand, and the 'understanding' forgiving sanction by the state of the male criminal.

Such responses to domestic murder do at least two things. First, they demonstrate the lack of seriousness with which some judiciaries view woman murder in a domestic setting, which sends a clear message to other men that they will escape serious custodial sentencing. Second, they trivialize the life and value of women in general. Structures of power and domination derive and maintain their status from beliefs legitimized in their historical longevity, which continue to be transmitted through 'cultural' mores perpetuated in formal and informal education and social-ization. They are thus learned values and experiences and, while they are unlikely to be 'unlearned', other beliefs more favourable to equalitarian principles can be encouraged to replace them over time. These argu-ments will be discussed in greater detail in later chapters, which focus on structural causes of global violence against civilians.

Conclusion

Prontzos reminds us that 'while less dramatic than military violence, structural violence actually accounts for far more deaths than does war'. He adds that 'the number of deaths in an average year from all structural causes is a matter of conjecture, but it probably totals over 50 million' (2004: 300). The UNDP estimates the figure at half this: 'only' 25 million (2003). In contrast, the World Health Report of 2002 estimated total war-related deaths in 2000 at about 310,000 worldwide (WHO 2002: 242). Of these, it has generally been accepted that between 80 and 90 per cent are civilians, of which the majority are women and children. Mack et al. (2005) conclude, however, that most of those people die from what might be termed the detritus of war: food availability and accessibility decline, increased exposure to disease with diminished sanitation capacity, or unexploded ordnance (this is quite distinct from institutional determin-ism of human insecurity. One might suggest Mack's work focuses on war-caused social destruction). Furthermore, the total war-death estimate is falling: 'battle-death' figures in conflicts that included a government stood in 2002 at 'just' 20,000, compared to nearly 700,000 throughout 1950 (ibid.: 4).

One problem this book is concerned with is the relative emphasis placed on resolving narrowly defined conflict when its contribution to the global annual human insecurity toll is minuscule by comparison with the numbers that die from violence defined in a more nuanced, sophisticated and complex interpretation. Despite the chasm between the differing complexities, those deaths are every bit as real for those who bear responsibility or suffer the associated grief and other consequences that accompany global structures of violence as those caused by the gun or the bomb.

The figures below offer a tabulated comparison to demonstrate the differential between war and war-related deaths, on the one hand, and deaths from U5MR, infanticide and maternal mortality, on the other. It is difficult to present a conventional table precisely because of the distinction between direct and indirect violence: the former is intermittent and figures may vary significantly from year to year or may not be estimatable, but the latter is chronic and persistent, permitting reasonable and consistent averages to be derived. In general, that distinction is enormous: while figures are estimates it is their disparity which demonstrates the gulf between the two conceptualizations of security. For the year 2002, most estimates of battle and battle-related deaths, as well as terrorism and the wider issue of 'political violence', suggest the total number of fatalities lies at approximately 222,587. Adding to Mack the victims of genocide and other forms of direct death for that year increases the figure only marginally. In contrast, the figures from indirect violence from human-built and operated structures are phenomenal. The estimates below are drawn from totals of figures from the sources used in this chapter. In each case, they represent 'best' case scenarios. In other words, they use the minimum figures where a range may be apparent. Estimated infanticide figures have been halved to take into account the Johansson and Nygren hypothesis.

TABLE 3.1 Global deaths, 2002

1. Direct, periodic, reflecting 'minimalist' perspective of human security

Battle deaths	Battle-related deaths	Political violence	Terrorism	Total (c.)
20,000	172,000	27,587	3,000	222,587

Mack 2005: 29–44

2. Indirect, chronic, reflecting 'maximalist' perspective and human insecurity definition

Intimate murder	U5MR	Maternal mortality	Infanticide	Total (c.)
5,000 + outside Asia (see above)	c.10,000,000	c. 529,000	est. 500,000	11,000,000

Amnesty International 2001: 12; UNDP 2005: 27; WHO 2005: 10; Watts and Zimmerman 2002: 1236.

Conventional and dominant models and approaches to security consider a maximum lethality of around one quarter of one million deaths in 2002. In contrast, the human security agenda may be faced yearly with approximately eleven million fatalities per year, of which more than two-thirds do not have to die (assuming a maximalist interpretation). As long ago as 1974, Kohler and Alcock proposed that structural violence caused 'almost 1,000 times the violence caused by civil conflict' (1976: 344); the lesson has taken a long time to learn. Global structures and institutions existed then and still exist, causing widescale human insecurity and accounting for an incomparably larger proportion of unnecessary and avoidable deaths than their direct counterparts. The second set of statistics is representative of structural forms and international institutions, and human beings are responsible for the creation, existence, execution and persistence of these entities. They were formed not by magic, but by man.

FOUR | Institutions, the U5MR, infanticide and maternal mortality

Mortality of children under five, infanticide and maternal mortality have been shown to be among the most pressing human insecurity issues of our time. These deaths far outnumber those in military conflict. In the following chapter, I examine the role played by social institutions, national states and International Financial Institutions (IFIs) in shaping conditions that compromise human security in general, and how the most vulnerable people dependent on state subsidies for essential resources are further marginalized by structural changes to basic human security provision. The chapter overviews general institutional economic instruments connecting developed and developing worlds, assesses how national social policy in the South reflects the will of Northern IFIs, and then reviews how the human insecurity discussed in the previous chapter, already threatened by uneven development mechanisms in general, is specifically aggravated by national social policy forged by international institutions.

Institutions take differing forms. They may be formal, constituted entities that labour to an agreed goal, staffed by people who mostly share that vision. They may be national or international and may be members of accredited bodies that share their common aim. They may also be informal and, while also constituted of rules of behaviour, they may not be legally recognized by public bodies. Institutions may carry beliefs and act to transmit those beliefs at the behest of a wider organizing architecture. They are normally, then, self-interested bodies, or interested primarily in their overarching objective, like the UN, which is tasked with preventing war and other forms of violence. As we shall see below in a fuller discussion of institutions, however, some formal and informal institutions' roles and objectives may not be considered in such a benign fashion as the UN's and have become the subject of fierce debate. Some view them as forces for good, while others are concerned that they perpetuate asymmetrical power relationships and are therefore not necessarily well intentioned for all.

Neoliberal financial institutions and global inequality

A fundamental conundrum of inequality in development is how poorer countries can replicate the success of richer states. Advocates of neoliberalism and its predecessors have long argued that the impersonal market will replicate Northern development if the same rules that enriched the North were applied to the South. Inevitably, this means their using IFIs and bowing to market discipline. If developing countries could create their own wealth, they would then be able to disconnect from the dependency relationship that continues (from the imperial era) to bedevil them. Some four decades after independence from the colonial authorities, however, and with numerous experiments carried out regarding the nature of development, healthy economic status still eludes many states in Africa, the Middle East and Asia.

Growth eludes many states because the IFIs that helped create stable and wealthy economies for the North have done so by maintaining an exploitative, uneven asymmetry of disequilibrium. That is, the rules of economic development and the historical conditions of the post-war period facilitated Northern growth under specific conditions which would not later be in place for growth in the South. Furthermore, colonialism extracted resources and transferred them to the North with uneven advantage, while debt accumulated owing to the conditions of the cold war and sustained massive and impoverishing corruption in many states of the South, much of which persists to this day. And while various infrastructures were created by imperial states, many of them had little impact for indigenous peoples at the time, and may be of questionable utility today. This brief overview does not consider the unimaginable damage done by the civil wars of independence, which were propped up by superpower interventions that raged across Africa and Asia and which, in some cases, are only just reaching a conclusion. Thus, the conditions that created wealth for Northern states after the Second World War are quite different from those that exist today, or existed at decolonization. Furthermore, the Northern industrialized states have created an elaborate set of rules for 'shared' growth that appear impartial and fair, especially in the discourses that surround them, but which disadvantage the South in many ways. Of these, the illusion of the 'free' market is the first to be addressed.

The 'free' market is a myth. It can in fact be better characterized as a heavily distorted market, with a 'free hand' guided by institutional divination derived from the most influential members of the IFIs (see below). Part of what sustains poverty and human insecurity is 'discourse dominance'. This means that neoliberalism can create the illusion of propriety by dominating debate, responses and logic. This is achieved in part by its ability to maintain that concepts like the 'free' market are valid, when the evidence shows quite clearly that the market is not free. To begin with, the World Trade Organization (WTO) and the G8 group of eight richest nations are two institutions that effect neoliberalism around the world. The WTO derives from the General Agreement on Tariffs and Trade (GATT) and sets tariff rates and other limits on national imports and exports. The G8 is an international forum that is in denial about an economic system that quite clearly in many instances puts profits before people and the natural environment, a theme that persistently runs through capitalism and neoliberalism as an 'impartial' and 'objective' resource allocator. The G8 is fully aware of trade and protectionism that favour wealthy states and business and impoverish further the poor, but denies that this is a Western issue, preferring to identify intra-regional examples of protectionism in some instances and in others urging that there is no other way of elevation from poverty (Lang and Hines 1993).

It was initially expected that those joining GATT would lower tariff and non-tariff barriers to trade and treat each trading partner as an equal (Barratt Brown 1993: 80; Mihevc 1995: 165–74). The use of Most Favoured Nation (MFN) status is now regular, however, and the GATT's descendant, the WTO, is dominated by the decision-making powers of the United States and Europe, even though, hypothetically, poor countries could outvote the richer (Harvey 2007). One Indian delegate complained that this economic institution for fair trading instead represented a 'one way street'. Delegates and representatives could metaphorically 'drive down it from the North, but the road was blocked from the South' (Barratt Brown 1993: 80).

This institution is part of a process that ensures that rich and powerful Western trading nations can protect their own markets from external competition, but which permits Western trading companies to penetrate the markets of developing countries and dump cheap goods, so undermining the value of local production and returning profit to the West (Harvey 2007). Examples include the practice of subsidizing agricultural produce in the USA and Europe and paying farmers in the developing world not to produce various foods in order to keep supply down and price up.

Conversely, produce sellers in North Africa, for example, have tariffs applied to their exports to southern Europe which make them more expensive than the same food grown and sold from Europe. The net effect can be that cheap and better-quality aubergines exported from Morocco, for example, are taxed at entry into Europe so that sometimes inferior, European aubergines are less expensive and therefore sell better than their North African equivalents. Simultaneously, IFI rules that propose mass exporting of raw commodities from countries in the South inevitably drive down prices because competition inevitably increases, pushing supply up. This economic instrument creates and maintains, through its rule-based neoliberal determinism, a thoroughly uneven playing field.

At all levels, export capacity is diverted to harsh debt repayment; the environment is degraded by excessive agricultural production; commodity prices fall and devalue local stock; land is given over from private subsistence to international export; state subsidies and welfare provision decline; and vulnerable populations have essential services and incomes reduced beyond the point at which they can survive. The commodities in question are subject to significant international market value fluctuations and reliance on mono-cropping has substantial negative consequences for the environment. In general, this policy does contribute to debt repayment, but with the effect that export profits directed to debt repayment are then unavailable for inward, internal investment in development and social support.

Hence, basic 'laws' and rules derived from ideational concepts of development dictated through IFIs ensure outward capital flows to service questionable debts; but they also mean that there is reduced capital inflow to nourish vital, human security protection (for example, state welfare). In a different system, where debt was cancelled or negated, the limited return on exports could be channelled to internal needs such as a health system; better informal and formal social health education; more essential and cheap basic health interventions like mosquito nets; more district and provincial hospitals and more mobile ('barefoot') nurses and doctors (to make returns more effective would require a genuinely free market; this would not necessarily be the best way to empower humankind, however). The WTO remains an unpopular body with many of its members, in no small part because of its role in preserving unfair agricultural exchange regulations.

In conjunction with other IFIs, the World Bank and the IMF endorse market mechanisms but furthermore provide various types of external financial provision: soft loans at low interest; capital loans for large infrastructure investment; or bridging loans to manage short-term deficits from exchange rate fluctuations, and so on. These loans are subject to approval; they pass through the ideological filter of neoliberal beliefs.

They are generally less favourable to wide-scale public health initiatives and public utilities investment and maintenance, and prefer private provision in these spheres because of their significant costs, because of inefficiencies in state provision, and because there is no shortage of evidence to suggest a long and continuing state misappropriation of such funds.

In the bid for efficiency, however, the human cost of not providing social support is not factored into the lending equation. As well as not funding essential public welfare themselves, the IFIs actively discourage state social interventions. Neoliberalism lauds the private and minimizes the state; business is first and foremost profit, not person, oriented. No honest assessment could argue otherwise. The global economy is composed of a socially constructed structural disequilibrium of power maintained by hegemonic neoliberal institutions. These institutions and their beliefs are important to understanding social welfare in developing countries, and human insecurity.

Institutions, social welfare and human insecurity

National social welfare policy, inaugurated comprehensively in Britain after the Second World War, was an early manifestation of the view that the state had a responsibility to protect its citizens from the worst effects of impoverishment. Social security 'from the cradle to the grave' became a mantra for acceptable government provision and few Western states are entirely without it. It is broadly accepted that, because of differing levels of access to essential development necessities, different regional influences and different life experiences (among other things), the state has some responsibility to protect its vulnerable citizens. Under social contract, states defend their citizens from external threats such as foreign armies; but it is also broadly understood that they will extend that security to internal concerns. This is why many developed states provide, with varying degrees of reluctance and enthusiasm, income support for the unemployed, tax credits for less wealthy families, free emergency care and protection, pensions, and so on.

Across the developing world after decolonization, however, there was little agreement on social responsibility or even capacity. In many places, the state had been quite an alien concept perceived negatively as a thief by peasants and as a means for self-enrichment by those appointed to it. What few development specialists rejected, however, was that the authoritarian nature of many post-colonial states, mirroring their colonial forebears, was much less likely to consider state provision of social welfare as a legitimate requirement of their leadership (Kamrava 1993: 15–29; Jackson and Rosberg 1984).

In addition, the general relative poverty of the former colonial states disallowed a comprehensive or effective means of state welfare provision, especially far outside the capital cities. Corruption became a byword of personalized rule, aggravated by the well-documented abuse and squandering of billions of dollars of financial aid throughout the cold war on tyrants and kleptocrats. While developed and developing states took quite different approaches to the notion of the social contract, taxation and welfare provision, then, it was broadly the case that whatever the type of welfare provision, it remained the jurisdiction of the domestic, sovereign state in Europe. This has changed considerably as IFIs now combine conditionality and prescription that turns domestic welfare policy over to distorted markets.

IFIs, the market and international social policy

Institutions are vital to understanding human insecurity, because they are the vessels that express the ideas of economic growth. Institutions in the international relations literature are often presented in two positive ways. First, in realist terms, they represent 'forces for good', because they are essential tools for managing the unpredictable forces of the international system. Second, as 'forces for good' they are also essential ingredients of liberal and idealist thinking. For the latter, they are presented as offering opportunities to extend and spread ameliorating mechanisms of peace and cooperation. Contemporaneously, this might be seen in the spreading of the (Western-conceptualized) human rights regime enshrined within (Western) democracy and its globalization through (Western-dominated) peacekeeping, peace-building and state-building. For the former, they represent instruments for the management of confrontation and disagreement. In the past these have included NATO and the Warsaw Pact, or the anti-ballistic missile (ABM) regime. More recently, institutions have been used to harmonize global policies in particular issues such as whaling, and have been shown to be influential on the issue of landmines, among numerous others.

Other literatures, however, suggest a different interpretation of the role and purpose of international institutions. It is this literature which has great importance for human insecurity. Cox, for example, sees institutions as 'a means of stabilizing and perpetuating a particular order' (1984: 271). In other words, while the discipline of international relations generally views institutions as restraining violent tendencies or developing some form of peace in an impartial manner, others view them as a means of creating and/or perpetuating inequalities desired by more powerful actors or groups of actors through the creation or preservation of asymmetrical power relations. Cox argues that 'institutions reflect the power relations prevailing at their point of origin' (1981: 133–7), while Williams takes the view that institutions 'often play key roles in the creation and maintenance of regimes [and] regime outcomes' (1994: 39). That 'point of origin', at the end of the Second World War when the West still maintained imperial colonies, was intrinsically biased against the colonized countries and in favour of the imperial forces, unsurprisingly. It is this original global power imbalance which IFIs currently perpetuate.

Conditionality is the means by which neoliberal IFIs compromise whatever social policy exists. Neoliberal philosophy maintains that the state must not influence provision of goods and services because it is inefficient; the market should take on supply in all areas. It is on this premise that lending is offered and, because developing countries have only a small number of public international lending bodies to choose from, they must acquiesce to these demands. In short, poor states seeking loans must surrender their economies to the rules of neoliberalism which insist on privatizing and deregulating basic welfare provision. For Deacon, it is clear that 'social policy activities traditionally analysed within and undertaken within one country now take on a supranational and transnational character'. He adds that 'supranational and global actors need to be given more attention in explanations of changing social policy' (Deacon et al. 1997: 1–2; Williams 1994: 83). Deacon et al.'s model and approach provide a useful framework for considering the relationships between globalization and types of human security provision or suppression. They also serve to contextualize and organize much empirical evidence in terms of a connected 'whole'. In much the same way that intimate murder around the world is not the product of discrete, unconnected forces, so too may we consider the neglect of state social provision and concomitant human insecurity globally as being interconnected by broader forces and beliefs.

Deacon is not alone in identifying the role of international neoliberalism and domestic welfare provision and their impact upon human insecurity. Yeates claims that 'the integration of a global perspective in social policy' means it should be considered in an international economic context. 'Globalization', she continues, 'emphasises both the international dimension of human welfare [human security] and focuses attention on international institutions as social policy actors in their own right' (2001: 18; 2005). She contends that 'people's life chances are ... being fundamentally affected by decisions taken in international forums' (Yeates 2005: 168; Hall and Midgely 2004). Furthermore, some extreme models of globalization advocate social policy intervention 'only ... when human capital stock is inadequate to sustain economic growth or when the depth of inequities and discrimination prevent good governance' (Ratinoff 1999: 45). In this context, human development takes a secondary place to this process because its security is mostly considered only when declining human input threatens state stability or profit maximization. This is perhaps a consequence of considering economics as an impartial and gender-neutral process.

Such concerns have not escaped the attention of IFIs. Latterly, some have recognized that without welfare intervention of some kind, economic development may not proceed to plan without damaging people. The shift is slight, however, and although the World Bank has accepted that states could provide welfare support, it advocates only minimum levels of assistance. Another major IFI, the Organization for Economic Cooperation and Development (OECD), has advocated similar basic interventions, and the WTO has argued for market provision in essential human security areas such as healthcare and social insurance (Lipson 2006: 47–50; Robinson 1999: 86–8). There is also further study of the possibility of regional and transnational social welfare intervention frameworks (Yeates 2005).

Despite at least sixty years of robotic economic imperatives which have failed to yield the promised 'trickle down', however, and despite multiple international forums' and bodies' voluble and vociferous public objections, there are few signs of changed outcomes for human security in the welfare context. As Deacon notes, ideas criticizing the virtue of globalization 'have had a hard time of it in the last decades' (2005: 20; Giroux 2004: 106–24). The market prevails, but as we saw from Chapter 3, many humans who might otherwise live and contribute to global society do not. Indeed, Colgan maintains that life expectancy in Africa has declined since the 1980s by fifteen years, while the post-independence decline in child mortality partially as a consequence of World Bank and IMF policies has been 'reversed' (2002: 1; Kim et al. 2000; Turshen 1999). For George and Sabelli, such lethal downturns allow 'forces other than human reason to determine what constitutes the desirable society' (1994: 108). The result is debilitating and immensely worrying for the relationship between resource availability and the lack of will to distribute those resources fairly, which have led to global poverty and mass human insecurity. Seabrook comments that this poverty, 'the poverty of [the twentieth century] is unlike that of any other. It is not, as poverty was before, the result of natural scarcity, but a set of priorities imposed upon the rest of the world by the rich' (Seabrook 2004: 3). In other words, the resources exist but millions die because of how they are disbursed.

Institutions, maternal and under-five mortality

We have established that Northern market dominance and priorities are responsible for economic adjustment and for the flight of cash resources to international banks through debt repayment and corrupt leaders' capital flight. Similarly, it is clear enough that external IFI lending conditionality stresses the role of the market in vital welfare provision for vulnerable groups. Services essential to the preservation of human security become inaccessible for the poorest, most vulnerable people, creating human insecurity on a massive scale in quite general terms.

More specifically, pregnant women need special care in prenatal development. Their unborn infants exert extra demands for basic nutrition on their often already weakened mothers' bodies, denial of which increases maternal susceptibility to immune system decline and thence vulnerability to ordinary diseases sometimes communicable through breast milk. This in turn exacerbates the consequences of their exposure to unclean water, prevalent in rural areas but problematic also in the world's booming urban slums, where unaffordable private water turnpikes are set to replace public provision. Already fragile and uneven health service declines further with marketization and state subsidy withdrawals due to international diktats; immunization programmes cease or are left to local or foreign NGOs, which are often unable to provide comprehensive coverage, and which attract criticism for replacing state health roles; subsidies on basic staples are withdrawn and nutritional intake declines; and so on. Pregnant women suffer the consequences greatly because of the additional medical and nutritional needs for their own bodies and for their infants, while their familial responsibilities may remain unchanged, adding to the onerous burden of the 'double day' in paid labour and home work.

At a later stage of pregnancy, cuts in subsidized public transport, where they exist already, result in pregnant women being unable to attend already sparse health clinics and access professional healthcare. Privatization often leads to the closing of field health clinics, following the general pattern of subsidy withdrawal for essential services. Illnesses contracted during pregnancy, heightened by decreases in health provision, may exacerbate the chances of complicated pregnancies and deliveries; that health situation will be made all the more extreme and dependent on professional, affordable expertise in the case of pregnant women who have suffered female genital mutilation. In essence, the supply of those resources essential to sustain a safe pregnancy is undermined by market-determined priorities and state domestic choices. Mostly, that supply is determined at end-user point by the market and its priorities; many states have domestic policies dictated by IFIs. Inevitably, pregnant women suffer from neoliberal diktat. The greater the availability of competent health provision in terms of doctors and nurses and in terms of physical infrastructure investment in roads, hospitals and clinics, the greater the likelihood of pregnant women surviving maternity. But the removal of essential cheap or free services, as a result of neoliberal conditionality and social sector privatization, debt repayment, cash crop exports and diminished and unstable returns in international commodities and susceptibility to rapid fluctuations in currency values, leads directly and indirectly to maternal mortality.

A similar chain of events affects children under the age of five, the most vulnerable of humans to avoidable death, who are dependent on interventions to grow and develop safely. A wide range of literature, both recent and from the earlier stages of global marketization, persistently documents the impact of market reforms in developing countries on vital child development and provides evidence of the consequences of these reforms on the U5MR (Isbister 2003; Kothari 1993). Access to essentials for safe infant development is determined increasingly by the relationship between social provision and global economic practice, as Deacon, Yeates et al. have suggested.

Neoliberal institutions and state governments are indirect determinants of infant survival rates. Most years, roughly ten million infants die before they reach the age of five, and, according to a wide range of reputable and reliable sources, most could be saved by cheap, low-level health interventions that could be provided by the state or local and international NGOs. Since the market dictates the availability of such interventions through its prioritization systems, the market must be held accountable to some extent for those deaths; it is not an objective model of distribution and to argue so is to deny the evidence of its subjective, constructed nature. And since international institutions emphasize, project and introduce the market around the world, it is those institutions which must bear responsibility for these avoidable outcomes. What becomes quite clear from considering these complex causative chains and recognizing and understanding their roles in human security and insecurity is that they are all human in ordination, management and legitimation. They are therefore quite changeable. These acts of international finance and social policy formats have consequences for which their perpetrators should take responsibility. Indeed, this may be one useful avenue to consider, in the sense that if 'development' is conceptually recast in terms of people's human rights, a trend for which there is already early evidence, then policies that consequently and evidentially fail to prevent avoidable deaths may break international human rights laws. If the right to life is a fundamental underpinning of human rights philosophy and legislation, then there are a lot of laws already being broken.

Infanticide

As we have seen in Chapter 3, infanticide is a practice most recently associated with India and China, although it can be found in many other places over time (Sen 1993; Klasen 1994). In some instances, it has been practised in war with the intention of ending an identity line; this type of ethnic infanticide, or genocide, is quite different from socio-economic child killing. The infanticide considered here is normally practised by members of a child's family concerned not with the eradication of lineage, but with the child's economic cost, its future dowry and its inability to provide parental care in old age.

Current figures suggest an average of around half a million per year, and it is aimed almost exclusively at girls (Penn and Nardos 2003: 26; Sen 1993: 1297). The manner of its euphemism, 'son preference', opens the door to complex explanations relating to the structure and bias of the international economy and society as well as welfare provision for those unable to work, either through old age or infirmity. In dissecting the causes of infanticide, however, it is often argued that it is in some way 'cultural' or determined by one's 'culture'. This defence is one of a number of social institutions surrounding the practice which must be dispensed with first.

The social institutions of 'culture' and 'cultural defence' are used to legitimize infanticide; they do not explain it. Its exclusion from scrutiny, through association with notions of local ownership, privileges it and implies that it is in some way innate to a particular culture and is invulnerable to criticism. A similar defence is also applied to 'honour' killing; in both cases, avoidable female deaths are defended by the use of the word 'culture'. Cultural specialists have maintained that the culture of others should not be subject to intervention, in part because such interference represents arrogant imperialism little different from the European adventures in Africa, Asia and elsewhere in the last century. In such a view, interventionists have no right, moral or otherwise, to challenge these practices (Steans 2007: 14–15).

Part of the problem with this argument is that the practice of infanticide is specific to no one culture, and no singularly deterministic process that marks it out as located in one identity, for example. It is to be found in quite different national cultures and at different times in history and in differing geographies. Various critics have, over the last fifty and more years, argued that 'culture' is a learned experience which translates into social practice that shifts over time and responds to various internal and external stimuli. It is not fixed and can thus be changed. Some human rights advocates and libertarians take this argument a step farther and argue that infanticide should be stopped because the rights of the child must be protected regardless of 'cultural' practice or sovereign inviolability. And, given that the practice occurs in the largest 'democracy' in the world (India), it is yet further at odds with the underpinning principles of individual liberty and the right to life.

At least half a million girl children are killed every year because of their sex. If this were conducted by soldiers in a war, it would be considered mass murder by some and genocide by others. Fundamentally, it would not be tolerated; there would be global outrage (MacKinnon 2006; Francis 2004: 65). Because, for the most part, it is poor parents or other family members who commit the fatal act; because it is normally not recorded and remains largely invisible to outsiders; and because when it is known of external agencies are unwilling to intervene in the internal affairs of China and, to a lesser extent, India, it continues. The reasons defy simple explanation, and involve to varying degrees, in various regions, the nature of global and national economies; the relative status of women to men; the social and gendered division of labour; and marriage practice and perspectives of female roles in the private and public arenas.

Infanticide is rarely what mothers desire, as one woman made so clear in Chapter 3. Few adults would relish the thought of killing their own child. To suggest it is solely culture or solely misogyny is to miss multiple and complex determinants. Infanticide currently reflects social attitudes to the relative economic value of females, but this also has to be set in the context of the restriction of female roles to the home/private sphere, as well as marital practices such as dowry that restrict the social role of women to the economically redundant but dependency-reinforcing domestic arena. Males, on the other hand, are directed to the paid labour environment. As such, they generate the income upon which their spouses and daughters are dependent and over which the females often have limited control.

This situation does not on its own result in girl baby killing. To these complex social and economic rules must be added the problem of poverty. Because life-preserving human security in modern economies is often governed by factors outside many poor people's control, they can be vulnerable to inconsistent supplies of essential goods like food, shelter and so on. Furthermore, because the socially determined roles of females in the home do not easily attract visible revenue, the females are considered a 'double burden' in relation to the revenue-generating capacity of males. Not only do they not bring in cash or other tradable commodities, they subtract from the sum total of household income because they need to eat, be clothed and may require costly medical attention.

Institutions and infanticide

There are many institutions, national and international, social and economic, involved in the promulgation and sustenance of female infanticide and they all bear relationships with poverty and the domination of politics, society and economics by male-favouring rules. These may be divided into two categories: those that act on the process, and those that, by act or omission, do nothing to curb the practice. In the first instance, there is direct violence by human act (the killing). This cannot, however, be divorced from the essential social and economic underpinnings of broader causative elements including sex subjugation and institutionally maintained female dependence. In the second instance, the cause of death may be personally denied and then informally concealed by formal institutions. For example, a child's birth and murder may be denied by the parents when birth occurs at home. State health institutions may kill the children in clinics and hospitals, or disguise murder as an accident. They may also not record a death or falsify its cause in official records.

Other state institutions are involved by omission of act or by act. Infant female deaths in unusual or suspicious circumstances do not automatically trigger constabulary or judicial inquiry, partly because it is rarely legislated for (because it is an 'accepted' trait) but also because the practice is understood and socially condoned by actors within state institutions. Since constabularies are subject to similar social indoctrination as the society they are tasked with serving, their attitudes routinely condone social practices and any intervention may be considered unpropitious and unwarranted. Demonstrating the interconnectivity between statutory bodies and received cultural practice, *The Times* reported in 2006 that despite sex selection ultrasound scanning being banned in 1994 in India, it is 'is widely ignored and no case has come to court' (26 December 2006: 36).

The international economy is a principal, and unintentional, institutional cause of infanticide. Insofar as the market itself deliberately discriminates against no one person or group (except the relatively weak), the functional by-product of infanticide is only indirectly dispensed. No individual operative causes this deliberately. Infanticide happens neither because all those parents hate their children, nor by accident, nor by act of God. It happens because international financial institutions combine to shape market activities such that they cause disproportionate disadvantages in certain areas of human production that have been unable to integrate with that market to a sufficiently beneficial degree. In many respects, the international institutions that 'guard' the functioning of the market are responsible for excluding from fair participation the people and communities that are forced into such levels of financial deprivation that the only choice they have if their newborns are girls is to kill them.

Sexing institutions, gendering infanticide

As a rule, the axiom that the moderated market – that is, the one controlled through human-led choices framed in international institutions – works to the advantage of the most powerful while it exposes the weakest to the greatest danger is not unreasonable. These relationships are ordered. Thomas contends that this arrangement 'is not a product of bad luck, but rather of existing structures which can be changed' (2000: 9). Similarly, Pogge maintains that 'the fact that a quarter of all children are born into [extreme poverty] is not bad luck but bad organization' (2002: 531). Infanticide is a product of a wide range of structured relations and failing expectations.

It is no coincidence that gender is also structured and maintained by male rules and decisions. As we shall see in more detail in later chapters, a core issue in poverty, the state and the global economy is the relative worth of men and women in a world led by men. A short overview of male domination serves to introduce global sex disparities for later chapters, and also sheds some light on why it is girls which are killed at birth in infanticide. To begin with, we must critically reconsider the assumption that sexual liberation has created broad, deep and meaningful equality between the sexes at institutional levels.

Historically, women have been politically marginalized and subsumed so that their status is second to that of men (de Beauvoir 1988). The literature examining and describing this phenomenon is important, but the evidence of contemporary marginalization is self-evident. Female national leaders currently constitute a short list, from which might be subtracted those who attained their status through their male relatives (Sonia Gandhi, Benazir Bhutto). The notion of a woman or, come to that, a black person becoming leader of the United States has only recently been the subject of serious debate. On the African continent, only one woman, Ellen Johnson Sirleaf, leads a nation-state (Liberia), and there are no female leaders currently in the Middle East, although there have been a number in eastern Asia.

Even where there have been female national leaders, female participation in parliamentary or other political processes reveals an obvious discrepancy in male and female representation. In England it was 1997 before a noticeable female component of Parliament became the norm, and even in such an 'advanced' democracy, this fluctuates. In the USA, roughly one quarter of elected state legislators were women during the last decade, and only 14 per cent occupied Congress (Palmer 2006). In 'advanced' Westminster-style polities between 2003 and 2005, in Australia, Canada and the UK, women occupied less than a quarter of elected seats (Sawer et al. 2006: 241). Such composition engenders unrepresentative human and security priorities. In other words, males determine most political and economic priorities in their policy choices and they also decide what is 'important', which is why 'hard security' almost always outranks human security issues and related policies.

The gender biases apparent in political elites are also, unsurprisingly, to be found in civil service departments, the military and most public service bodies, representing an anomaly in terms of political representation compared with male-to-female population ratios (Mazurana and McKay 2001: 136–7). In criminal prosecution cases, alleged rape of women achieves a conviction rate disproportionately lower than all other crimes, and there are more women in English jails for non-serious offences, including non-payment of TV licences, than there are men (Kelly et al. 2005). In the commercial world, nearly all of the largest businesses are run by men; sex discrimination in globally recognized business is evident in the cases taken before courts; and women are paid less than men for doing the same work almost everywhere. In England, government offices were still unprepared in 2007 to deal with equality of pay for males and females doing the same work despite having been given ten years' notice. The UNDP shows that no country in the world offers women equal pay for the same work (2005). In the developing world, literacy among females is almost always lower than that of men; school attendance is almost always better for males than females; and women are almost always the victims of sex crimes rather than men.

Women's public under-representation is matched in the private, unpaid household domain. Traditionally, women have done home chores and raised children, cooked, cleaned and otherwise maintained the private domain while men fulfilled their potential in the much more variegated public arena of paid work. This fundamental divide reinforces the difficulties for mothers of leaving their prescribed, 'natural' role raising children in the home, which marginalizes female personal development and preserves their economic dependency on male partners. It is to be noted that this has changed enormously since female suffrage facilitated other public roles for women. But despite incremental changes at grassroots level, in job and career access, in crèche care and so on, structural impediments to full equalization remain firmly in place. Indeed, social structures that place women in the home with the child remain quite firmly in place in many parts of the world, so that while women's access to paid labour is argued to have empowered them, they face the 'double burden' of having to work both inside and outside the home. These are quite general conventions which apply, more or less, globally, to varying degrees. They impact most deleteriously upon females in polities least supportive of legal rights that constitutionally enshrine female independence from males, and which are recognized and accepted in social practices and by male elites. Emancipation rarely develops and takes hold in societies led by elites whose political and social practices are governed by sexist assumptions and behaviours. Examples might include Japan, where the Japanese health minister described women in 2007 as 'birth giving machines' (*Independent*, 29 January 2007: 27); and Hungary, where in 2004 the prime-minister-in-waiting declared that 'men should be free to trade in their wives ... Anyone whose wife is getting old deserves a younger one' (*The Times*, 16 September 2004: 35).

Negative attitudes to women are built on ancient foundations but are sustained by contemporary institutions and beliefs. Infanticide occurs in China and India because extremes of devaluation of females collude with severe poverty and occur as a result of dominant and as yet ineffectively challenged institutional beliefs and outputs. Each element of the formula that creates infanticide should not be seen in remote analysis, but as part of a complex and conjoined system that results in the killing of girls because they are socially valued below boys, in part because of their relationship to productive capacity in a gendered economy and in part because of social rules that exclude women from equal or fair participation. China and India are significant examples of how this constellation of forces combines to produce infanticide.

If it could be halted, social and economic institutions and their prerogatives combine to ensure it is not. State and social institutions may do little to help and much to exacerbate female marginalization generally and infanticide specifically. In India and China, there is limited challenge to systemic patriarchal predominance, reinforced by varying degrees of Islam, Hinduism and Confucianism, which ensure the prioritization of men above women. Sexism is as yet largely unreconstructed and is rife in social attitudes to women's sex roles and sexual behaviour and to women's choice of apparel and public voices. Various forms of employment are proscribed by male institutional diktat, and social segregation can best be described as 'traditional', a euphemism for crude control. Social proscription is routinely mirrored in state obstruction of women's challenges to 'tradition'. The legal system is invariably male dominated with masculine values enshrined in legislature by male-led parliaments; in some legal systems, a woman's voice counts for one half of a man's; and women are prosecuted for adultery and stoned to death while the male adulterer is often given much lighter – if any – sentencing (in not dissimilar ways to women in the West being prosecuted for prostitution while their male clients are rarely forced to court). These issues are only the tip of an iceberg.

Conclusion

Essential social provision for basic human security is increasingly determined not by basic grassroots needs but instead by globalized gender prejudices and distant, disinterested and 'impartial' economic models based on human beliefs. The market alone does not determine that it is girls which die at the hands of their families, rather than boys, in infanticide. It is beyond dispute that those families themselves select the females, although often with wider social condonement. The economy again has much to answer for, but it is not the only determinant of the relative economic value of males over females. That relative value was prescribed and formed through political and other power institutions long before the market appeared in its current form. It is clear that there is a structural determinism in the elevation of men above women, and there are human-constructed barriers to women's progression towards structural equality.

More specifically, state behaviour in financial terms is now governed to a large extent by international institutions projecting the policies and priorities of neoliberal assumptions and beliefs. This extreme form of capitalism, based on competition and exploitation, inevitably cannot generate even outcomes because its functioning cannot take into consideration relative strengths and weaknesses, and how they permit or prevent people's potential engagement with the market. Although its proponents consider its mathematics an objective science, this belief cannot take into account the disparate conditions of those who have little choice in engaging with it on uneven terms. Furthermore, given that its primary international institutions convey inbuilt advantages for those who benefit most from it, and who established its working rules, those in weaker positions are yet further distanced from equal opportunities to engage with its mechanisms.

There are, inevitably, commonalities and differences between infanticide, on the one hand, and maternal mortality and the U5MR. The U5MR and maternal mortality differ from infanticide in at least one important respect; that is, children and women die from what would otherwise be considered indirect and often avoidable causes, rather than by directed, deliberate killing. Furthermore, while social welfare provision in terms of pensions also determines whether a child lives or dies at birth for all three groups, these decisions are also influenced by the nature of the labour sector as well as familial expectations and the social limitations of women.

Underlying influences on all three categories are to be found in international financial institutions and the ideologies they project. But in addition, they are shaped by, to different degrees, state institutions and their national policies, which reflect male priorities that routinely marginalize women's opportunities by relegating them through socially institutionalized and condoned prejudices. Linking the national and international institutions and policies are compromise and corruption. IFIs compromise the ability of states to determine their own policies by rejecting state social subsidies. The record on corruption in developing countries legitimizes this compromise, while corruption itself directly marginalizes vulnerable people in general and codifies state responses to infanticide, the U5MR and maternal mortality by dispensing with formal recording processes, often through corrupt practices.

A parallel is appearing. The most vulnerable in society appear to have least representation in government. Exclusion from representation seems synonymous with relative denial of human security and also explains why it affects women more than men. Children, of course, are not represented formally in the apparatus of government except through maternal care preferences, which are in turn disproportionately advanced in government circles because women normally have only limited authentic representation.

Human insecurity in the areas discussed above is directly and indirectly connected to national and international institutions that are inscribed with, and dominated by, masculine priorities. Vulnerable and marginal groups are almost always under-represented in governments globally, in a process that determines their access to key foundational elements of human security on the basis of cash, rather than by health and equality. Relative vulnerability caused by gender and inability to participate in market functions, regardless of cause, is a key determinant of a marginalization that is often first formalized in state under-representation reflected in and reflecting societal gender values.

It could be worse. If the evidence truly suggested that these conditions, rules and institutions were biologically determined and genetically fixed, then realism would have had its roots confirmed and there would have to be a grim and regrettable acceptance of a truly unjust, violent world. But the evidence does not suggest this at all. It suggests quite clearly that the majority of the experiences, conventions, institutions and ideologies are in fact man made and expressed through socially constructed bodies that stem from the minds of humans. They can therefore be transformed over time by increasing public consciousness of the way in which it has been misled by propaganda and the power of andrarchy and neoliberalism (to which we will turn in later chapters).

FIVE | Institutions and intimate murder

This chapter is concerned with the relationship between different types of intimate murder (lethal domestic violence, 'honour' and dowry killings), on the one hand, and the extent to which these are learned behaviours that are institutionalized to create lethal human insecurity, on the other. I examine how each type of partner killing is connected by learned expectations on the part of males that they hold the right to subliminally and/or overtly control female behaviour through violence and other sanctions. These behaviours I codify as Direct Control Violence (DCV), drawing on the control violence work of Radford and Russell (1992). Its global prevalence and commonality of purpose identify it as an international institution and, because the rules of DCV are rarely of the written variety, it is conceived as an informal social institution. This particular institution serves conscious and unconscious hegemonic male domination, in the same way that contemporary international financial institutions serve pre-eminent neoliberalism. Both these sets of formal and informal institutions conform to the models outlined by Payne (2005), Cox (1984, 1981) and Williams (1994), for whom institutions perpetuate a particular asymmetry of power and advantage. We may consider this to be institutional instrumentality; the institutions are instruments of belief. The chapter argues that such violences mutate in response to social challenges to legislation to different degrees in different locations, demonstrating the acquired (learned) nature of the process, variegating institutional impact.

Intimate murder: changeable social or permanent biological origins?

Conventional explanations for intimate murder have normally revolved around whether they are cursed by biological programming, or caused by social learning. In the first theory, our experiences and actions are a product of our genetic make-up and reflect biological evolutionary necessity ('survival of the fittest') and are, therefore, relatively unchangeable. This view underpins much of the realist literature in international relations, which argues that while biological determinism may mean that we have a predisposition for violence that cannot be changed, the provision of regulating institutions such as the rule of law will constrain this behaviour.

Goldstein, for example, posits that our general behaviour is the product of 'pathological predispositions ... [from] heritable traits that influence individual behaviour' (2002: 32; Sheehan 2005: 121). For Goldstein, social and cultural explanations of violence against women are weakened by their global extent. He argues that 'a right to kill unfaithful or disgraced women represents not the culture-to-culture proliferation of misogyny but the culture-*by*-culture expression of a biologically evolved behavioural pathology ...' (2002: 28). Such examples of violence against women share in their origins the same genetic programming that explains other, worldwide, forms of violence, as a general rule. It is immutable but its impact may be limited through institutional mobilization.

Social constructivists and other social determinists, however, are less inclined to surrender the debate to science (Francis 2004: 68–77). Most critical feminist argument also considers bio-determinism both facile and convenient, divesting men of responsibility for their violence against women (and against other men and boys and girls, also). Others who challenge the biological determinist perspective, such as anthropologists like Leacock, have long argued that such behaviours are not fixed by a static biologically fixed human nature. Indeed, for Leacock, human nature is:

> A mix of potentials and propensities that are expressed differently under
> different conditions; at the societal level, social-historical processes are
> of an altogether different order; in between, mediating the two, at the
> individual psycho-social or behavioural level, the person operates at
> a nexus of social-economic relationships; and at the ideological level,
> people's perceptions of their relations to each other and to nature are
> patterned by traditional concepts, in part spontaneous and in part ma-
> nipulated, and with a certain lawfulness of their own that arises from the
> nature of language as a symbol system. (1983: 267)

In this interpretation, and in the interpretation of many others who challenge immutability in human behaviour, violence against women by male partners and relatives happens because of learned expectations, presumptions and behaviours, both of men and women, which derive from older attitudes (discussed in Chapter 9).

Another body of scholarship which challenges the monocausal bio-determinist perspective is concerned with the nature of 'culture' (Bayart 2005). For cultural theorists like Borhek and Curtis, 'culture consists of learned (as opposed to innate) and shared (as opposed to truly idiosyncratic) ideas (as opposed to physical artifacts) which permeated time and society to create norms of social behaviour that accrued an unchallenged legitimacy' (1975: 48). They add that 'the process that accounts for the acquisition of culture by individuals is called socialization and consists of regular schedules of reinforcement' (ibid.: 48). Wherever what we thought of as 'culture' affects human security, it is learned and therefore it is adaptable. Mead argues that:

> Humanity rests upon a series of learned behaviours, woven together into patterns that are infinitely fragile and never directly inherited ... Long before [a child] is strong enough to deliver a blow, the angry gestures of the human child bear the stamp not of his long mammalian past but of the club-using or spear-throwing habits of his parents. (1977: 185–6)

Bayart also addresses repeated acquired behaviours reinforced over time and argues that, universally, culture is a learned belief set that is responsible for traditions of all kinds. For Bayart, they derive from human agency, repeated storytelling, socialization and legitimation over time. In some instances, they may be quite harmless; Morris dancing in parts of England physically harms no one intentionally. But others, such as those explored below in terms of female control and punishment for aberrations, belief killings, dowry murders and so on, are learned rationales that kill intentionally and avoidably. Imparting a sense of the extent of such behavioural patterns globally, Bayart comments that:

> From the hills of Beaujolais to the land of the Bamileke, from the Deep South to Liberia, from Lusaka to Rome, from the canton of Vaud to the land of the Ovimbundu, in short, from one space or historical landscape to another, the intersection of the processes of inventing tradition, which has been constitutive of the general movement of globalization for more than a century, reminds us that there is no culture that is not created, and that this creation is usually recent. (2005: 59)

This work takes the view that, in the long distant past, bio-determinism may well have guided and dominated a range of prioritizations and a division of labour to match such priorities and needs. When our external environmental conditions were not controlled by humans owing to limits in mental and technological evolution, for example, some factors in biology almost certainly were at the fore. While biological factors may take millennia to change, however, humans have reshaped their surrounding environments far more quickly, such that the earlier divisions of labour and priorities that evolved in very harsh and unforgiving environments are no longer necessary to the same degree in the more 'tamed' environment humans generally inhabit. In other words, 'as human culture [has] developed, there [has been] growing control over instinctual impulses' (Connell 2000: 213; Clamp 2005: 20–21). On the assumption that we are learning creatures with the obvious capacity to evolve beyond the constraints of our natural environment, we can learn quite different relations between men and women that are not based on domination, control or violence and which underscore improved human security.

Furthermore, with intellectual evolution and some degree of enlightenment, humans have challenged fundamental propositions regarding equality and justice in different places and at different times. This is evidence of their impermanence, malleability and social construction. In some regions, characterized by political systems determined by the secular state legitimized by substantial democracy, challenges regarding relative status between the two main sexes of male and female have drawn the conclusion that, ethically, humans should be considered equal regardless of sex, ability, race and so on. In conjunction with this social evolution, the growth of political, legal and economic institutions and procedures promoting equality as necessary has accompanied the more basic intellectual conclusions of equality in principle between males and females (Reardon 1996: 315). This process differs across geographies. In South Asia, particularly, women's rights are deeply challenged by males of all ages. But in other areas, women's rights are legislatively enshrined; this is not to suggest they are necessarily respected, however. The issue is far more complex than simple legislative endorsement, as we shall see.

An essential point is that attitudes to women's equality differ; they can therefore not be purely biological. Difference demonstrates social conditioning. In other words, whether social or biological determinism best explains intimate murder or not, the continuing practice of partner-killing globally affirms its social construction while institutional responses also vary, demonstrating their own social amorphousness. In different parts of the world, institutionalized sexual equality has been attempted, while in others attitudes towards it are indifferent or entirely absent, suggesting quite different global, religious or political perspectives on the matter. It is the position of this work that such violent practices are not explained by reference to 'cultures' because intimate murder happens everywhere in all forms and stages (to date) of socio-economic development and among all religions (although the methods of killing may vary). Accordingly, a universality of treatment exists which reflects asymmetrical gendered relations. This does not, however, infer biological determinism, because although intimate murder is geographically universal, not all men behave violently, and social reactions differ in terms of condonement and condemnation. Once this view is firmly established, we may now examine how relative human insecurity is constructed and therefore may be changed.

Having rejected both biological and cultural explanations and justifications for the global breadth of intimate partner-killing, this book considers a different, ideational and institutional determinism which explains all three types of woman-killing. We proceed on the reasoning that there was almost certainly some degree of early biological influence that led male and female behaviours, and that the environment determines this, in line with most theories of evolutionary biology. Human genius has, however, tamed the natural environment to the extent that 'adventure seekers' tired of mundane, secure living may now have to travel many thousands of miles to seek out an environment that challenges their security. Furthermore, that is a choice, not a necessity. We are able to master our domains or change our locations to those of greater security, given access to the right resources. Because of these changes, the social rules we learned to generate biological and social security are no longer relevant and do not have to be sustained. Indeed, what sustains social behaviours like 'honour' killing is often to be found rooted in a tradition that few recall the origins of and for which the context has also changed over time. More normally, social behaviours that perpetuate particular advantages are relocated randomly into myths, or are the subject of contested interpretations of religious tomes. In other words, early biological imperatives and practices in male control of females are routinely perpetuated by adherence to learned practices that are no longer relevant or necessary, but which have been perpetuated and institutionalized by male-led institutions to preserve assumed superiority and advantages.

Relationships as possession and control environments

Much of the literature that examines domestic murder locates it on the same continuum on which rape is placed. It is considered as control behaviour based on expectations derived from socially constituted experiences (UNIFEM 2003; Davies 2004; Watts and Zimmerman 2002). The many different forms it takes, outlined in Chapter 3, are deployed with similar intent. That is, to ensure that partner behaviour conforms to what the male has received consciously and subconsciously throughout the course of his life. The sources of these social messages are mutually reinforcing and reflect male domination around the world. Sex (the biological identity of men and women) is associated with and converted to gender roles (the roles associated with men and women).

Aberration from these roles leads to confusion for men who have been steeped in traditions of distinct female roles that are reinforced from the moment a male is born (Faludi 1999). Early-years biological sex differences are accentuated by the attendant gender reinforcements in toys, games and other routine and unchallenged socializations, while early sexualization of females through fashion is blatant. This is so routine that it appears normal, which it is. It is therefore not hard to argue that men and women have different expectations of sex equality (MacKinnon 2006; Runyan and Peterson 1991). Traditionally – and it is definitely changing – men believed in the home as their domain to control – especially as only they could own houses. Men and women's socialization ensured this and public institutions preserved and protected those rights. Women who transgressed such expected behaviours could expect to be, and were, punished. Most punishment stopped short of killing, and some killings have been accidents (which would probably not have happened were not some forms of violent control already being exerted). In parts of the developing world, wives and girls are still stoned to death for social transgression in acts of extreme barbarism.

These relationship expectations are also deeply influenced by the notion of 'rights' and 'possession'. Around the world, men who have killed their partners have done so to stop other men 'having' 'their' woman (Wilson and Daly 1992: 89–93). The defendant's refrain of 'if I can't have her, nobody can' is common. Such behaviour reflects an undesired and unacceptable loss of control over the woman's behaviour and a second loss of face and masculine status when another man 'possesses' her. His humiliation is twofold: first he is rejected by a woman over whom he is expected to have dominion; and second, another male assumes control and demotes the first in masculine hierarchies. Males may not be conscious of such conditioning, but it exists nonetheless. Furthermore, after divorces or separations, men will often still hound their former partners. Indeed, the time of handover of shared children is a very dangerous point for female ex-partners.

This construction of control 'rights' is reinforced in unconscious social practice. Windsor notes that 'in every form of marriage in every society, until the West invented the Registry Office, a woman has been given to a man by another man' (1988: 455). This 'giving' is still symbolically evident in many Christian weddings, where the bride passes down the aisle from her biological father (who had initial authority) to her new husband, who assumes the protective/control role from that point. This allows the new male to legitimize the woman's social status by ensuring she does not remain single and out of the control of an 'appropriate' male. In this way, she will not be a 'threat' or a 'lesbian' or 'frigid' or in some other way not compliant with masculine-institutionalized requirements. While barely felt in Europe, Australia or Canada, these types of institutions transmit social rules and expectations in parts of South Asia quite overtly. They are so normalized that they are rarely noted or challenged; this normalization is the source of their resilience and of the tenacity of male control, and the target of various critical feminist works designed to make males and females more aware of sometimes relationship-damaging influences.

Possession and control, authorized through the husband's status, are common experiences of wives. In some societies, the post-wedding arrangement may be varilocal, meaning that the new wife moves out of her biological family's home and in with her new husband's family. Here, it is normal for her to play a subservient role to that of her mother-in-law. Christian wedding ceremonies also often stipulate that only death should part the couple, hence further theological justification for possession. Of course, a female or male may depart from the wedding bonds. Women have, however, traditionally been punished to a greater extent than men for leaving a marriage and this act may also impact on any children, who will most usually remain with their mother, who, as a woman, is normally paid less than a man. Women may be run out of their own villages; demonized and verbally and physically berated, castigated and punished; excommunicated from their own families; and despised for the choice they make in leaving abusive relationships in which they are violently beaten, humiliated and subjugated as a matter of routine. The experiences of such women in rural Asia today are not far removed from those of women in Europe but a hundred years ago, and more recently in many cases.

Possession is also related to the bride's virginity at the time of the marriage, hence the usual white attire; but not for the groom. This was commonplace in Europe and the USA until quite recently. But the attitude towards female sexuality in supposedly 'developed' countries continues to reflect historical conditions. Possession, then, remains a part of social ruling over women. In many parts of the world, a woman is still expected not to have been sexually 'taken' or 'possessed' by another man before her betrothal. In Turkey, for example, female virginity may be monitored by the state, a process it denies. Human Rights Watch

(HRW) has, however, identified state and constabulary roles in forced virginity exams (1994: 23). This intervention is a social control process. In other words, the information gathered has wider social consequence than simply a police record. As in many other countries that persistently protect male domination of and advantage over women, the information can be used to discredit the female or her family. Long-lasting social penury, marginalization and ostracism may then be the instruments of punishment and control for women who do not adhere to male dictates of ownership, custody and subservience.

'Excessive' sexual activity by females before marriage is still socially castigated by both men and other women. The open damning of a woman for an independent sexuality is reflected in the implicit condemnation to be found in sexual harassment and rape cases. There, women's choice of underwear and outerwear can be used to try to influence juries, as if indicative of bad character or deterministic of guilt. Precisely how many sex partners a woman may take before marriage is unclear because of its subjective nature; what matters as much in this context is that the same social ruling is not applied to men's sexual behaviour and a woman's security is established by social rules transmitted by males.

Such domination, possession, punishment and control of wives is evident before and during marriage, with 'after marriage' being a key problem for men and women, in different ways. In Jewish law, the 'Agunah' tradition means that men can refuse to grant divorces to their wives, leaving the woman literally 'chained' (Sassoon 2005). It also occurs when a husband dies prematurely or naturally. In various parts of the world, where a husband has died, his widow may be forced to marry the brother of her husband (Lamb 1999; Harlan and Courtright 1995). In this way, she remains socially 'protected' in the embrace of a male related to the husband. Without this intervention, her prior possession and questionable and 'dangerous' sexuality distress males and females and render her of low value to other males. She may be socially condemned to a harsh life of being single in societies that mistrust single women over a certain age. Her social legitimacy is ensured only by her marital submission to another, 'respected' male. She may also be burned to death after her husband dies, on his funeral pyre, because her role is contextualized in relation to her location with a respectable male (Weinberger 1999; Banerjee 2003). His passing nullifies her *raison d'être*; her utility is negated and her existence often means extra cost for her community while that community perceives her as sexually threatening, in accordance with deeper fear and suspicion of female sexuality generally.

These fears are also causal in FGM and other methods of minimizing female independence.

Thus, the sexual and social independence of women before and during marriage is governed by socially developed rules that reflect masculine priorities and expectations descended from times when nature remained untamed and unpredictable. Human development and ingenuity have overcome many of the challenges of the natural environment, however, rendering such social rules unnecessary as far as women are concerned. Male adaptability to such social transformation, however, remains painfully slow for the women whose social rights have been determined in order to sustain male domination and advantage. It is this global social institution, of Direct Control Violence, which leads to thousands of avoidable deaths worldwide and is thus a key contributor to human insecurity. It should be noted that a common defence of communities that overtly physically control and punish women is that such measures are taken for the woman's safety. The problem with this argument is that it is males (and often other females) who create conditions of insecurity that make women insecure in this way in the first instance.

Domestic murder

Although intimate partner murder remains common in Europe and the USA, there has been notable change in assumptions regarding the perceived rights of males to control women through violence and other forms of coercion, given that marriage is no longer the social, economic and legal control mechanism it once was. This in itself is suggestive of the construction and reconstruction of social dynamics in gender relations. Society in many parts of Europe and the USA has become openly intolerant of male partner abuse; men's groups have formed to represent men opposed to male violence against women; the judiciary's attitudes towards rape victims and survivors of domestic violence have modernized (to an extent); and legislation has been passed concerning the rights of women abused in the traditionally private sphere to have their cases considered in the public legal arena. Furthermore, public and political institutions have accepted women's right to 'invade' some of the last bastions of female exclusion, even if they remain dominated by men, and revised rape prosecution procedures now mean that women cannot be directly cross-examined by their alleged attackers. Encouragingly, as a liberal rights regime gathers momentum in conjunction with changes in economic development and other factors; as the propriety of violence as a means of social transformation is increasingly challenged; and as state independence from religious control (secularization) declines, the liberal polity recognizes and concerns itself with women's rights and male-to-female behaviours, even if change can sometimes be sloth-like in speed.

But despite such changes, partner murder persists. In 2005, 866 women were murdered, suggesting that more than 600 died by their partners' hands. This data comes from the six countries that differentiated male from female murders and responded to an ongoing research programme in 2007. A very crude extrapolation suggests that at this rate, a global estimate for 2005 could be as high as 20,000. This extrapolation does not include estimates of dowry and 'honour' killings; nor does it consider variables such as corrupt, involved or absent constabulary and successful concealments and non-reporting. The figure is likely to be much higher. Partner killings are routinely carried out as punishment for leaving a male; for damaging his public persona and reputation ('honour'); for disobedience; for challenging domestic or financial authority, and for many other quite trivial 'offences'. Constabulary and judicial (institutional) reform is characteristic of numerous northern European states and the USA, South Africa, Thailand and Canada, Australia, New Zealand and an increasing number of other states around the world. Females are increasingly supported by appropriate institutional responses to allegations of violence and death threats. Northern Ireland, a relatively patriarchal environment also influenced by church attitudes that have in the past condoned male violence in relationships, has an increasing number of police stations equipped with domestic violence units staffed by both Protestant and Catholic female officers. Such changes are evidence of transformation and progress, which in turn is evidence of the social construction and therefore impermanent nature of domestic murder. They also reveal the degree of formal institutional challenge to informal institutional beliefs and the extensive role of institutions per se.

Belief/'honour' killings

'Honour' killings are referred to here as belief killings in an attempt to disconnect a positively held social construction (honour) from the illegitimate violence of partner murder. They occur, as we discussed in Chapter 3, as a result of female 'betrayal' of male 'honour'; another socially constructed, transformable determinant of violence and human insecurity. Women often accede to these rules because they too are part of a broad socialization through male domination of contemporary institutions, the governing rules of which were formed in much earlier times but which still enshrine and sustain the priorities of men. It should be noted also that, complicating the matter further, women are killed by men for reasons that may have little to do with 'honour'; but 'honour' may be used to defend or explain the action (Welchman and Hossain 2005: 8).

Historically, such violent control of women's social and sexual behaviour has not been limited to Asia, the Middle East, Latin America or Africa. Victorian England was noted for strict 'ladies' etiquette', the breach of which was likely to bring public criticism upon a male relative or husband for failure to control 'his' female. Similarly, national legislatures did not necessarily accommodate the right of women to act independently of a legal consort in principle. Indeed, women's suffrage is less than a century old in the UK and beating of wives was common and either ignored or, if publicly cast, not subject to particular laws protecting women in the private domain of the male home.

Belief killings are social acts, in the sense that they are conducted within societies conscious of the processes involved and which choose not to reject their validity. Furthermore, they occupy a space between informal (social) and formal (public) institutionalism. This may be described as a grey area in which social condonement for belief killings may persist in contrast to its legislative outlawing; but where the formal constabulary and judicial interfaces consist of humans socialized and inscribed with private beliefs that contrast with their public duties. This situation is common in areas with limited and socially recruited constabulary and militia, and ineffective metropolitan influence, where social prejudices overcome professional responsibilities.

Furthermore, legislation is only one aspect of institutional transformation. While parliaments may change formal laws that outlaw violence against women, other institutions and processes may interpret them in a number of ways. Again, until quite recently, British courts relied on juries composed only of men, whose socialization regarding women influenced how they perceived an alleged victim and her assailant. Particularly where the issue was domestic violence, even where the male perpetrator was found guilty, sentences were determined mainly by male judges and were sometimes unduly lenient. In some elements of sharia law, a woman's account of events is equal to only half a man's, meaning that two females' matching accounts would be required to equal one male's. Factored into this must be the consequence in societies where male partners are the sole breadwinner, forcing a battered wife, for example, either to not report violence, or to plead for leniency in sentencing because any children involved would suffer if the main earner were incarcerated. In general, institutional imbalances are clearly in favour of males in belief killings. They have been informed by personal experience and storytelling; females learn from other mentors of their socially prescribed relationship responsibilities; their distance, both geographically and politically, from legal remonstration influences the degree to which men may enjoy immunity for the use of violence; and the formal structures of law are unevenly distributed and often only arbitrarily effective. Female human security is directly damaged by a combination of informal-social institutional predominance and formal-legal institutional incapacity.

Dowry murders

As we noted in Chapter 3, dowry killings have much in common with 'honour' killings. If the compensation package owed to the family of the groom by the bride's family is incommensurate with the groom's family's demands, the 'honour', or status, of the groom and his family has been damaged and violent retribution is routinely exacted. Our concern here is the role of institutions in determining this form of human insecurity. Clearly, dowry killing, like its belief counterpart, is a social familial arrangement. Neither rationale for killing female partners is biologically necessary and they are therefore better understood as constructs that sometimes take the guise of 'custom', 'tradition' or 'culture'. They are not, however, the only institutional determinant of sustained, structured violence against women by partners and partners' families and friends. Socially institutionalized and predominant practices merge with political, legal and civic institutions such as the constabulary, the rule of law and the legislature. While these institutions do not normally deliberately kill women directly (except in the cases of judicial executions or renegade actors), they play an important role in mitigating the social condonement of dowry killings and, through this, the condonement of the individual acts.

It is impossible to separate the earlier socializing experiences of individuals in societies that routinely subjugate women from the influence those experiences have on the carrying out of official, state duties. Those experiences may be positive or negative; but either way, they penetrate public official institutions and influence institutional impartiality. That is, the informal values that people learn may be transmitted into formal institutions that are designed to protect different value systems. For example, while a parliament may pass equality legislation in a very formal environment, where the values associated with such an institution are at odds with extant social practice, and where institutional transparency and oversight are questionable or absent, due process may not be the outcome. The man arrested for burning his wife for failing to produce sufficient dowry may be interviewed by constables of either sex who themselves believe the assailant did the right thing socially and that the law is in fact inappropriate. If the case goes to court, the sitting judge may take the same view and dismiss the case.

This presupposes a constabulary presence. Police representation may be entirely absent in some rural areas that lie beyond a capital's authoritative reach, as Tambiah made clear in his galactic polity model of traditional and developing countries (1977). Conversely, police activity may be present, either in the form of regular constabulary or distantly appointed local authority or militia, but may side with the groom's family because of their own socialization and learned attitudes towards women and marriage. Or it may simply be vulnerable to bribery because of poverty or non-payment by their state. Illustrating these relationships, Penn and Nardos note that:

> In many instances, policemen have been known to refuse to enforce laws against dowry because they themselves do not want to give up demands for dowry as a source of income from their sons ... [They] are easily bribed by the groom's family to disregard criminal evidence and to terminate investigation ... The police do not immediately collect evidence ... because they wait to be bribed. (2003: 99)

Murder may also be reported and ignored or parried; or the police may punish a woman for reporting an attempted murder (Gaag 2004: 27). Institutional change towards an impartial, legal-rational model with all equal before the law is less likely to develop where family and community have not been affected by social atomization and rural–city migration; where metropolitan geographical oversight is not comprehensive and where its neutrality is compromised by familial ties; and where social networks of patronage and clientelism are vital to manage life-threatening instigators of human insecurity such as storms, crop failure and drought. In other words, it can easily be the case that the traditional rules of hierarchies, patronage, female subordination and other social mechanisms vital to the management of potentially devastating threats to human security, such as starvation and waterborne illness, are also the rules and expectations that lead to lethal human insecurity in dowry and belief killings. It may be the case that some societies that routinely dispense belief and dowry murders may also be routinely vulnerable to far greater threats that render whole communities insecure. While certain

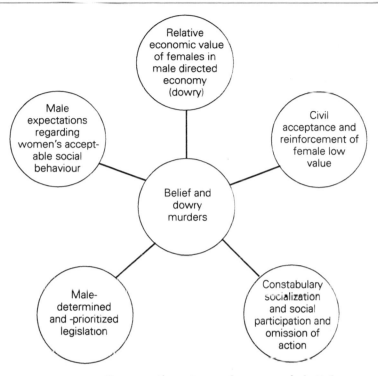

FIGURE 5.1 Key causative actors and processes in belief
and dowry killings

processes may be unavoidable for broad community protection, however, the same cannot be said of belief killings: they are all illegitimate, avoidable and unnecessary.

What is quite clear, however, is that the rules of dowry persist as a result of poverty, greed, male dominance and the advantages involved in having male children in a male-dominated economy. This in turn encourages sex selection, which stimulates infanticide, which in turn damages the perceived value of females. Dowry becomes related to infanticide, complicating the vicious circle of violence against women. It is all but impossible to ignore institutional processes and social rules in belief and dowry killings.

Linking intimate murder, institutions and human insecurity

Intimate murder on a global scale does not happen by chance. It is not independent action by crazed males between whom there are no connections. The violence is linked by socially constructed attitudes that originate in male-driven belief-systems that have been socially codified

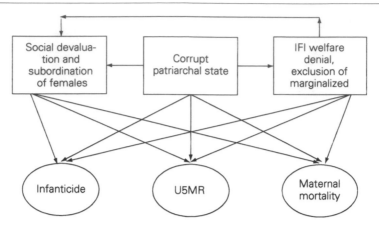

FIGURE 5.2 Mapping institutional roles in infanticide, under-five mortality and maternal mortality

and institutionally normalized. This process is accorded informal institutional 'status' because of its clear objective of controlling female behaviour and punishing aberrations from socially constructed rules, its commonality across regions and its persistence over time. It is equally important, however, to consider the role of other formal institutions in condoning, defending and perpetuating this practice, even if they were promulgated with the intention of arresting intimate murder. This section draws together parallels between each form of violence; discusses institutional reform and resistance over time; and plots a model of positive, if unduly and unacceptably slow, social reconstruction to undermine this global human insecurity.

Conclusion

Dowry, honour or other, unclassified 'domestic' partner killings share a common link. They occur when the females involved challenge their male partner's or his family's perception of male 'honour', most normally constructed around his perceived 'right' to control and direct females in his jurisdiction, and the status this creates within shifting male hierarchies. Marriage as a social institution endorsed by religion has traditionally been a vehicle that places women under the juridically endorsed control of men. In such arrangements, women's rights have been subsumed to the male; this is why until very recently in parts of Europe, including the UK, wife abuse conducted in the home remained the private business of the pair, rather than the public responsibility of the courts and constabulary.

Similarly, again until quite recently, it was the 'conjugal' right of a husband to force his wife to have sex with him when she didn't want to. The same behaviour between strangers is rape. Women thus surrendered their rights to sexual privacy through marital vows; it seems most unlikely that those vows were created by a woman. Furthermore, it has been the case that women were and are, in different societies, relegated to the private sphere and excluded to varying degrees from the public arena that men dominate. Until these arrangements were publicly challenged by women and men opposed to the broad control of women, wife beating and killing were socially constituted and legally condoned by indifference or denial. The greatest advances in changing these conditions have tended to occur at the points at which multiple institutions and processes have clashed and merged.

In the northern European and North American models, in very broad and general terms and trends, one of these clashes emerged from demands for equal political rights for men and women, which in turn translated into growing, if troubled, access to employment that undermined economic dependency on spouses and parents. Increasing democratic secularization and distance from religious power over state legislation also prompted the gradual but ever-challenged 'habituation', or normalization, of the belief that women should not be beaten by partners and should have rights that protect them, set in an impartial and ever more professionalized and neutral legislature, judiciary and constabulary.

The evolution of such formal institutions, however, outstripped the desire of key informal institutions to reform accordingly, creating further tensions and confusion in adult male expectations regarding gender relations and male power and rights. Furthermore, transformation of the social rules that young males learned also failed to keep pace with legislative change. Thus, while the external, legislative order was forging ahead, social rules were not. This created confusion; for centuries, formal institutional attitudes had matched their social equivalents, but increasingly the two drifted out of sync.

This in itself created yet further tensions. Legislation persisted in understanding violence as physical, and banned men from beating women; increasingly, men took to other forms of oppression and control that took time to be reinterpreted as the same control and domination mechanism. For instance, while direct violence was outlawed, indirect violence was not considered. Bullying, verbal abuse, financial manipulation, intimidation, indirect threats (such as to a couple's children), threats of leaving a female spouse with no money, threats of having her put out of the house, constituted male responses to their removal of a traditional 'right' to exercise control and authority by easier, more instant means. These forms of violence, which reflect the broader conceptualization of human insecurity, are also now legislated against, but in various parts of the world, males have found other means of abusing their spouses when control is diminished by external factors.

Two notions may be developed here. One is that it is hard to deny the range and depth of social construction involved in the creation of human insecurity for women in terms of intimate murder. Another is that institutions have both caused and sustained that human insecurity, but have also been transformed (to certain degrees, and with much more room for improvement) through direct challenges. Wherever it occurs, intimate murder happens when males perceive female challenges to their 'rights' of domination and when males are humiliated and 'dishonoured' to the extent that they must exert violent retribution to re-establish their social status in their society, however defined. That these codes of conduct are so evidently human constructions carries with it the inevitable conclusion that they can be further transformed in Europe. It also suggests that this form of human insecurity in other parts of the world, such as South Asia and Africa, may be susceptible to similar transformation. A crucial variable, however, is wealth in general, and women's independent access to financial security through the reconsideration of women's right to equal participation in the public sphere and their removal from subjugation in the private domain.

The institutions of power and domination involved in female human insecurity derive and maintain their status from beliefs legitimized in their historical longevity, which continue to be transmitted through social mores perpetuated in formal and informal education and socialization. They are thus learned values and experiences and, while they are unlikely to be 'unlearned', other beliefs more favourable to equalitarian principles can be encouraged to replace them over time. Conceptually, however, these are matters of power and control. How they differ is essentially reflected in the extent to which women's rights have been codified, legislated for and openly protected by the law and by social attitudes; the degree to which the economy has developed; and the extent to which legal codifications encourage, facilitate and sustain female rights and abilities (including from education) to participate meaningfully in the broad public sphere. Without formal and informal social, economic and political institutional reform, female human insecurity is likely to remain vulnerable to the brooding will of institutionalized male domination.

SIX | Human and realist security

Given the scale and extent of human insecurity demonstrated in Chapter 3, statistically, geographically and conceptually, is there any reason to suggest that there may be a connection between the creation of human insecurity, on the one hand, and, on the other, the creation of more obvious realist security concerns? In loose terms, this is referred to as the 'security-development nexus', which conceptualizes a relationship between political stability, on the one hand, and levels of economic development, on the other. It is an area that has been of some interest to realism, unlike human security as an abstract concept, because the kinds of security involved relate to state stability, failed states, civil war, contagions of failed states, states in which terrorists may operate with impunity, and so on. Given these valid interests, and the general assumption that some form of relationship exists, is there reason to believe that human insecurity as we consider it here also has a deleterious impact on state stability, perhaps leading to state collapse, contagions, civil war and vulnerability to terrorist penetration? This should also be considered in the context of emerging multilateral aid policy from the West, which the USA projects as a tool for minimizing the migration of external threats to the USA from external, contemporary international threats to the US homeland (Cooper 2006; Mueller 2006).

Human insecurity and anti-state violence

The relationship we are concerned with here, then, concerns traditional violence triggered by conditions of human insecurity: riots in response to poverty and disease. Such clashes between state and society over impoverishment and its causes are numerous and widespread. Ferraro and Chenier claim that 'between 1976 and 1994, violent protests against IMF actions occurred in 26 countries' (1994: 288). The *Intercontinental Press* also identified many such violent confrontations, including, for example, the deaths at the hands of the national constabulary and military of sixty anti-IMF protesters in 1984 in the Dominican Republic (August 1984: 296). The World Development Movement's *States of Unrest III* survey records: '238 separate incidents of civil unrest involving millions of people across 34 countries. Many of these incidents ended with the deployment

TABLE 6.1 Civil, anti-state resistance to increased human insecurity, 2003–07

Location	Date	Instigating event	Human insecurity	Political insecurity	Deaths
Zimbabwe	Jan. 2003	Food price hike and distorted allocation	Hunger/starvation	Food riots, constabulary violence against civilians	
Bolivia	Feb. 2003	Tax hikes	Impoverishment and all derivatory consequences	Constabulary and civilian violence against state	33
Switzerland	June 2003	Anti-G8, anti-globalization protests	Impoverishment and injustice	State (25,000 troops and police) vs. society: 9-hour running battles	
Nigeria	July 2003	Oil price hikes	Impoverishment and all derivatory consequences	General strike escalating to rioting	10
Chile	Aug. 2003	Decline in working conditions	Lower income and poor job security	3,000-strong march leading to rioting	
Bolivia	Oct. 2003	Gas exports for perceived elite benefits	Diversion of national wealth and further impoverishment	4 weeks of street riots	58–74
Mexico	May 2004	Reinforcement of unfair trade practices	Social injustice, unfair trade and poverty	State constabulary vs. rioting and looting	
Uzbekistan	Nov. 2004	Regulation of informal economy	High unemployment, state appropriation of private goods	State constabulary vs. 2000–3,000-strong demonstrations, rioting, destruction of state property	
Uzbekistan	May 2005	Religious repression, economic deprivation and corruption	Removal of basic human rights and income opportunities	State vs. society riots	169–745
Argentina and Uruguay	Nov. 2005	International deregulation and market biases	Exposure of national producers to hostile and unfair market forces, large-scale impoverishment	Anti-constabulary rioting and violence close to international summit meeting; banks and US symbols burned, 20 injured	

Location	Date	Instigating event	Human insecurity	Political insecurity	Deaths
Hong Kong	Dec. 2005	World Trade Organization	Negative impacts of unquestioned globalization	Up to 4,000 people rioting, leading to 1,000-strong assault on police; 135 injured (61 police)	2
France	Oct. 2005–Jan. 2006	Government-led youth employment marginalization	Immediate and long-term denial of potential for dignified life and opportunities	State of emergency declared; anti-state rioting, looting and violence; 2,900 arrested	
India	Jan.–July 2006	Land expropriation for private industry	Landlessness, unreliable income security	Armed state–civilian conflict; lethal guerrilla warfare	374
Bangladesh	Aug. 2006	Land expropriation for private industry	Landlessness, unreliable income security	Armed business/paramilitary–civilian conflict: 300 injured	6
India	March 2007	Land expropriation for private industry	Landlessness, unreliable income security	Armed police against farmers over land prices	14

of riot police or the army, resulting in almost 100 documented fatalities, with arrests and injuries running into thousands' of which 'over half [were] directed specifically at the IMF and World Bank' (WDM 2003: 1–5). The report reviews, among other factors, the impact of IMF-dictated VAT increases on milk, sugar, flour, water and electricity in Niger. The capital city, Niamey, was 'shut down'. Strikes also took place outside the capital and citizens were arrested after demanding food price reductions.

Neoliberal adjustment and violent public responses

Protesters may target a wide range of concerns, and they may be spontaneous or organized. Sometimes, people's frustration at unaffordable prices of essential goods is directed at icons of the state: public buildings, limousines, state officers and police. At other times, critics may target actual projects and international institutions' workplaces. In Assam, India, a World Bank workshop was disrupted by 'social activists opposing ... large dam and river linking projects [as part of] a strategic vision document' prepared by the Bank. And in Nicaragua in late 2005, the IMF stipulated that the state raise electricity prices by a quarter before lending would commence (WDM 2003). The International Confederation of Free Trade Unions (ICFTU) has also charted political insecurity and instability caused by the IMF and the World Bank as they direct economic change in many developing countries (ICFTU 2006). Their report surveyed Argentina, Croatia, Indonesia, South Africa, Tanzania and Uruguay, examining the impact on social provision, social justice and social stability of various IMF-induced activities. These included, among many other documented cases, privatizing freight rail, water supplies and postal services, and employer-friendly work contracts.

What is the relationship between economic structures and institutions, on the one hand, and human insecurity and direct violence, on the other? The direct violence is often, in these situations, a response to price rises in essential goods and services. State agents remove subsidies on foodstuffs and utilities (these might include basic staples like maize, bread or rice, and essential services like clean water provision or electricity). There are various reasons why this might occur. Sections of society may become targets of state oppression, for instance. But the incidents discussed above and tabled below were caused by external, rather than internal, challenges. The state removes subsidies and redirects utilities when it is told to by the IMF and other powerful and influential international actors. Such decline in state provision is associated with the rules of Structural Adjustment Programmes (SAPs). In essence, SAPs are introduced with the intention of rendering efficient failing national states and economies by disciplining them. Often, poor countries' states are run on extensive bureaucracies normally overstaffed owing to social phenomena like common social patronage, elite patronage and cronyism. SAPs dictate that such bureaucracies are cut to improve economic efficiency and save money. They also insist on ending state subsidies of essential resources like clean water, electricity and basic foodstuffs.

For the directorship of key IFIs like the World Bank and the IMF, the application of SAPs to all poor states will lead, it is argued, to the global conformity of state with market, generating an efficient global wealth production system that 'lifts all boats'. SAPs, however, are only instruments of the wider neoliberal economic structure that predominates in the twenty-first century. Neoliberalism in practice relies on quite brutal extraction of profit with limited serious or neutral reflection on longer-term damage to the natural environment and human opportunity. It is the rapaciousness with which neoliberalism dictates the application of SAPs in 'inefficient' countries which leads to sudden marketization 'shocks' which escalate the price of normally more affordable (state-subsidized) essentials such as food staples, water and electricity. Responses have unsurprisingly taken the form of violent citizen challenges.

Convention has explained these eruptions of violence 'as "populist" reactions to a painful but generally progressive process of transformation and capitalist development' (Walton and Seddon 1994: 4). They represent 'not a structural feature of the world economy, but merely a lag in the catch up of the poor world to the prosperity of the rich world' (Wade 2005: 291). In other words, sudden shocks are a necessary part of state and economic restructuring and have little meaning or consequence. The ongoing relationship of dependency, debt and structural adjustment in the development and otherwise of countries in the developing world, however, led Walton and Seddon to consider the notion of structural causation and connectivity to direct violence. They argue that these problems were 'intrinsic to the international capitalist economy' and that 'popular struggle [was] linked to class struggle'. They extended this analysis and noted 'an exceptionally wide range of social forces, both responding to, and ... shaping the process of global [capitalist] adjustment' (1994: 5). They argue that structural adjustment creates 'severe economic hardship' from external and internal economic policy choices that 'betray the moral economy' (ibid.: 52).

Walton and Seddon are not alone in their conclusions. Rapley writes that 'it has become almost axiomatic that material inequality and political instability go together ... [Furthermore] policy changes that ... withdraw state protections for the poor in Third World countries have begun a wave of political protest' (Rapley 2004: 3). Nathan is also concerned that 'structural adjustment programmes have aggravated poverty; [IFIs] are accountable more to their Northern "shareholders" than to recipient governments in the South; and they are not held accountable for their mistakes and failed policies' (2000: 188). Willetts also considers these issues and finds 'the failure of neoliberal policies' at the root of 'current patterns of violence and conflict' (2001: 36). The shock of SAP restructuring was responsible for direct violence. She notes what she calls 'the dark side' of neoliberalism, the consequences of which involve economic 'shock therapy, rapid market liberalization and onerous structural adjustment programmes [which] might be part of the security problem rather than the solution' to inequality and instability (ibid.: 36–7). Goldstein concurs, adding that SAPs bring 'rioters into the streets demanding the restoration of subsidies of food, gasoline and other essential goods'. He claims this is because 'terms are too harsh, and it results in mass unemployment and the abandonment of any kind of social programme' (1994: 539). Criticism comes also from the Central Intelligence Agency (CIA) of the United States government. It declared in 2000 that:

> The rising tide of the global economy will create many economic winners, but it will not lift all boats. [It will] spawn conflicts at home and abroad ... Regions, countries and groups feeling left behind will face deepening economic stagnation, political instability ... They will foster political, ethnic, ideological and religious extremism along with the violence that often accompanies it. (WDM 2003: 5)

In other words, while many will benefit, not all can: neoliberalism's man-made rules are governed by predatory exploitation, through uneven competition, for finite resources via an unfair trading system preserved by asymmetric, man-made international financial institutions. Those who cannot compete reasonably will be relatively marginalized, and the greater the marginalization, the greater the potential for violent responses to failed state and international economic and political policies. The evidence does not suggest, however, that states fail or become susceptible to terrorist presences or that civil wars routinely break out owing to human insecurity or economic underdevelopment. There exists, then, a security-development nexus, but this could be more usefully qualified as a 'human insecurity-economic development' nexus. The normal conception of security-development does not affirm, from the evidence assessed here, a critical mass of political instability that reflects realist priorities. The security-development nexus as it is probably most widely understood identifies a relationship between human poverty and domestic political instability. This is assumed at some point to be capable of mutating into international crises based on medical contagion – the political theory of contagion, where as one state is infected by a political problem, neighbouring states also contract the political 'virus'. It is also, however, a cipher when applied to human security in the developing world, because there is a disjuncture between whose security is created by whose development. That is, while the common perception of the nexus implies stability and safety for humans through economic growth in the South, its actual application since 9/11 has been to secure the USA and other Northern states through selective wealth enhancement of particular states considered at risk of subversion by unsavoury elements who are imagined to exist, or are imagined to pose a threat to US homeland security (Wilkin 2002; Stewart 2004).

Relative deprivation and direct violence

Nafziger has identified further correlates that generalize about outcomes from relationships between poor states and international economic sponsors like the IMF and the World Bank, on the one hand, and disempowered citizenry, on the other. He maintains that violence is to be expected because:

> Economic decline and predatory rule that fail to provide state services lead to relative deprivation ... Relative deprivation spurs social dissatisfaction and political violence. Poor economic performance undermines the legitimacy of a regime, increasing the probability of regime turnover. Political elites use repression to forestall threats to the regime and capture a greater share of the population's declining surplus. Repression and economic discrimination trigger further discontent and socio-political mobilization on the part of the groups affected, worsening the humanitarian crisis. Protracted economic stagnation increases the probability of population displacement, hunger and disease. (2002: 162)

Winter and Leighton also note this relationship. They argue that 'those who are chronically oppressed are often ... those who resort to direct violence ... Often elites must use direct violence to curb the unrest produced by structural violence'. They add that 'huge income disparities in many Latin American countries [for example] are protected by correspondingly huge military operations, which in turn drain resources away from social programs and produce even more structural violence' (2006: 1). For Nafziger, the performance of the state is tied to relative content or discontent where essential services are concerned. It is accepted by most that credit is determined through economic and political conditionality. It is also accepted that there are good reasons for describing IMF and other approaches as 'austerity measures'; but those upon whom austerity is forced are almost always the most vulnerable to declines in essential services. It can be of no surprise, then, that there is a direct relationship between the IMF and the World Bank, on the one hand, and discontent and violence on the other.

Further evidence of structural influences in these processes comes from the developed world. Europe was alerted to impoverishment and human insecurity when 'race riots' reminded observers globally of the gap between employed indigenous French and poorly employed immigrant populations. Parts of Paris burned for several nights. Furthermore, Britain has, according to UNICEF, 'one of the highest child poverty rates in the rich world – 15.4 per cent of the child population', whose life chances are undermined and whose insecurity is exacerbated by these conditions (2007). And in the USA, 46 million vulnerable citizens do not have access to free health provision (Kaiser Foundation 2007). It is this commonality of polarities and spread of human insecurity which point towards similar structural determinism and institutional commonality across regions. There is thus little doubt that structural, indirect violence does indeed lead to direct violence. This seems to occur on a limited scale, however, in the sense that there is little evidence to demonstrate a connection between structural economic intervention and wide-scale, continuous direct violence that spreads contagiously to other states and destabilizes seriously the international environment. Goodhand advises that while there is a relationship between poverty and insecurity, 'chronic poverty by itself is unlikely to lead to conflict' (2001: 4). Furthermore, this form of violence remains a minority killer compared to the lethality of diarrhoea, malaria and structural femicide, poverty and starvation.

State failure and direct violence

The relationship between structures of violence and direct violence does not, however, cease at the most obvious and immediate confrontations between the normally unarmed citizenry without institutionalized use of weaponry and the state as the instigator of anti-human security policies. Willetts postulates that there is a relationship between the rules of neoliberal growth and the rise of extra-state challenges for and

claims to political legitimacy. In this view, the long-term economic decline experienced in some African states (for example) as a consequence
of deleterious economic intervention, coupled to domestic corruption
and incompetence, has eroded the legitimacy that governments need
to maintain authority.

When this happens, authority may be transferred to often competing
groups led by 'warlords' who provide or withhold, through the rule of
arms, the social services civic society requires to prevent a decline in
human security. Willetts suggests that when 'state legitimacy and the
rule of law have all but broken down ... authority is increasingly divided
between what is left of formal institutions, local warlords and gang or
Mafia leaders' (2001: 40–41; see also Rapley 2004: 116, 120–21). Rapley
adds a connection between the neoliberal economic order and religious
affiliation. He claims, for example, that:

> All over the Arab world, in the midst of growing shortages of jobs, hous-
> ing, education, and services, not to mention a widening pattern of in-
> come distribution that is fuelling a resentment of the privileged classes,
> many people – particularly young men, who are left idle and without
> appreciable prospects – have gravitated to the support networks of
> Islamist organizations, be they clinics, schools, day-care centres, welfare
> distribution programs, investment companies, or even banks (ibid.: 129).

Thus, whereas violent citizen objection to state policies may constitute only sporadic opposition to specific policies and issues, it may also
prompt more organized and/or more broad-fronted opposition to state
authority, which results in regime change or the formation of extra-
state institutions that have civic legitimacy or which control citizenry
in ways similar to the state without necessarily having been legally sanctioned.

Smith maintains that 'when privileged elite defends its too large
share of too few resources, the link is created between poverty, inequality
and the abuse of human rights. The denial of basic freedoms ... forces
people to choose between accepting gross injustice and securing a fairer
share by violent means' (1997: 15). Sandbrook and Romano conclude
that humanity is governed to a large extent by markets in flux which can
have devastating consequences, as well as producing problematic riches.
These polarities and fluctuations require 'strong, coherent states to take
decisive defensive action and mediate domestic conflicts; yet these new
tensions, combined with externally influenced austerity programmes and
anti-state ideologies, challenge the legitimacy and coherence of already

weak states'. The resultant credibility vacuum is fertile ground for violence (2004: 1008).

The WTO, IMF and World Bank are key instruments of globalization and the tensions and violence Sandbrook and Romano refer to above. Those roots may not be readily evident to all, but Thomas argues that 'the fundamental causes at the root of hunger, poverty and inequality must be addressed, or the achievement of human security will be impossible' (2000: 9). Causation is structural and institutional.

Willetts then examines the argument from the other end. Given structural and institutional determinism, she is concerned that 'global security will not be enhanced until such time as the existing economic orthodoxy is challenged and replaced ... neoliberal policies constitute a form of structural violence that places the greed of the few above the basic human security of the many' (2001: 44–5). Such commentary is likely to be labelled as hyperbole partly because it is not entirely fair to blame the greed of the few for all the ills of the world, especially as so many people benefit and enjoy solid human security without excessive or unreasonable consumption. But the point remains that there are consequences to the neoliberal top-down model that must be taken seriously as it relates to human insecurity.

Scholarship and research must, however, also be attentive to structural and institutional changes from the bottom. Harris maintains that the frequency and geographical range of civil challenges to states and institutions in developing countries (discussed in detail above) appear to have diminished since the turn of the twenty-first century, to be partly complemented with political demonstrations in the developed world against neoliberalism. He argues that:

> Since Seattle [December 1999] ... anti-globalization demonstrations have, if anything, intensified. They have different characteristics to the IMF riots and the global social movements involved have broadened their activities and agendas. The protests have been generalised to question the policies of these organisations, usually their neo-liberal agendas, and to criticise the processes of decision-making in the institutions which they argue demonstrate a 'democratic deficit' in that they are not transparent and accountable. The activists in these demonstrations have also become much more centred in the developed countries rather than primarily in developing countries. (2002: 1)

O'Brien et al. (2000) also identify a range of protests in other developed states against various IFIs specifically, and destructive neoliberalism generally. In both the developed and developing worlds, however, given that the state is normally armed, it is not uncommon to see violent civil agitation and confrontation. This is also a 'hard' security issue. It involves complex government policy-making regarding financing security organs such as the constabulary and the military. Often in developing countries, this function may be tendered out to privatized security forces that may or may not be subject to the same legislation and oversight that regular state organs usually face in Western democracies. Where this happens, and when the line between the state and non-state use of 'legitimate' violence blurs to undermine civil society relations, yet greater insecurity can develop. The reaction of the Ogoni people in Nigeria to Shell Oil's use of the state security apparatus to protect their foreign private investments at the expense of the natural environment is well documented (Frynas 1998; Wheeler et al. 2001). It is an example of a spiralling cycle of violence beginning with grassroots resistance to damaging foreign direct investment made immune through the 'renting' of state agencies such as the police or army to protect the 'investors' from the indigenous people they are harming or robbing.

Conclusion

The question posed at the beginning of this chapter was, 'Does human insecurity cause political insecurity and direct violence that may or may not result in mortalities?' The answer can only be yes. There is no doubt at all that the causes of human insecurity are international institutions and structures, as well as corrupt, nepotistic and kleptocratic governments. But the two are in fact inseparable in some ways. Globalization, or the subjugation of all states and markets to market discipline in order to generate payments from South to North and open Southern markets while closing their Northern counterparts, has aggravated conditions of human insecurity. People have responded with direct violence against both their governments, for implementing structural financial reforms that undermine their access to basics and essentials, and IFIs, which compromise sovereign economic independence by making loans conditional upon the strict market reforms that compromise human security.

But there are relatively few fatalities caused during anti-state, anti-reform rioting and protesting, and few states have recently been overthrown on these grounds alone. States have been temporarily destabilized but have normally retained external IFI support as long as reforms are maintained. In very few cases have such instances resulted in contagious 'knock-on' effects with neighbouring states. The numerous outbreaks of violence noted above have not resulted in continental decline or widespread warfare, and there is no comparison with the humanitarian disaster in the Democratic Republic of Congo (DRC) that retains the interest of conventional realist security specialists. There is a clear 'security-development nexus' in the DRC, but there are also innumerable other factors that have contributed to the catastrophe in the Congo.

Statistically and relatively speaking, the impact of human insecurity alone on political stability is marginal, although not to the people it affects. In contrast, however, the role of civil institutions and human ideas in the creation and perpetuation of epic human insecurity is colossal.

SEVEN | International institutions

One of the most encouraging aspects of research into human insecurity is that, once the central causative agencies, institutions and structures are identified, the extent of human determinism and social construction is readily apparent. A second encouraging aspect is that such social processes are not permanent, as realism suggests, but are in fact socially transformable through ordinary processes of challenge and reformation. Finally, it is encouraging that, rather than having to institute a wide-ranging social transformational process from inception, challenges to all the structures, institutions and agencies are already well under way and, in the case of critical feminism's insights into male domination, have been ongoing for centuries in various forms. Similarly, current social protest regarding poverty and vulnerability is also only the latest version of already long extant processes that challenge the institution of unnecessary impoverishment, vulnerability and death. This chapter briefly reviews the limited success of external challenges to individual elements of the international economy, and then discusses potential and problems in externally challenging the IFIs' intellectual rationale. The second half of the chapter treats the institution of Direct Control Violence similarly.

International Financial Institutions and human insecurity

If it were reasonable to argue that the global economy has been determined and is managed primarily by rational men whose faith lies in the impartiality of the objective market system, then human responsibility for outcomes in this process would appear to be a non sequitur. It would be the case that an objective system would have no role or ability in favouring one group above another, so explanations for disadvantage and large-scale human insecurity would have to be sought elsewhere. There would be no expectation that the beliefs and values upon which both resource distribution and power-seeking rest should be fundamentally challenged. But this is not a reasonable argument.

In the process of its being, the neoliberal market massively enriches some and indirectly kills and marginalizes many more, and its competitive nature reinforces negative elements of human interaction. One may construe 'the market' as raptorial, greedy and warlike, little removed from the marauding and plundering ways of the imperial era of conquest and domination; Cohen (2001: 74) calls it 'predatory', as does Gelinas (2003). Given that the central difference between now and then is that the asymmetrical power relationship is now legally condoned and socially legitimized through institutionalization, Cohen's characterization seems apt. He concludes that human efforts 'to get beyond predation ... thus far have failed' (2001: 74). Agathangelou and Ling are similarly pessimistic when they remark that:

> Socialism's retreat ... allowed ... owners of corporate capital – the 'Wall Street-Treasury-IMF Complex' – to abrogate an earlier, social contract with workers ... for a rapidly globalizing market system ... High income inequalities and polarities now afflict the world, especially [for] those who are neither white, male, professional, nor Western ... The international financial institutions ... seek only to fatten their own treasuries rather than improve people's lives ... Such violence inheres in neoliberal globalization. (2004: 531–2)

The nature of neoliberalism is unavoidably rapacious, increasingly competitive and hyper-masculine. Its predatory character necessarily invokes winners and losers, and the asymmetrical power and opportunity advantages enjoyed by institutional policy-makers, public and private, and state leaders to varying degrees, ensure shifting hierarchies of identities that generate great and moderate riches for some, but which in the process inevitably also ensure that lower participants and those excluded from effective participation in this hierarchy of masculine perceptions, beliefs and priorities die in their millions.

But the evolution of the concept of human security is evidence of a humanist recognition that, whether or not one approves of neoliberalism, it is deleterious to hundreds of millions of people and lethal for many millions more. Hayden maintains that:

> The injustice of global poverty arises from the fact that it is produced by shared global institutions with which, under conditions of economic globalization, we are all engaged in some form ... We are all connected to extremely powerful institutions such as the IMF, the World Bank and the WTO, which determine and mediate our relationships to one another ... insofar as they govern markets, trade and foreign affairs. (2007: 288)

Human intellect and compassion continue to evolve in constructive ways and reject predation of one group upon another. Kofi Annan iterated this point as UN secretary general when he set out his stall regarding human security in 2000. He urged that: 'No shift in the way we think can be more critical than this: we must put people at the centre of everything we do. No calling is more noble, and no responsibility greater, than that of enabling men women and children ... to make their lives better' (Annan 2000: 7).

Contemporary external challenges to IFIs

Thomas's survey of ongoing social challenges to neoliberalism identifies three strands of thinking. First, it seems increasingly unlikely that a global revolution is imminent, undermined perhaps by the hegemony of the neoliberal discourse, the apparent invulnerability of its international institutions to external and internal criticisms, unparalleled wealth and crass consumption (jewellery for mobile phones) in the states that host neoliberal power. The days of heroic workers storming various strongholds of capitalism imagined by various thinkers did not materialize (this is not to suggest that they won't in the future). Second, this approach seems to have been replaced with demonstrations around the world aimed at specific incidences of excessive and lethal neoliberalism rather than confronting neoliberalism as an organic, holistic whole. Third, it seems to be the case that reining in neoliberalism is more likely to happen in response to activities 'at the sub-state level' (2000: 111).

While there has been only limited transformation of IFIs, and while promises on debt reduction have been inadequately translated into repudiation, to a certain extent critics of structural adjustment interventions have been heard. Poverty Reduction Strategy Papers (PRSPs) have introduced a number of reforms designed to compensate for the shock of adjustment for the poorest. Critics maintain, however, that these have been ineffectual. Johnston argues, for example, that PRSPs continue to reflect neoliberal tendencies and that the reforms are 'not a significant departure from previous arguments'. The results of the reforms are so limited that economic policy will continue, argues Johnston, 'to obscure the development of policies that will have a positive effect on the poorest' (2005: 135).

Only limited changes have been made to trade regimes. The unevenness and inequality evident in many trade arrangements have become the subject matter of many public challenges to various problems in development. However, Deraniyagala notes that while some trade reforms have been introduced, they are destined to produce similar outcomes to lending reforms because the problem-causing biases inherent in the institutional vessels of the world economy remain (2005: 99–103). In other words, these inputs are not challenges to the institutions' underlying conceptual determinants. They are adjustments made at the fringe of the system which inevitably have only a very limited impact on the outcome of the policies, when it is the institutions of the structures which require attention and adjustment. In a sense, they miss the bigger picture.

Other solutions for economic development and vital human security have focused on debt, but again with only limited success. Adams (1991) invokes the legal concept of 'odious debt'; others have maintained that poor people should not pay for loans from which they did not benefit. Yet others maintain that the debt has been repaid many times and it is the interest which accrues (George 1989, 1992). Cancelling debt would therefore not hurt lenders because they have already reacquired most of the capital. Furthermore, most lending institutions maintain funds for emergency contingencies and would cover their losses satisfactorily (Riley 1991). Yet others maintain that debt cancellation by public lenders would have only the tiniest effect on the global economy, which would shake off the impact quickly (ibid.). Various other approaches to debt cancellation and debt remodelling have been advanced, but these share with those noted above the problem that they do not represent structural revision. They address only one component of the wider structure and its institutions which ensures that independent development is out of the grasp of the most vulnerable. Once debt is repaid or cancelled, more loans would be required for the necessary infrastructural development and system creation to facilitate a developing state's intermeshing with the international economy. Once this occurred, however, development would still be elusive if the other elements of institutional asymmetry remained in place.

Another approach to dealing with inequality considers redistributing cash, credits, taxes and debts. Some have proposed a Tobin Tax on profits made from, for example, international currency speculation (Tobin 1996; Patomaki 2002). The tax would not have to be very high to yield significant results which could then be diverted to various schemes to alleviate poverty and human insecurity. Redistribution would achieve little, however, and is like aid. It does not address the root causes of inequality, impoverishment and immiseration which are central determinants of terminal human insecurity. Redistribution of resources might provide temporary respite for some poor people in some places, depending on where the distribution occurs, and it might save some who would otherwise have died. But it would have to be permanently repeated, because the structure of distribution is already determined in favour of the richest and most powerful countries. Once redistribution ceased, the situations that lead to lethal impoverishment would remain. Other proposals also tend to address the peripheral consequences rather than the central causes, akin to using a sticking plaster for a decapitation.

Thus, although a global Marxist revolution seems unlikely at this stage (which may or may not be a good thing), and while states seem unwilling to engage at a level that creates effective changes to human insecurity globally, ordinary, concerned human beings have mobilized with speed, passion and technological efficacy to challenge the institutions and processes considered to be most dangerous to human security, even if the concept is not yet publicly or widely referred to as such. Significantly, however, this has 'yet to cohere into a collective demand for fundamental change in the world order ...' (Payne 2005: 5). That is, there is no holistic approach that identifies institutions and structures that determine the practices of the various individual aspects of the modern economic system and the assumptions upon which they rest.

In other words, while human security as defined here originates in the ideational and ideological beliefs and constructions inherent to andrarchy and neoliberalism, the targets of scrutiny noted above are only the institutions and specific practices that derive from their ideas, beliefs and value systems. They are only physical and psychological manifestations of belief structures that are rarely ever considered broadly. The WTO, the IMF, the World Bank and the G8, among others, are but extensions of the greater structures that contain the programming for the institutions, which then translate that programming into actions conducted through human agency and acceptance of the ideational reliability of the structures from which their orders come. This is perhaps why independent 'strikes' at specific singular issues like debt, while raising public and political awareness and inducing limited reform, are limited in their ability to effect wide-scale changes in human insecurity. If structures are likened to radio transmitters, then the institutions are the radio waves and transmissions that tell people what to do. Currently, opposition is focused on the equivalent of 'jamming' radio waves while leaving the transmitters intact. Those that diminish human security by whichever agency are still receiving their orders, and there are no other transmitters currently online, to draw the analogy to a close. In essence, it is intellectual decapitation which is absent. The fundamental idea must be challenged at the same time as the 'bottom-up' methods are invoked.

Institutional challenge from within

We have noted that challenges to institutions have had only limited impact. One of the reasons for this is that the characteristic inertia in the face of public challenges from movements such as Oxfam, Save the Children, the Fifty Years is Enough campaign and Greenpeace is in part due to a lack of challenge from within the international financial bodies themselves. In the study of international relations, opinion is divided over most things. But few would disagree that *people* communicate the beliefs and associated will of an institution; without people, institutions would be moribund and meaningless. They require voluntary participation by rational-acting, conscious people, often in their thousands, who agree with, or at least do not find morally repugnant, the goals and methods of the institutions they work for. It requires a perception of legitimacy for most people to work for an IFI: of rationale, existence and conduct. IFIs are operated by people who, for the most part, believe in the propriety of their conduct and that their actions represent a 'force for good'. If individual and group intentions are sound, as they almost certainly are, why the dissonance between intention and outcome?

In her study of Adolph Eichmann, the notorious Jew executioner, Hannah Arendt pointed out that under certain circumstances, people may carry out actions remote from the consequences of those actions and of which they may claim to have no realization and therefore no real culpability for negative outcomes. Arendt recorded that Eichmann 'could see no one, no one at all, who was actually against' the plan he was implementing (1964: 116). Eichmann claimed that 'there were no voices from the outside to arouse [his] conscience' (ibid.: 126). In his case, the end state of his acts and decisions remained invisible to him (he claimed). Arendt described this not in terms of an abstract 'evil' but instead as banal thoughtlessness, in the sense that Eichmann 'chose not to exercise the capacity to think about and judge his actions in the light of the ends of the social system within which he functioned as an agent' (1978: 245).

This attitude is fairly common in global institutions because of their organizational culture, which is maintained when there is external acceptance of their mandate or task and a minimum of internal dissent to the policies involved. In the case of IFIs today, few of their employees are exposed to the negative consequences of their institutional outputs. Nor, in the absence of first-hand exposure to problems their institution creates, do they absorb external reports of negative, deleterious or lethal outcomes. But it is fairly safe to argue that, were they to make connections between their acts and mass lethality, they would not want this to remain the case. They would, one may posit, seek to redirect the resources of their organization towards more thoughtful actions that resulted in more positive benefits.

Various forces (none of them extra-human) combine, however, to minimize critical exposure of large institutions' outputs. External challenges are often abnegated by employee loyalty generated by institutional propaganda and 'mission statements', for example, and perceived or real threats to job security. Resistant employees may be isolated by their own colleagues who cannot, because of their own families, risk association with criticism. Employees also attempt to balance the claims of external agencies against constant internal ideological reinforcement. Capitalism is, after all, the dominant, hegemonic belief and practice for resource distribution on earth, and it is considered value free, so it cannot be wrong (see below). The culture within Nazism underpinning the execution of the Final Solution was one of undeniable faultlessness that brooked no survivable opposition or challenge. External criticism was denied and rejected, and few of its members had the inclination to challenge it from within.

In similar scenes of belief suspension and denial, ongoing, lengthy, valid, accurate, reliable, competent accretion and representation of evidence of immiseration as a result of IFI policy are rejected by the IFIs involved. This attitude and behaviour have since been presented as common within large organizations with specific objectives they believe to be largely unassailable. Examining organizational culture, Weaver and Leiteritz identified comparable behaviours on the part of the World Bank. Such arguments as follow apply also to the IMF, an institution underpinned by a very similar ideological ethos. Although quite clearly the IMF employs different tactics in managing economies, it shares with the World Bank the objective of sustaining the free market framework within which, they believe, development for the poorest will occur (internal contradictions notwithstanding).

Weaver and Leiteritz argue that internal challenges or questioning in the World Bank were subject to what they described as the 'tenacious survival capacity of the Bank's dominant organizational culture'. They discuss 'the extent to which reform initiators are able to go beyond formal structural and rule change to disrupt the underlying informal values and incentives and incite meaningful and sustainable changes in organizational behavior', and conclude that this would not happen unless any proposed change was already in line with the expectations and values of the organization. They argue that the

[c]atalyst for reform within highly autonomous and powerful international organizations such as the World Bank hinges upon a convergence of external and internal factors. Specifically in the case of the Bank, change in the interests of the [World Bank's] principal member states in conjunction with paradigm shifts in the broader international development regime and the 'whistle-blowing' activities of visible and vocal NGOs cumulated in a resounding external demand for Bank reform. Yet because the World Bank is a relatively autonomous international organization, a comprehensive reform initiative did not emerge until a change in organizational leadership and a core coalition of internal reform advocates pushed for reform from the inside, articulating explicit targets and the strategies for getting there. (Weaver and Leiteritz 2002)

Young describes the requisite forces as simultaneously 'endogenous and exogenous' (1999: 144–5). In other words, any push for change from without needs to be accompanied by an acceptance of the validity of such demand from within; and vice versa. Furthermore, this needs to be accepted by the institution in question.

A key problem with such approaches is that an institution must accept reform to initiate it. A dual 'endogenous and exogenous' approach may test the credibility of the institution's operating systems, but institutional inertia may reduce the effect of internal and external criticisms. In the case of the IFIs that project agency from the ideology of neoliberalism, ideological legitimacy and the absence of equivalency may for some time transcend challenge. The World Bank and the IMF derive great legitimacy from the compelling and internally legitimizing inevitability and dominance of the Bank's 'ideology [of] economic neo-liberalism', which itself is essentially a 'technocratic' and objective mission with universal 'value-free' truths (Williams 1994: 110; Balaam and Veseth 1996: 29). This belief is further emphasized by the absence of a 'legitimate' alternative; the cycle thus becomes self-reinforcing, and claims to the contrary may be treated with McCarthyesque suspicion (Caulfield 1996: ix).

Furthermore, it is normal to be suspicious of the monumentally obscene, so that human beings' entire intellectual and emotional frameworks do not collapse. The gross inequities around the world, visible to those involved in and constantly exposed to the evidence in the development, poverty and globalization debates, force humans to draw on 'enormous psychological resources to ensure [that poverty does] not interfere with our "normal" life by burdening us with a crippling sense of guilt ... through blatant use of the ego defence of denial' (Nandy 2002: 112–14). In other words, it is part of our psychological 'immune' system designed to prevent us from being so emotionally overwhelmed as to render us unable to function. Pasha and Murphy maintain that the historical problem of poverty and destitution is evidence of a persistent capacity in humans to remain blinkered to real causes of real inequality. They maintain that only when 'released from the fetters of an ego defence [may] a real recognition of ... inequality ... ensue' (2002: 5). It was long maintained in development circles in the 1970s that 'De Nile ain't jus' a river in Egypt' (Mark Twain).

With this validation of the Bank's legitimacy and authority, coupled to basic human psychological subroutines, few people inside the Bank and other parallel organizations have an incentive to critically challenge underlying claims and assumptions or their modus operandi. This reluctance is, however, further underpinned by World Bank protocol dictating that a majority of its operatives do not see the consequences of their actions at grassroots level, and internal dissent from the neoliberal line is seen as 'an indication of a desire to find alternative employment' (Caulfield 1996: ix.). Rich also points to the control the Bank exerts over the ideological reliability of its staff (1994a: 198). In this sense, then, there is little reason to expect that a neoliberal international 'development' organization like the World Bank would deviate from its line while the internal environment passively and actively discourages dissent and compromises employees. These characteristics are in general terms shared with the IMF (Williams 1994: 111), as inevitably they will be with most large-scale neoliberal IFIs. Ideological supremacy coupled to compromised employees is the powerful adhesive maintaining a set world-view against supporting external public challenge.

Recognizing dogma and challenging intellectual legitimacy

For scholars such as George and Sabelli, institutional dogma is underpinned by adherence to a creed bordering on fundamentalism. That is, the institutional capacity of neoliberal financial institutions to withstand a veritable barrage of criticism and demand for change from the external public and a few internal dissenters derives in part from hubris and absolute faith in the structural, ideational underpinnings in ways not dissimilar to religious fundamentalisms. Hayden maintains that such 'ideological beliefs tend to ossify into commonly accepted opinions and standards, into conventional categories that are elevated to supreme wisdom and which compromise the ability to think, to explain, to understand, and to judge from an enlarged mentality' (2007: 295). An unshakeable faith in neoliberalism explains institutional refusal to reconsider policies that are considered by many outside their organization to be fundamentally flawed and actively lethal for millions. This said, ossified bodies may also crack with age.

References to religious undertones have been commonplace for some time. Rich describes the World Bank as the 'Vatican of international development' (1994a: 195). Mihevc identifies intolerance to opposition and argues that 'the strategies employed by the World Bank to guarantee the hegemony of its ideology and to deal with dissenters ... correspond to those of fundamentalism' (1992: 4, 12). George and Sabelli (1994: 96) maintain that for the Bank the 'operations of the free market are assumed to be value-free, efficient in allocating resources and socially neutral' and their legitimacy becomes inviolable. The IMF has been referred to by one observer as 'International Monetary Fundamentalism', which involves 'the imposition of identical prescriptions on all countries ... no matter what conditions prevail locally'. Seabrook continues that everywhere 'the advice, exhortations and orders are always the same; and the consequences, for the poorest, the same' (1992: 12; Kothari 1993: 8). Continuing the supernatural theme, Carmen claims the outcome is 'a carefully cultivated mystification: it allows the developed to continue to indulge in a dangerous self-delusion while the underdeveloped [internalize] the myth that they are indeed incapable, incompetent and "the problem"' (1996: 1; Rapley 2004: 126). George and Sabelli refer to key financial mechanisms as 'supranational, non-democratic institutions ... with a doctrine, a rigidly structured hierarchy preaching and imposing ... a quasi-religious mode of self-justification' (1994: 97).

Continuing the theme of dogma and fundamentalist extremism, the authors equate such organizational ethos with the worst characteristics of the most flawed communist polities of the cold war. IFI organizational ethos is, they claim, 'reminiscent of a centralized political party characterized by opacity, authoritarianism and successive party lines' (ibid.: 5). They also compare the World Bank with the medieval church system (ibid.: 5), while Rapley refers to a 'fundamentalist' attitude (2004: 126) and Rist describes IFIs and neoliberalism as a 'global faith' (1997: 56). The absence, then, of viable alternatives and the resistance of the neoliberal IFIs to internal and external criticisms despite a surfeit of evidence are underscored by a fundamentalist mentality akin to the worst we have seen from religious zealots and bigots around the world and the brutally dictatorial Stalinist regimes of eastern Europe. Intellectually, the conundrum is vapid because debate and challenge are effectively stymied by uncritical faith. Neoliberal IFIs and their foundational beliefs should be subject to as much criticism as any other institution or body charged with the global responsibility of creating wealth and ending lethal penury, just as any influential faith system should be, including Christianity and Islam.

Despite the apparent limitations to change, there are reasons to be optimistic. Such transformation rarely happens overnight but instead springs from a kernel of thought upon which others may build. Institutions and empires rise and fall unpredictably: publicly institutionalized slavery is a thing of the past and the 'communist' empires of eastern Europe collapsed with little resistance from their ideologues. The structures of violence that constitute the title of this work have been identified not as inevitable, immutable consequences of a savage human nature but as responsive, flexible and shifting mental processes of human beings and their subjective perceptions of insecurity.

Evidence has also been proposed of causes of institutional inertia from the bottom up; and while great sway is held by some employers in IFIs, there is little reason to believe that internal unionization and changes to transparency rules might not accommodate and protect internal challenges. There is no good reason why the employees of global IFIs should not be entitled to comprehensive union membership. Furthermore, many of the instruments required to mount challenges exist already in the form of International NGOs, which come very well equipped to express dissent. Worldwide communications systems such as the Internet can spread such debates. But it seems that the most effective approach is a simultaneous holistic, top-down, bottom-up model that accepts the social construction of global structures of violence while simultaneously internally and externally challenging the institutional transmitters of belief and perception that unwittingly cause such global, and avoidable, human suffering without a shot being fired.

Intellectual challenge

It seems that the institutions transmitting ideological values rest on some problematic assumptions. One of these is the claim that economics is an impartial and objective, value-free science. In the natural sciences, from which social sciences borrow methods and approaches, generalizations can be made from given, consistent data. Each time water is boiled at sea level, it boils at the same temperature, allowing predictions to be made. It is also devoid of human factors influencing the environment in which it boils. But every economic calculation must involve an almost unending range of human variables, from the sublime to the ridiculous, all of which are largely unpredictable. For neoliberal economists to claim that this is a value-free science seems to deny key aspects of human economic behaviour such as taste (and how that taste may change on any day); choices made in terms of limited opportunities; external shocks such as unpredicted supply or demand collapses; and so on.

Related to this is the intellectual problem of economic models and generalizations. Considered for what it is, the argument is made that, like democracy, capitalism is a transferable asset that can fit anywhere. But the conditions that gave rise to and sustain democracy, like those that make capitalism effective, are not necessarily present everywhere. Neoliberal institutional legitimacy seems to rest in large part upon the assumption that if social, political and economic conditions are changed in poor places, market capitalism, like democracy, will take root and flourish. But this neglects some very important factors regarding different historical conditions and trajectories, and different physical environments and their sustainability and relationship with resources.

This is before we even consider the innate advantages enjoyed by Europe in the form of imperial extraction and oceanic exploration, the latter of which was made possible by technological innovation in eastern Asia and the Middle East. In other words, the innumerable variables present in social science intellectual explorations mean that neoliberal economics as a science based on human consumption cannot share the same foundations as the natural sciences. Furthermore, the 'science' of economics seems to rest on an ability to create generalizations of which social scientists tend to be suspicious. Rist puts this well. He argues that 'when economists assert that certain "principles" or "laws" are valid everywhere and for everyone, they are engaging in a piece of deception, because it is illegitimate to deduce a "general theory" from particular cases. This, no doubt, is why most economists come to grief when they talk about "development" ...' (1997: 106).

Economics involves subjective decision-making on the part of millions of people; it cannot decide which model should be used where; it is massively divided at most levels, as one would associate with a social science like international relations or politics. It is therefore neither reliable nor acceptable as a universal approach; but neoliberal economists are still maintaining that what seems to work in the West can work elsewhere. This cannot be true realistically and, given that globalization's assumptions rest on this misnomer, there are wide grounds on which to challenge the ideas and the institutions that animate them as central causes of human insecurity in so many domains. Such claims are fundamentally false, but their regular iteration is an element of the neoliberal discourse from which its hegemony and seeming invincibility derive. But again, it is not all bad news. The greater degree to which social construction can be demonstrated in these equations, the greater the awareness of the possibilities for change.

Direct Control Violence and institutional reform

Perhaps because of its distastefulness and its tendency to be practised in private, it has been difficult for some to comprehend male violence against females in institutional terms. Let us remind ourselves how institutions are considered in the literature, and then consider this institution against other, perhaps more familiar, examples. For Goldstein, an institution is 'the tangible manifestation of shared expectations' (1994: 341). This description suits 'cultural' behaviour; it relates to behaviours of humans in relation to what they have learned over time and what remains socially legitimate in its own context. Other notions of institutions concern organizations involved in directing and coordinating various policies. This is perhaps the more commonly held notion, which many realists consider as essential for managing power inequalities and disputes.

Additionally, we noted that scholars such as Payne (2005), Cox (1984) and Williams (1994) present institutions as maintaining disequilibrium, rather than being impartial or neutral mechanisms. Thus, in the same way that economic institutions like the WTO and organizing bodies like the G8 maintain advantages for secondary refining economies above primary exporting states, we might suppose that male-built social institutions like politics, law and economics may seek to exercise a form of authority that uses various forms of control to preserve male dominion (Ahmed-Ghosh 2004: 94). This might explain why institutional change has been so slow in the most basic of rights areas, such as suffrage, or equal pay for the same work, and we may therefore expect similar challenges in dealing with institutional entrenchment and resistance to change that various scholars have identified with regard to the IFIs outlined in previous chapters (ibid.: 95).

In terms of the control by men of women, Direct Control Violence (DCV) fits these definitions. It is a long-extant practice considered socially acceptable where it occurs and is thus normal and legitimate in a society or across a broader environment. Part of its essence is that it is shared and hence has broad legitimacy. When we consider DCV as an institution, it does indeed maintain and perpetuate (through expectation and fear) the systemic advantage of males over females in a range of environments, including the private, the social, the economic and the political, in different places. Not all forms of violence are obvious, but the threat of damaging consequences from a female's actions by a male 'superior' would also act as a means of control. In these senses, then, DCV is the institution connecting and transmitting the beliefs and values of andrarchy. This too fits the model under development in this book. Not every discrete act of male-to-female violence would constitute an institution. But by demonstrating the similarities of purpose of different types of intimate partner killing ('domestic', 'honour' and dowry), and by illustrating their global extent, we are able to query the origins of such behaviour. We are also able to reject it as solely biologically determined, because it does not happen to every woman, everywhere, all the time. Not all men beat their partners, or are misogynistic or controlling; and those who do have normally observed such behaviour early in youth, in private and in public, and have internalized the practice. DCV, then, is an informal social institution that seeks behavioural propriety on the part of females based on assumptions of male superiority and expectations of female submissiveness to male authority.

Institutions and change

Unsurprisingly, some of the approaches considered in relation to economic institutions may also apply in the case of the institutional control violence experienced by millions of women. For example, it seems reasonable to assume that pressure on male behavioural patterns will work better when applied from within as well as from without. Already, various male groups such as 'White Ribbon' have orchestrated campaigns to educate males against violence against women, while women's groups have fought the external battle for hundreds of years. But perhaps a key priority is identifying institutions at work. Because these are much less formal and in many cases are entirely illegal, this process of revealing institutionalism is harder. Public challenges to the most obvious discrimination conducted by formal, legal bodies have been the subject of criticism for centuries and, as with their economic counterparts, their susceptibility to change confirms their social construction. Can the same be said of other forms of violence and discrimination?

One of the key problems in considering global institutionalized violence against females is its hidden character. Domestic violence and partner-killing were sanctified behind closed doors that were originally owned only by men, codifying the acceptance of violent control behaviours by males in the home. But whereas these concerns are now more within the jurisdiction of formal public offices such as courts, the informal consciousness that socially orients male attitudes to females in the private sector is far more evasive and, perhaps, far more violent. But again, as per its public counterpart, violent outcomes for females are determined predominantly by money and men's socialized assumptions regarding female legitimacy.

'Are women less than men?'

The control 'rights' that have long accompanied male–female intimate relationships, along with various institutions that have underscored such perceptions such as traditional marriage vows and associated property ownership, the churches and law, obviously pertain more widely than in mere intimate relationships. In the formal commercial environment, women are routinely paid less than men, have glass-ceiling barriers to promotion, are discriminated against in male-dominated environments such as financial markets, are exploited in low-paid casual work like their male counterparts, only more so, and are also discriminated against in childcare provision. If this may be considered indirect violence, in the sense that it is unreasonable and unjustifiable discrimination on the grounds of sexual identity in an 'impartial' market, the informal commercial environment is responsible for shocking degrees of direct and indirect violence against females. This environment combines perhaps the worst of all human attributes: brutal dehumanization of females with rapacious and violent greed. The key institutions that control, dominate and murder females in the illegal sector are only a shade removed from their formal, legal counterparts, and for this reason the same institutions should remain the subject of concern. The key difference separating the two is really enforceable regulation/non-regulation of free market principles.

In the formal arena, the market is more widely legally regulated. In the informal sectors, it is not regulated at all. The unregulated commercial arena is ugly in many ways because it allows for any demand to be provided for, including recordings of 'snuff' killings. But the gendered barbarity and pitilessness that accompany the viciousness and inhumanity involved in supplying, managing and controlling the illegal trafficking of females globally reflect the capacity to dehumanize girls and women. In many respects, trafficking for sex-working or other slave duties demonstrates the types of inequality that prevail when regulation of male beliefs in sex superiority is absent. This perhaps speaks volumes for the extent, breadth and depth of socialization of women as 'less than' men. This is visible to those who are prepared to look. The way in which the informal sector works with regard to female selling utterly gives the lie

to notions of meaningful equality between males and females, the roots
of which lie in social attitudes and the construction of the 'traditional
family' (Giddens 2002: 54). While some degree of change has repealed
gender inequality, it has been mostly at the 'grassroots' level: a new law
that allows women to compete in legal firms, a different social view that
recognizes prostitute women as human beings with families. MacKinnon illustrates clearly how structural change – that which underlies all
inequality – has eluded suspicion and confounded challenge. It is well
worth quoting her at length. She asks:

> If women were human, would we be a cash crop shipped from Thailand
> in containers into New York's brothels? Would we be sexual and repro-
> ductive slaves? Would we be bred, worked without pay our whole lives,
> burned when our dowry money wasn't enough or when men tired of us,
> starved as widows when our husbands died (if we survived his funeral
> pyre), sold for sex because we are not valued for anything else? ... Would
> we, when allowed to work for pay, be made to work at the most menial
> jobs and exploited at barely starvation level? Would our genitals be sliced
> out to 'cleanse' us ... to control us, to mark us and define our cultures?
> Would we be trafficked as things for sexual use and entertainment world-
> wide in whatever form current technology makes possible? Would we
> be kept from learning to read and write? If women were human, would
> we have so little voice in public deliberations and in government in the
> countries where we live? Would we be hidden behind veils and impris-
> oned in houses and stoned and shot for refusing. Would we be beaten
> nearly to death, and to death, by men with whom we are close? Would
> we be sexually molested in our families? Would we be raped in genocide
> to terrorize and eject and destroy our ethnic communities, and raped
> again in that undeclared war that goes on every day in every country in
> the world in what is called peacetime? If women were human, would our
> violation be *enjoyed* by our violators? And, if we were human, when these
> things happened, would virtually nothing be done about it? (2006: 41–2)

MacKinnon might also have asked: if females were considered human,
would tens of millions be murdered at or before birth because they
were valued less than males because the economy is grounded in male
labour divisions and priorities? Or would gang rape of young girls count
as a 'legitimate' 'cultural' pursuit to enhance the masculinity of young
men in the USA and elsewhere? Or would women be denied access to
female sanitation in sweatshops across the globe, or be enslaved by rich
businessmen in London and New York, or kept indoors and forbidden

male contact unless it is with a family member who was entitled anyway to rape her with little chance of incarceration? Or, on multiple levels of breathtaking, unspeakable tragedy, would they be stolen from loving parents and sold as four-year-old virgins to rich Asian males for sex acts claimed to cure them of their lethal infections of HIV/AIDS, and then, if they survived the agony of rupture, would they then be imprisoned in undefined living deaths as incurable HIV sufferers and then blamed for their own circumstances?

In the illegal sector, then, prevailing social attitudes towards females are magnified when regulation and constabulary oversight are absent or partial. There will always be criminal capitalism, in the sense that large-scale crime in drugs, weapons, young children and so on work to the same principles of supply and demand as do house sales, new cars and hedge fund acquisitions. Where treatment of females in the two capitalisms varies in degrees of exploitation and violence, it shares the origins of both in the subliminal and overt association of females with a wide range of negativities that attend them from birth: from socially constructed variations on original sin, through their representation as sex objects, their economic relegation behind men, social control by male rules, punishment for social 'aberrations' of sexuality, private legal 'ownership' in marriage, public legal discrimination in employment, public exposure, sexualization and commodification in 'art' and global pornography, exclusion from various public institutions, social endorsement of intimate partner brutality, relegation behind boys in schooling, media representation of female 'victimhood' and dependence, legal forgiveness of brutal male violence, humiliation of survivors of alleged rape and other sex crimes, disproportionate exposure to sexual violence in war, and so on. There is no shortage of provocations of female 'lessness' that leads to different forms of chattelization. The main instrument of separation between legal and illegal trading is the presence of legal scrutiny; and even this varies from country to country, border post to border post, rich man to poor man. Such widespread negative social public and private attitudes have been determined by ideas derived from now redundant biological imperatives; and institutions have formed and in some cases been perpetuated around those ideas from which in turn human agency derives. Reconstructing from the present miasma of values attached to females requires social acceptance, not biological surgery. This is not rocket science.

At the heart of these forms of violence and control are global institutions. IFIs and markets combine with male internalization of the 'lessness' of females to create a female cattle market fulfilling the demands of both regulated and unregulated markets. The scale and audaciousness of these forms of violence must be properly understood in order to identify institutional determinism and to formulate legislative responses and social awareness. These, and MacKinnon's vital observations and arguments, are not rhetorical commentary. These acts diminish and end women's lives, but they also darken men's lives. Andrarchy robs men of the potential for very different, and better, lives with women; and it robs women of equality and opportunities to enjoy peaceful and enriching lives with men. Despite superficial and sometimes substantial reformation, it is hard to escape from the evidence that andrarchy ensures that males continue to dominate almost all aspects of all societies, while dominant institutions perpetuate this asymmetrical inequality to the extent that casual, socialized female subordination has become normalized so that, like most normalized subject matters, it is not treated with the critical scrutiny it needs to render it a visible anomaly. But combining them are social attitudes which are malleable, not fixed.

The brutal dehumanization of women, according to MacKinnon, has become so much a part of our 'normalcy' that we may reasonably conclude that it self-institutionalizes through its endemic pervasiveness in much the same way that the dehumanization of black people became both normalized and legitimized on spurious racial supremacist grounds. Indeed, substitution throughout much of MacKinnon's quote (above) of 'black slaves' for 'women', along with a few mild contextual changes, demonstrates the normalization and socialization involved during imperial conquest and in structural sexual domination. Hanmer and Maynard conclude with regard to structural male domination that 'so perfect is its system of socialization, so complete the general assent to its values, so long and so universally has it prevailed in human society, that it scarcely seems to require ... implementation' (1987: 13–14). As a consequence of this deep-rooted social evolution and institutional and structural reinforcement and maintenance, Mazurana and McKay remark that 'we often do not notice [the] sex-based injustice' that accompanies these institutional and structural formations 'because we are so accustomed to seeing males with more power, prestige and status than women' (2001: 130). But perhaps because it is so visible, its dominance is easier to prove.

Conclusion

Various social commentators query whether feminism has been rendered redundant by the increased opportunities some women experience, especially in the rich world. In early 2007, a female social commentator excoriated women's rights in Iran and lauded the progress and equality of women in the UK. She berated critical feminists and asked, 'Is there really anything left to march for?' The answer quite clearly is yes. The social determinism of female status links punishment, control, theft, violation and commercialization. Marching has worked for change before, is still used in a wide variety of social circumstances and will work again. But the greater the information regarding semi-visible or invisible control mechanisms, and the closer these can be tied to the social formation of female value, worth, status and rights, and the more these can be demonstrated as malleable concepts derived from social construction, the greater the possibility that other institutional beliefs, values and attitudes will expand. In answer to the social commentators' question, of whether there was anything left worth marching for, we might suggest the right not to be beaten to death by male partners, chauvinists and misogynists; the right for a third of women not to be sexually abused by a male in their lifetime; or for effective judicial reforms so that completed rape prosecutions are proportionate to rates of prosecutions for other crimes.

People might also march to raise awareness that many women are forced to stay in violent relationships because they are dependent on their partner's income and because he threatens the children to silence her. We might also march because there are still too many men who think drug-rape of women and girls is acceptable. People might take to the streets because they don't consider global sex trafficking of women as representative of an equal or just world. Perhaps some people might march so that females are represented proportionately in politics and religious office; or receive equal pay for the same work. Women are far from equal but inequality is masked by normalcy deriving from the pervasive conditioning of boys and girls, men and women, all around the world, and it remains a key determinant in perpetuating the relegation of women in relation to the institutional and structural domination of andrarchy and, with it, neoliberalism. The invisibility and durability of this process are testament to the extent of masculine domination of global social institutions and social normalization over many millennia, which would suggest that public airings of these phenomena and their root causes have as yet been inadequate to the scale of the task. It would appear that the greatest illusion that male domination has conjured has been to convince so many men and women that it doesn't exist.

EIGHT | Andrarchy and neoliberalism

The institutions discussed in the previous chapters – from the IMF to dowry and honour – are not the end of a one-dimensional causative chain that simply terminates millions of civilian lives unnecessarily, devoid of an organizing architecture. Rather, the financial and domination institutions that convey violence, directly or indirectly, are instead vessels for ideational *structures*, or social, political and economic organizing ideologies. The notion of 'structure' in international relations is not a new one; it is considered in a variety of ways and differs, as one might expect, according to perspective. This chapter outlines conventional, realist understandings of 'structure' in the world system, and then introduces the notions of global structures of andrarchy and neoliberalism. I propose that it is these formations which not only account for the human insecurity outlined throughout this book, but which also clearly display the extent of human, social construction in mass human insecurity, thereby confirming their vulnerability and susceptibility to change. This is in contrast to the realist model, the anonymity and impermeable innateness of which is said to preclude such transformation as might reduce violence and human insecurity on a global scale.

Realism and structure

A basic understanding of structure in realist thinking is expressed by Goldstein as 'the distribution of power' within the international system (1994: 76). This can take a range of forms and, of course, power itself can be defined in a variety of ways, including diplomatic, economic and military, among others. Jackson and Sorensen describe this notion further. Balances of power will exist in a variety of configurations (bipolar, unipolar) between states which react to the structure within which they themselves exist. In other words, 'the structure of international anarchy produces [the] effect' to which states respond (2007: 291). Clemens notes the influence of Hobbes on Kenneth Waltz, who identified 'anarchy and the distribution of power' as the 'underlying structure of the international system' (1998: 14). For Wight, the systemic structure of international relations is 'international anarchy: a multiplicity of independent sovereign states acknowledging no political superior, whose relationships are ultimately regulated by warfare' (1991: 7). Neorealists, or structural realists, take a slightly different view of structure and state, but essentially, and ontologically and epistemologically, the distinctions are in roles. The international system itself forces states into power-acquiring behaviour which in turn creates the seemingly arbitrary nature of the system, or, in the words of Mearsheimer, 'it is the structure of the architecture of the international system that forces state to pursue power' (2007: 72).

Though ideologically very different, this model finds not dissimilar expression in Wallerstein's 'world-system' structure. In this version, 'the system more or less determines what happens to individual states' (Cochrane and Anderson 1986: 217). The authors conclude, however, that this system is dualistic and reflects relations between states that create the system and the system that shapes states (ibid.: 230). In other words, 'states generate ... structure through ... mutual interaction [and] the structure influences the behaviour of states' (Griffiths 1992: 80). It is a reciprocal arrangement involving mutual, continuous reinforcement as long as the existing rules and beliefs of that system of states remain largely undisturbed. Translated into a real life scenario, this means that current security outcomes, as perceived from a realist perspective, will remain as they are until the paradigm they represent is itself challenged. In this model, violence is inevitable periodically. For many realists, it is because of this that human interaction through states and associated structures must be moderated by 'neutral' international institutions that manage their intrinsically violent 'disorder'. These institutions mirror national-level bodies such as law enforcement agencies. They differ, however, in the sense that there is no supra-state constabulary with universal authority and legitimacy to enforce penalties for non-compliance.

Realists are reluctant to consider transformation of the system from violent to non-violent. Clarke observed of realism that it:

> Denies the possibility of progress ... [because] the parameters of realist thought are set by the boundaries of historical experience ... This feature of international politics is permanent and since states and statesmen cannot rise above it, there can ... be no significant progress in international life. (1980: 56–7)

In other words, for realists, looking back historically proves the nature of the system; war has been a constant throughout history. Realists are disinclined to consider seriously the notion that the violent nature of the international system is in fact a product of the way states are organized locally and internationally. Nor do they consider that the priorities

incumbent upon a hierarchical, masculine, confrontational and competi-
tively ordained male-dominated global environment contribute to the
nature of state and system. In short, for most realists and neo-realists,
state and system are codependent and fixed in behavioural terms as
a result of a particular interpretation of a monolithic human nature.
The world is structured within international anarchy, with states as key
actors and international institutions regulating largely indiscriminate
and unstoppable clashes in an unregulated systemic chaos.

In this system, humans are less responsible for the routine and violent
outcomes of unpredictable international political and economic turbu-
lence than the nature of the system itself. Human security is, therefore,
not of appropriate concern for the field of realism, nor is human insecurity anything other than the product of a constellation of forces
deriving from the unchangeable 'state of nature' in which we all exist. Not
only does the international system sustain itself by its own nature, but
realist interpretation sanctions this conceptualization and so reinforces
the violent composition and consequences of its interpretation. In short,
this is the way the world is. It is not constructed deliberately to function
in this manner but, because states reflect human nature and the system
reflects states, it is unchangeable and therefore resources are better allo-
cated to understanding and implementing regulatory mechanisms to
make the best of a poor situation.

While these views regarding international structures form the basis of
the dominant school of international relations, they are not without an
expanding counter-narrative. Fierke, for example, considers structures as
'a product' or constructed system or entity composed 'of the assumptions
we bring to day-to-day interactions'. She writes that 'states, democracies,
international institutions, power politics, humanitarian interventions, or
economic sanctions only exist by virtue of the social, ideological, cultural
or political structures by which they are given meaning and imbued
with legitimacy and power' (2007: 3). For Fierke, structures contain and
direct dominant beliefs. The more dominant the belief, especially in
the absence of an alternative, the stronger and more self-perpetuating
the structure and its supporting discourse. It is to this type of structure
that we now turn.

Alternative structures

I refer here to a structure as an overarching concept or ideological
'engine' derived from a combination of biological traits and learned behaviours, desires and expectations developing in a fluid social environ-

ment that formulate priorities for varied needs and wants. This type of structure forms from human design, either from biological determinism or as a result of social construction, or from a combination of the two. This model assumes varying degrees of both inputs. Humans are fully responsible for structural composition, and its prolongation and longevity are their liability as well. From structure derive rule-governed institutions designed to communicate, project and convert the structure's values and beliefs into policies designed to achieve the objectives of the structure. The transmission and conversion of beliefs into functional policies are enacted through human agency. For Dessler (1989), accepting this was essential to understanding the reproduction of structure, whilst structure created agency. That is, humans choose to enact, ignore or reject the ideological will of the structure by participation, exclusion or challenge. Equally, many humans may remain uninformed of undesirable consequences of structural outputs as a result of ideological predominance. Either way, human choices cannot be seen as ignorant of, or detached from, structural and institutional processes and outcomes. The institutional elements have been a bone of contention for realists and social constructivists alike (Gould 1998: 87).

Structure is, therefore, connected to agency outcome by rule-based institutions that translate ideology into practice. In this understanding of structure, the emphasis is on human participation based on adaptable and transformative ideas. It is from this process that life-ending outcomes derive. Human insecurity, then, can be seen as a product of human-created interrelated structures of belief and organization. Furthermore, unlike realist-based schools of thought, this model involves multiple structures functioning simultaneously, mutually reinforcing one another, both enmeshed and overlapping. In the same sense that we now understand there to be more than one universe (a multiverse), it seems unlikely that the international system should be so simple as to consist of only one structure.

Andrarchy and neoliberalism

Booth maintains that 'different political theories conceive the structures and processes of human society' (2005: 13). This can be extended quite diversely: different world-views, different attitudes, different experiences, different sexes, different constructed identities, may all conceive of security, structures and processes relating to any topic. I propose that, taking a different approach through human insecurity as it has been defined here, reveals quite different structures and processes at work. There are, then, two connected, dynamic, socially and mentally constructed (man-made) formations, *andrarchy* and *neoliberalism*, which constitute the binary structure that determines, through formal and informal international institutions, the mass avoidable deaths that constitute human insecurity. These may in effect be the 'deep structures' that are 'more solidly sedimented' that Waever refers to when he notes the limits to social reconstructivism (2002: 32). Andrarchy and neoliberalism are mutually reinforcing and complementary structures composed of, and generating, values that drive and prioritize favoured outputs. The andrarchal-neoliberal structure is a composite of self-legitimizing values and beliefs underpinned by socially condoned and normalized discourses, behaviours and expectations. It is a self-sustaining association constructed from a shared belief in the importance of particular concepts and their relative priorities, needs and capacities which has been constructed and reconstructed over time, and which has altered in accordance with dynamic factors such as control of the external natural environment and access to and domination of others.

Andrarchy Andrarchy is the gender-partisan ideological domination and rule structure that determines and sustains the general relative power of males over females globally. It is an ideological, ideational structure of domination by rule and rule by domination, through institutions, learned behaviour and rejection of challenge. It enjoys passive and active social endorsement by both sexes, in that it is rarely conceptually identified or challenged as globally destructive, and it draws on active enforcement of values through myriad social sustenance mechanisms developed over millennia. It does not mean that all males dominate all females all the time. Nor does it imply that all men are equally influenced by the values associated with andrarchy. Each male responds to such ideational influence in the same way that he would respond to any other idea, or concept, that determined his behaviour. Andrarchy may be conceived of as a governing architecture, or structure, to which all males respond to different degrees, but which many males are also unaware of at the conscious level. There are, however, dominant elements, such as machismo, competition and hierarchies, to which most males subscribe in various forms of business, adventure holidays, promotion-seeking, sports and maintenance of 'honour', to name but a few.

While its influence is almost global, it is embedded in and relates to different political spaces to different degrees. It has been absorbed into male and female consciousness globally but has been restrained by differing perceptions of the rights of men and women. Its manifestation can be quite obvious in political spaces that do little to condemn violence and control of all sorts against women; but it may also take more subliminal form in other societies where men and women are less conscious of structural, indirect violences against women and other men. More overt, direct and aggressive andrarchy contrasts with its indirect, more subtle but equally controlling counterpart. It is expressed through all forms of multimedia, but direct violence and traditional hyper-masculine identities are more stereotypical in political systems that have not instituted female emancipation to the extent that gender equality is a habituated social experience. That is, in the same way that Rustow (1970) anticipated that the process of democratization would become more entrenched the longer politicians practised its rituals, we may also say that the farther societies move from gender-unrepresentative government and institutionalized inequality, so may the influence on women of andrarchy decline.

Contemporary andrarchy is a hegemonic organizing concept, the pervasiveness of which many are unaware. Like patriarchy, it is routinely labelled and rejected as feminist fatuity or misperception. This is partly because andrarchy is so deeply embedded in routine social, economic or political organization and behaviour that any challenge appears as a challenge against a widely accepted normality known as 'the real world'. For example, when the undeniable disparity between world female population and women's political representation is presented as a target for reform by critical feminism, responses are often aimed at discrediting feminism per se, rather than admitting the problem. This is partly because admitting the problem raises far too many other questions that are the undoing of so many masculinist arguments.

Critiquing male domination (andrarchy) also attacks deeply embedded subconscious learning shared by both sexes in the Western world. Most societies sustain myths, images and fabrications about the 'danger' of 'independent' women, whose behaviour may be represented as socially treasonous and to be punished. We noted earlier the universality of tales such as that of Adam and Eve, for example, which from the very earliest expression underscore other, more conscious understandings of the formation of the gendered world around us – although, as we noted earlier, this changes over time. The contrarian sexual objectification of females (contrarian because it is this which andrarchy seeks to control, while producing ever more versions of female sexualities) is hard to ignore. While it promotes fantasies of female sexual rapaciousness, it excludes females from spaces of power in proportion to their demography. To an imaginary external observer examining world newspapers, females will appear more often as sex objects and rarely as political agents, while our imaginary observer will see males in political roles far more than as sex objects. The division is quite clear.

Andrarchy not only determines sex bias and the domination of women, it also impacts seriously on males, because it is not a monolithic construction or concept. Andrarchy consists of multiple masculinities, some of which compete consciously for masculine status within the dynamic hierarchy of shifting, fluid masculinities known as hegemonic masculinities (Whitehead 2002: 88–94; Hatty 2000). Male domination globally has created similar structures of masculinity internationally. Connell refers us to 'the production of a hegemonic masculinity on a world scale ... a dominant form of masculinity which embodies, organizes and legitimates men's domination in the gender order as a whole' (2000: 46; Steans 2007: 15). Also, however, it ranks, rewards and punishes men who do not conform to the competitive rules of masculinity and who do not attempt to place themselves in rankings of andrarchy.

In this model, males compete for ranked status which is associated with various symbols of achievement. In a medium-level business, for example, it may be a high-end company car such as a Porsche. In higher-level business, it may be access to a private aircraft. In establishment circles, it may be membership of a particular private club. In other circles, ownership of the most ferocious canine in dog-fighting and cock-fighting tournaments confers status within hegemonic masculinities. The hierarchies are not restricted to adults and are to be found in the early stages of boys' development in school, demonstrated through their relationships with girls. The symbols attached to particular achievements identify the status, in a manner similar to promotion and ranking in the armed and civil services.

Males who do not interact in the conventional competition for such masculine status are ranked by others who do. The young male that does not follow football is a minority among his football-loving brethren; his 'masculinity' and 'sexuality' are often open to doubt and criticism, resulting in alienation and positioning within the feminine, or homosexual, 'Other'. The female 'Other' is normally excluded from these hierarchies, except where she is classified as a 'tomboy' and given 'honorary' membership of the masculine clans, opening space between the sexes and gender from an early age. Pettman maintains that these competitive hierarchies, intrinsic and central to hegemonic masculinity, inevitably revolve around 'establishing and maintaining power, which crucially includes naturalising or normalising power relations. The subordination of women, heterosexuality and homophobia are bedrocks of hegemonic masculinity' (1996: 94), and hegemonic masculinity is a fundamental bedrock of andrarchy. It is not coercive; it is a far more subtle process, as one might expect of something that has developed over millennia, and this explains why it is hard to detect and recognize. Von der Lippe explains this succinctly, writing that hegemony, or

> the authority of the dominant group, is not imposed on individuals, but offered to them in subtle ways. What is offered ... is not just an assertion of another value ... The twist is that hegemonic discourses are offered as something you already agree with, as a reflection, so to speak, of your own desires, needs and wants ... The subtlety is exactly this: whatever the values and interests of a dominant social, economic or political group, they are perceived as the values dear to everyone. Hegemony treats particular values as if they are universal. (2006: 64)

This is the essence of hegemony in neoliberalism: it is the ability to offer more and better of the same, which people believe they want or need anyway.

Hierarchies are far from fixed, and the fluidity involved reveals and demonstrates their social construction and thus their susceptibility to change as part of routine social processes. Recognizable examples of sources of tensions between male/masculine identities might include skinhead or Byronesque haircuts (the latter ironically not dissimilar to that of an earlier European icon of hyper-masculinity, Tarzan); aggressive or sympathetic business management styles; and rough or sedentary sport. Some masculinities embrace intellect above physical strength and displays of machismo ('the pen is mightier than the sword'). While some do not compete consciously, their self-exclusion may relegate them in the eyes of others of both sexes. Connell maintains that such groups 'are often culturally discredited or despised. Men who practice them are likely to be abused as wimps, cowards, fags' (2000: 217; Francis 2004: 70). In many cases, this stimulates male departure from masculine groups and a migration towards other groups they believe they may better associate with.

The social construction of boys and girls from an early age is well documented. Mangan maintains that from childhood many cultures are recognized as 'devoting considerable effort to prepare the boy to be a man'. This preparation involves 'an atmosphere of aggressive competition, personal assertion and inculcated self-sacrifice – to the perceived advantage of the group, the team, the nation' (2006: 3; Tickner 1988: 436). Differences in 'man-type', that is masculinity, derive from differing exposure to the range of social factors that surround boys and girls from the moment they are born. This is especially visible in the school playground, where young males jostle and fight for status and positions in changing and shifting masculine groupings as their masculine identities and claims take initial shape. Boys compete for inclusion in the 'in-group' or with a dominant, alpha-type male. Exclusion is confirmed by name-calling that reflects diminished masculinity, such as 'weed', 'runt' and other negative labels. In general, it is a trend shared globally (Connell 2000). Perhaps because of this ever-expanding range of areas in which males compete, girls in the UK and some other parts of Europe have advanced in academic ratings, prompting complaints that boys are falling behind and demands that action should be taken. No such action was called for by politicians during the centuries when girls routinely remained behind boys.

These elements of the social construction of gender, identity and life roles are evidence that masculinity is not solely a biological imperative. Furthermore, these social transformations appear at different times and in different places. Connell argues that:

> Different cultures and different periods of history construct gender differently. In multicultural societies there are likely to be multiple definitions of masculinity. Equally important, more than one kind of masculinity can be found within a given culture, even within a single institution such as a school or workplace. (ibid.: 216)

The fluid nature of masculinity and its regular reformation in social and mental construction have become more visible, and respectable, as major international media and sports stars' behaviour has forced social opinion leaders to try to define for mass consumption the behaviour of their sports and hyper-masculine heroes. The globally celebrated English footballer David Beckham and his complex and movable masculinities, for example, prompted suggestion of a crossover of sexuality and cosmopolitanism which found expression in his 'metrosexuality'. Beckham's obvious hyper-masculinity as a world-class international footballer merged with his 'feminine' urges for clothes shopping and colouring his hair, supposedly the domain of female behaviour. Clearly, if such a public persona could have changing characteristics referred to as masculinities, they could not be rigid.

Similarly, the US rapper Eminem, part of whose repertoire is associated in the media with guns and misogyny, also sings and raps about his love for his young daughter, Haley. He also refers to a traumatic childhood using violent and hateful lyrics ranged against his mother, which are paradoxically set against a background of classical strings including violin and harp. The hyper-masculine ('dangerous' rapper with guns and criminal record) converges with the hyper-emotional (visible and audible expression of love in front of a global audience), demonstrating a publicly visible example of the multiple identities and characteristics possible in any male – as well as the confusion this brings to many men. This differentiation reflects important influences such as early childcare, natural and built environment, education and mentors, among numerous others. Both examples (Beckham and Eminem) amplify and substantiate Connell's thesis regarding fluidity and change in masculinity (see also Hooper 2006).

Whitehead, however, expresses concern about the utility of the concept of hegemonic masculinity; he suggests it is as weak as 'patriarchy for understanding complex male social and positional structures' because it presupposes an 'innate drive for power'. He also maintains that most men are not party to its existence (2002: 92). But male participation in competitive masculinization is socialized from birth through normalized, unavoidable social conditioning from other men who have grown up knowing no contest to their positioning above women, and by women who have been similarly indoctrinated to their lower status. Males are as subject to shaping from birth as de Beauvoir's females (1988: 295).

Andrarchy's global extent and influence are hard to deny. The state is conceived and organized in the manner of andrarchy. The core of political power around the world is government and government-constituted international public bodies (Connell 2000: 41, 220; Steans 1998). No government in the world has its composition dominated by women, even to a simple majority. Almost all major power processes in the world are dominated by the rule of men (Reardon 1996: 315; Connell 2000). Public institutions such as the state are male dominated, as are its principal statutory bodies.

Such power and domination have in some places been diluted; but as a global practice, they are still the norm, despite the presence of what Eisenstein refers to as 'sexual decoys' (women whose presence in elite politics appears to confound the argument of male domination, but which in reality demonstrates the disparity yet more clearly). This does not infer by any means that 'all men are bad or domineering'. Rather, it is an argument that proposes that the rules men and women consciously and unconsciously live by and consider 'normal' and largely unchanging are in fact both constantly mutating and also damaging to both sexes at all levels. And rather than advocating a shift from a model of the world run by males to one ruled by females, or seeking the overthrow of all men, most critical feminists seem more likely to want to share, representatively, thoughtfully and cooperatively, a reformed concept of power that is more harmonious and more in the interest of both sexes and all populations.

Neoliberalism Neoliberalism is defined differently by its advocates and detractors. Armstrong et al., for example, consider it to be 'a firm belief in the efficacy of market forces and hence in the necessity of deregulation and privatization in economies based on some variant of state control or intervention, and a stress on trade-led growth rather than protectionism' (2004: 235; Balaam and Veseth 1996: 29). Most would agree that neoliberalism is a right-wing extension of general capitalist principles that articulates a view of development measured in numerical, 'neutral' economic terms (GDP, GNP, for example). This is based on a belief in the inefficiency of the state as an allocator of resources of all forms; and on the argument that as well as being inefficient economically, it is easily corruptible and, therefore, even more wasteful.

To compensate for the removal of state provision of traditional welfare, the market is proposed as the alternative with privatization of health and other services to take up the slack in state funding. In conjunction with this, the market provides the vessel through which exports of basic commodities like tin, zinc or coffee will realize profits that can then be used to pay off debts; an essential condition for independent national economic development in the South. The market is presented as an objective, impersonal mechanism, and so all states have equal opportunities if they rely on their 'natural' resources. The playing field is level, the gates to foreign markets are open, and independent development is a natural consequence of strict adherence to market disciplines. It will, of course, hurt to start with, but this is only a temporary condition.

There are a number of problems with this explication of neoliberalism. To begin with, any measurement of development based solely in economic terms reveals primarily economic growth in the first instance and, in the second, conceals impoverishment and other indicators of development that allow us to estimate improvements or deteriorations in human development. It is a narrow measurement of financial growth incapable of measuring in human terms the impact of neoliberal reforms on poor people. It is designed primarily by males using mathematical economics, and results in masculine priorities. It cannot detect or measure social evolution because it is a gendered measurement that derives from gendered institutional bodies and ideational structures (Griffin 2007: 225).

For Griffin, this neoliberal ensemble of institution, structure and consequence 'reproduces meaning through assumptions of economic growth and stability, financial transactions and human behaviour that are intrinsically gendered while presented as universal and neutral' (ibid.: 220; Tickner 1992: 73). That female children are killed because their gender-prescribed roles exclude work-age females from public office and paid employment, and restrict their economic and personal independence and devalue them, is not a coincidence. It can be causally traced and connected to the masculine ideational determinism and constructivism of the neoliberal economy and its andrarchal partner. Neoliberalism, as the means of exploiting natural resources and taming or controlling nature for man's benefit, is violent towards females, just as it is towards the natural environment. It is a harsh world indeed that divides man from the environment and from women.

A second problem with any view that projects neutrality on to neoliberalism lies in the suggestion that the state's role in welfare provision must be reined in because it is inefficient as an allocator and corrupt in management practices. While there is some truth in the second part of this claim, the essence of state provision is that it is free at the point of use for the most vulnerable (Harvey 2007: 38). That is, the poorest people have varying degrees of access to state healthcare and education, mainly in large towns and cities. In practice, it may not be free because government employees are often so poorly paid that they willingly take bribes or sell what are meant to be free goods such as medicines.

Ultimately, the problem with privatizing state health provision, or public utilities such as water and electricity, is that those with no money, no matter what the nature of privatization, cannot access essential services. This has a long and penurious knock-on effect: denial of access to clean water increases susceptibility to waterborne diseases which undermines health and leads to a downward spiral. It also sustains dependency on common social patronage systems, which reinforce social hierarchies quite antithetical to democracy. Furthermore, the 'efficiencies' associated with privatization derive from competition, which may take some time to establish before it drives prices down. Normally, initial privatization pushes prices above state-subsidized levels. If people have no money, they cannot buy privatized essentials. Invariably, this affects women more than men.

A third problem with an uncritical perception of neoliberalism comes in the form of a paradox. Debt repayment through exporting basic staples and other commodities in large amounts can depress global market prices of the goods in question. To maintain high export levels requires greater output of the same goods, which has a twofold effect. First, it depresses prices further and concentrates dependency on single cash crops that are vulnerable to fluctuations in demand. Second, it places greater pressure on the natural environment as people are forced to grow ever more export crops and, in turn, undermine the environment in a vicious cycle.

Even this approach might have some benefit, if the profits reflected fair rules and the returns were to be reinvested in national growth strategies. But the profits go abroad to international public and private creditors to repay debts that most of the present population of Africa and Asia were not responsible for generating in the first instance and have seen little or no benefit from such lending. George summarizes the complex debt-trade-market-protectionism equation:

> Debt is an efficient tool. It ensures access to other people's raw materials
> and infrastructure on the cheapest possible terms. Dozens of countries
> must compete for shrinking export markets and can export only a limited
> range of products because of Northern protectionism and their lack
> of cash to invest in diversification. Market saturation ensues, reducing
> exporters' income to a bare minimum while the North enjoys huge
> savings. (1989: 143)

Finally, the notion that there is a level playing field for fair competition is a fantasy, as we saw in Chapters 5 and 6. The WTO, like the GATT before it, ensures that Western markets are protected from competitors, and regional arrangements, such as the Common Agricultural Policy (CAP) in Europe, ensure that keenly priced North African produce cannot challenge more expensive and state-subsidized agriculture from Europe. This also means that European consumers do not benefit from the best-priced goods available. Armstrong et al.'s description, then, denies the degree of protectionism inherent in the WTO and the use of subsidies by powerful states such as the USA to exclude competitive goods from their domestic markets. It also refers to a 'firm belief' in the market, whereas various criticisms have likened this to a fundamental or extremist attachment to this form of distribution which denies the legitimacy of, and/or attempts to discredit, challenges to its functions (Peet 2007: 15; Rapley 2004: 126).

One might therefore view such 'firm belief' as at best insufficiently reflective and at worst crudely dogmatic. It brooks little opposition, as we have noted in previous chapters. Offering a more realistic perspective on capitalism and markets, Payne suggests that neoliberalism may be characterized by 'increasing profit margins, weakening trade unions, eliminating inflation ... and boosting growth by means of supply-side economics' (2005: 25). He also identifies the issuance of 'supply-side' economics, which is counter to the 'natural' demand-led market, and draws attention to the connection between increasing profits and decreasing employee representation by unions (ibid.).

As we noted in the introduction, polarities of wealth have in some ways reached obscene levels; and the promised 'trickle down' effect that suggested that as the developed worlds became rich the rest would follow has failed to appear. What we may discern primarily is that there is a gap between rhetoric and reality. The rhetoric consists of pro-market advocates of a free market and free trade who argue that rising tides float all boats. The reality is that the 'playing field' is tilted south and 'comparative advantage' is a latter-day extension of the rules of expropriation and exploitation of the imperial era. Foreign direct investment often offers poor returns for poor countries, and the gap between rich and poor is not closing at any rate that suggests that immiseration may become any time soon part of a distant history. Harvey argues that:

> The gap between rhetoric (for the benefit of all) and realization (for the benefit of a small ruling class) increases over space and time ... The idea that the market is about fair competition is increasingly negated by the facts of extraordinary monopoly, centralization, and internationalization on the part of corporate and financial powers. (2007: 42)

Neoliberalism does not engage all competitors on the same terms. It is in fact only the latest institutionally legitimized mechanism of unfair imperial extraction based on modern asymmetrical power relationships of domination and exploitation. Neoliberalism in action is a partisan ideological and hegemonic structure that dispenses resources from an uneven power base through institutions formed and driven by dominant or hegemonic states which perpetuate economic asymmetry, and sustain the poverty that influences under-five mortality rates in the USA as well as Equatorial Guinea, Borneo, Bangladesh, Peru, Mexico and Syria, to name but a few. Its commonality is testament to the near-universal election of neoliberalism (Murphy 2000: 792–3), whether it benefits poor people or not. Its primacy remains in part based on its association with science, a hugely problematic connection. This legitimizes its application, as we have seen, but given the extent of human interaction with and intervention in the process, there can be little doubt that neoliberalism, 'rather than deriving from the neutral findings of an exact social science', is more reasonably understood as an inexact social science (like all the others involving human behaviour), forming a 'cultural, political and social endeavour, rather than a study of the application of proven, scientific truth' (Peet 2007: 15). In much the same way as hegemonic beliefs have persistently mis-generalized women and 'the Other' as 'irrational', so too has the social science of economics been anointed with the legitimacy attached to exact science (Agathangelou and Ling 2004: 522). This myth-making, undertaken to present as 'common sense' notions that are in fact fundamentally flawed, has relocated the non-biological social behaviour of humanity in the domain of science, implying permanence when the mere presence of social change falsifies such a conclusion. The net result has been that basic challenges to 'normalcy' are effectively quarantined by the capacity of hegemons to restrict debate to what appears 'normal' while 'producing and enforcing silences on disapproved topics, terms and approaches' (ibid.: 15). This is sometimes referred to as a hegemonic discourse.

It is important to understand that progress in understanding the validity of these ideologies, and their impact on global human insecurity, is hampered by their domination of the surrounding discourses. This is in part because they dictate, through their apparent normalcy and longevity, the terms of any debate. In other words, their dominance and routine presence in the 'real world' reinforce our assumptions and beliefs about the 'real world', at which we may shake our heads in dismay, but which assumes some form of inevitability. Harvey tells us that for such a 'system of thought to become dominant ... require[s] the articulation of fundamental concepts that become so deeply embedded in commonsense understandings that they are taken for granted and beyond question' (2007: 24). It is this appearance of normalcy and permanence of men as political and economic leaders and capitalism as the 'proven' way, as if nothing else had ever been or ever could be, which shape our expectations, when there is a very real and imaginable alternative. But consideration of this alternative is subdued and limited because such life and world dominance determines 'the nature of truth' and justifies 'the established political and economic systems and make[s] people accept it as the only one that is legitimate, respectable and possible' (Gelinas 2003: 23). As the two structures of andrarchy and neoliberalism converge, combine and extend their authority, little space is left in which to construct alternative discourses. It is in this very social construction, however, that opportunity prevails.

Binary global structures: the symbiosis of andrarchy and neoliberalism

While realists have assigned a neutrality and anonymity to a fixed and inevitable unitary structure that disburses direct violence randomly in all areas over time, considering a binary structure constituted of andrarchy and neoliberalism allows us to identify particular relational processes that are neither neutral nor anonymous and which are also not fixed. By illuminating the interwoven nature of the two dominant, masculine global structures, we can identify the human ideational origin and determinism involved, and trace the communication of their beliefs and priorities to human insecurity via their global social and financial institutions.

Or, as Hayden suggests, 'it is the structural nature of global poverty today that makes it possible to trace back to specific institutional contexts the agents and policies responsible for continuing radical inequality' (2007: 289). But to better understand their functioning and the manner in which they have normalized processes and outcomes that kill millions of people yearly, we may benefit from comparing the shared values and beliefs that connect them and which reinforce one another. Close scrutiny reveals parallel doctrines and methodologies in domination and exploitation; competitive and sex-gender hierarchies; and self-legitimization,

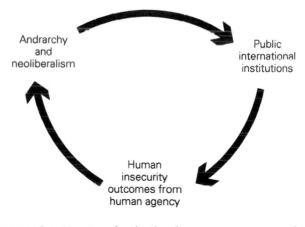

FIGURE 8.1 Structure-institution-human agency mapped onto human insecurity

among others. Many of these areas inevitably overlap and cross-connect; their values are shared and disbursed with similar objectives.

Andrarchy, neoliberalism and human insecurity

This andrarchal-neoliberal structure directly and indirectly determines a wide range of global human insecurities. The neoliberal element accepts that not everyone can win in a system that pitches infinite demand against finite resource access. It is tolerant of different opportunities which it represents as 'natural' and codifies as acceptable through the invoking of theories such as 'comparative advantage' which 'explain' why some states fare better than others. It presents its functional practices as impersonal, scientific and impartial and measures outcomes accordingly, for the most part, in terms of currencies, reflecting its gendered constitution. The andrarchal aspect within neoliberalism, as we have seen, ranks relative human performances and capabilities along hierarchical lines, creating scales of economic and social vulnerability compatible with perceptions of relative 'weaknesses'.

Inequalities are unavoidable but can be minimized by global adherence to market discipline. It will not accept a role in the staggering levels of poverty identified in Chapters 1 and 3 and normally locates large-scale suffering from resource shortage on actors other than itself. These might include a centralized and corrupt state administration; the policies of particular dictators, the consequences of which people must pull themselves out of through debt repayment; fiscal impropriety in state policy; corruption in general; and any other number of failures that exist outside of neoliberal international policy. That is, the human security deficit is not the responsibility of the structure that determines global economic policies. Neoliberalism does not accept a role in the deaths of millions from preventable and avoidable hunger and disease.

The andrarchal element of this structure relegates women to a lower position in most spheres and in many different ways. It projects an illusion of desire for equality through slow reform but maintains a fundamental support for notions that create and perpetuate inequality, such as the role of biology in sex and gender differentiation. It forces, through its social rules, confrontation and competition between males, creating hierarchies that persist through men's lives and which too often exclude them from enriching and emotional relationships with women and other men.

Andrarchal rules of behaviour strangle individual development in men and relegate them to crude roles that impede self-enrichment. They create codes of conduct and 'honour' that breed competition, tension and violence, between men and men and between men for women. They maintain repressive male–female relational limitations in all countries, and reinforce traditional, damaging and unnecessary gender stereotypes by their mass diffusion and constant recycling of destructive discourses of denial. They endorse and legitimize unnecessary violence and stimulate global arms sales that cause direct violence, while their conflation with neoliberalism reinforces competitive hierarchies and attitudes that relegate millions to penury and death.

These hierarchies are an essential element of both structures. They have been perhaps most evident since (but not formed during) the imperial era, when empire was built on armed violence, slavery and unregulated exploitation, although they are visible in all periods of male-formed human history. Uneven playing fields were a key characteristic of imperial domination, and what was undertaken by force of arms is presently legitimized through international institutions. The contemporary outcome in neoliberal terms can be seen in the rankings of GDP and debt service ratios. In human security terms, it finds expression in the Human Development Index: both are displayed in terms of hierarchies. Wealth and health ratings reflect advantage and disadvantage which andrarchy and neoliberalism sustain and strengthen through manipulation of the global asymmetrical status quo in economic wealth and gendered divisions of power. Relative rankings are functions of relative power, rather than coincidences, and their persistence is a product of the asymmetries maintained through institutions and structures.

Both systems' hierarchies are formed from and reinforce competition. Competition is a routine, normalized and deeply entrenched social behaviour to be found in the playground and in educational assessment, in rankings and promotion in business operations, across the armed and civil services and within government globally (Connell 2005, 1987; Messner 1992). Competition is the essence of the formation and reformation of fluid hierarchies and, like neoliberalism and andrarchy, inevitably creates winners and losers. It is the nature of the construct, but the fact that it is a construct means its permanence is not inevitable.

Both systems involve socially legitimized and endorsed aggression as part of the competitive process; in business, aggression is rewarded when it achieves profit, and in globally endorsed sports such as rugby or football it is a norm. Connecting the two, sport was used to prepare young English males to: 'Administer the Empire [because] team sports, based as they are on the twin values of dominance over others and deference to the authority of leaders, were valued as a means to inculcate initiative and self-reliance, along with loyalty and obedience' (Messner 1992: 10). Increasingly, especially in the West, corporate marketing strategy adopts sectors of society, such as sport, associated with masculinity and competition. In January 2007, David Beckham's appointment to a US football team made him the highest-paid sportsperson in history. But his importance here is less as a footballer and more as a commercial carrier; a recognized global symbol, identification with which is likely to produce mass sales while propelling the 'virtues' of competition and masculinity, socialized behaviours that result in a variety of forms of violence that are causally constituted in andrarchy, neoliberalism and human security and which we consider 'normal' and permanent. Connell notes this as a broader phenomenon: corporate bodies, run by males in an ultra-competitive market environment and staffed by ultra-competitive salespeople (mostly males), 'increasingly use mass-media images of the bodies of elite sportsmen as a marketing tool', repeating and reinforcing the merging of competition and masculinity (2000: 221; Griffin 2007). Moore maintains that this system is a reflection and replication of masculine traits: competition for resources; ranking between males within and between peer groups, and between males and females and heterosexuality and homosexuality; and violence and confrontation. He maintains in relation to capitalism that:

> Competition for place, power, sometimes even for survival, is the essence of the system. Those on high may 'lose their shirts' ... while some among the lowest of the low will rise to heights ... Those who make it to the top are likely to be the most ruthless. The system cultivates and rewards aggression, greed, selfishness ... Violent conflict is thus built into the system. (ibid.: 2)

Andrarchy and neoliberalism also share the relegation of women. Women are excluded from various businesses and levels of business in the private sector. Women are discouraged from joining the armed forces because it can render their male counterparts vulnerable (as a result of codes of 'honour' and 'chivalry' that demand they protect 'the weaker sex'). Those areas of traditional male employment that do accept females require particular behaviours from women in many instances. Jeong notes that for women to work in masculine appointments 'means accepting masculine standards and thus reinforcing dominant masculine values' if they are to succeed in the competitive-masculine world (2000: 79).

Integration with such male institutions and practices has the effect not just of requiring changes in female behaviour (where such behaviour has not already been adapted to fit into other male areas), but also of undermining female behaviours that are disrespected by masculine institutions. Female 'emancipation' in terms of equal opportunities in the male-dominated elite-competitive workplace comes at the cost of acquiescing to the very attitudes that exclude females from fair participation in the labour market. Furthermore, women are still trapped under the 'glass ceiling' that prohibits progress beyond a certain level. Dismissals and employment tribunals also confirm the reluctance with which andrarchy allows females into its dominions. Reflecting this balance, men mostly earn more than women for the same job and therefore have greater power in the home; women also normally sacrifice earnings when they raise children, exacerbating inequality.

Both andrarchy and neoliberalism accept and are coterminous with violence. LeRoy notes that 'hierarchical structures [hold] within themselves the potential for violence ... Competition for place, power, sometimes even for survival, is the essence of [both] system[s]' (RMPJC 2003; Messner 1992: 10; Connell 1987: 184). Their assumptions are undeniably reflective of masculinity, in this respect. Both systems maintain a belief in the inevitability of violence; war is unavoidable and casualties will eventuate, and death through impoverishment on a global scale is an unfortunate side effect that some will inevitably suffer. It is remarkably close to the system Galtung referred to when he diagnosed global organization as 'pregnant with violence' two decades ago (1985: 146). Each system feeds the other and has reciprocating male-oriented values that sustain their predominance and hegemony as well as their unassailability in a process of heteronormativity (Zalewski 2007: 309; Griffin 2007: 229). It is a lethal duality directly and indirectly responsible for massive and avoidable death of civilians. Andrarchal neoliberalism and elite (male) leaderships are premised on, constituted of and export and reinforce multiple masculine modes of competition and violence which are mutually self-reinforcing and perpetuating (Hooper 2001; Vasquez 1993). Human insecurity can be described as the collateral damage of the man-made binary structures of andrarchy and neoliberalism.

But perhaps most importantly, andrarchy and neoliberalism share hegemonic discourses of self-validation. They are presented and sustained in ways that make both socially constructed and mutable systems appear 'natural', innate, 'credible, legitimate, benevolent ... inevitable and irreversible' (Gelinas 2003: 98; Connell 2005: 45). Hayden notes that, despite the staggering levels of polarity and inequality around the world, the structural origins 'become normalized in institutional conditions that

TABLE 8.1 Commonalities between andrarchy and neoliberalism

Common elements	Andrarchy	Neoliberalism
Structural inequality	Masculine 'rational' domination over feminine 'irrational'	Exploitative neoimperialism vs. economically restricted neocolonies
Competition	Hegemonic masculinities and male identity formation	Basis of the market and the theory of the firm
Hierarchical power rankings	Physical strength; exam assessment; military ranks; job titles; sport rankings	GNP, GDP scales; Forbes ranking; 'Rich List'
Sexual inequality	Females subordinate to males institutionally and politically	Sale of females as chattels; lower pay for women; glass-ceiling exclusions of women; job exclusion
Legitimized and normalized violence	Boxing; American football; intimate murder and lesser domestic violences; dog fighting; fox hunting	Mass civilian mortality disconnected from neoliberal processes
Assumptions of rationality	Males 'own' the idea of rational and therefore objective behaviour, legitimizing dominance	Neoliberal markets claimed to be rational and impartial, transferring failure to 'irrational actors' deviating from neoliberal agenda
Wide social acceptance of self-legitimization	Male domination as 'natural' and 'necessary' biological division of labour; theological tradition and identity of deity; political and economic institutional domination	Absence of alternatives; demonstrable capacity to enrich; fundamentalist dogmatic attitude to challenges; discourse domination

produce or reinforce social, economic and political disparities' (2007: 290). Both are presented as permanent systems legitimized by necessity and propriety and both offer positive gains, while those most important in their preservation are also those that benefit most from them. That their proponents can universalize their viability through dominating and manipulating public discourse and denying the legitimacy of resistance and challenge, while perpetuating extremes of inequality, may be a function of unintentional ignorance, confusion or denial at all levels and in all countries. Peet maintains that neoliberalism is a social phenomenon that is able to assert hegemony and legitimacy by 'cross-dressing in the legitimating garb of science' (2007: 15). But whichever theory better explains the hegemony, legitimacy, lack of alternatives and destructiveness of the system, what is lacking, according to Hayden, is 'transferable perspective'. That is, if everyone in the world could see and feel everyone else's positions, there is a high degree of likelihood that the legitimacy and credibility of current global economic and political organization would be severely damaged (2007: 290).

Conclusion

Two structures, then, are prevalent globally, and reflect Cox's notion of a 'neubleuse', or constellation of ideologies from which international structures derive (Murphy 2000: 792; Cox 1996). This binary system is a coterminous conjoining of multiple global ideological influences creating and legitimizing global structures and institutions responsible for large-scale and reversible human insecurity. Neoliberalism is the male-dominated and -determined economic structure causing mass inequality around the world, within states and between the sexes. This fluid, adaptive, dynamic, social, political and material process is driven by andrarchy. Andrarchy may be considered as competitive rule by males seeking perceived needs resulting in and sustaining dominant male hierarchies as a result of which female marginalization occurs all but globally.

The process of globalization, to which few are ideologically or otherwise opposed, is an essential conveyor and articulator of the masculinity that underpins andrarchy, and andrarchy of masculinity, because globalization, since its most obvious expression is in imperialism and colonialism, transits from the West to the 'rest'. Western politics, economics and business are ineluctably masculine arenas. In other words, ideational export accompanies economic transfer through the international institutions of neoliberal globalization and contains within it messages of masculinity from Western and masculine economic and political institutions. Connell elucidates unambiguously and lucidly: 'The conditions of globalization ... multiply the forms of masculinity in the global gender order ... [which] ... provide new resources for dominance by particular groups of men. This dominance may become institutionalized in a pattern of masculinity which becomes, to some degree, standard' (Connell 2000: 46; Zalewski 2007: 309).

Modern globalization, driven or dominated primarily by the old imperial metropolises and the United States, involves the perpetuation and export of male-created institutions that embody and sustain masculine behaviours, especially competition, as well as beliefs about gender roles and divides. This male-dominated process is informed by masculine priorities that in turn both legitimize and reinforce the andrarchal power source that underscores the functional elements of neoliberal globalization. Or, as Zalewski considers it, 'heteronormativity [the reproduction of masculine domination] is ... constitutive' of neoliberalism (2007: 309). In so doing, the male-led metropolises export and replicate and/or reinforce the gendered power structures in the peripheries, mirroring structures at the centre. The two power distribution structures are intimately connected by the institutional and institutionalized disequilibrium they are built upon and sustain with direct and indirect agency. To view the two structures as disparate would be to ignore the fact that they are mutually interdependent and reinforcing entities that govern and dictate the public and private, local and global outcomes of human in/security.

NINE | Global structures

Given the scale of the kind of global human insecurity we have covered in this book, one might imagine that while millions die quite needlessly, their protection would be afforded a greater presence on the top table of security studies. Why is this debate marginal, when the scale of death is staggering? A conspiracy theorist might propose that this is because, were the bull grabbed by the horns, some of the fundamental assumptions upon which realism rests would be pilloried and ransacked, because human insecurity tells us that the international system is not how realism presents it and is quite transformable.

In fact, no such conspiracy theory is needed: the evidence speaks for itself. Tackling honestly the global trauma of human insecurity does far more than this. As well as upsetting critical realist shibboleths regarding the inviolability and fatalism of global security structures, it identifies and names the institutions and structures involved in devastating millions of vulnerable lives every year. It tells us also that these structures and institutions are neither fixed by biology nor set by chance, but are instead created from human ideas, sustained by human-populated institutions, and enacted by human endeavour. Crucially, this implies they can be changed, over time, with improvements in global human insecurity following. This important debate might not have been possible without feminism's decades-long engagement with a masculine-dominated and feminist-hostile realist security sector.

This chapter draws on critical feminist challenges to the masculine orientation of realism, explaining why its sex composition prioritizes some security issues and marginalizes others. I then apply the evidence of socially constructed human insecurity (social constructivism) to realism's claims regarding global structures (inflexible and permanent) and international institutions (neutral and fair). Finally, I look at how these developments may influence the global security debate in the future.

Critical feminist challenges

The mainstream security debate that currently occupies centre stage is predictably, and not entirely unreasonably, dominated by issues such as terrorism and nuclear proliferation, or missile shields designed to manage both problems. These are 'hard' and 'important' security matters; and there is little doubt that both ought to be fully engaged with. They are also 'masculine' issues, according to much critical feminist literature; less 'critical', less 'important' issues such as migration and refugees, global warming and human security are considered reflexively opposite as 'feminine' concerns. Sylvester argues that international relations (IR) is 'implicitly wedded to an unacknowledged and seemingly commonplace principle that international relations is the proper homestead or place for people called men' (1994a: 4). There is no doubt that IR is dominated by males; this composition is evident in the literature and at large IR conferences around the world. The normal response is that this is an accurate reflection of the world. Another way of thinking about that claim is that the world is like this because of masculine domination. For much critical feminism, and many others, the masculine domination of the discipline, its trust in structures as being fixed, its claim to authenticity through its 'scientific' approaches, is what defines and limits how we can think about security. This hierarchy is an entirely unsurprising product of masculinity's elevation above the 'feminine', men above women, and is in fact an extension of broader male domination globally, as we have seen in previous chapters.

This would not be the first time feminism has confronted a male-dominated global institution. Critical feminism has been lambasted, misrepresented and misunderstood, deliberately and through unintentional ignorance. It has been demonized, marginalized and accused by neo-feminism of creating its own limitations through the 'wound of gender' and by not considering sufficiently male suffering (Zalewski 2007: 303–8). Feminism has invoked fury and vitriol and provoked whispered malice and sly, patronizing commentary from middle-class white men and women at international conferences. It has caused some men to lament the days before 'political correctness' prevented them from disbursing 'just a little fun' to sometimes vulnerable women and girls. It has provoked 'incredulity' and has been accused of having failed to 'undo' or transform IR (ibid.: 307). It has been disingenuously represented and imagined, caricatured, ridiculed and labelled 'radical', a term that tends to result in the ostracism of whatever it is applied to.

But throughout, it has challenged some of the most fundamental beliefs men and women hold dear. It confronts inequality with complex arguments that suggest enormous change is required in extant social, political, religious and economic organization. It asks us to think in ways that force us to confront and question global conventions. Zalewski charges that 'feminism ... haunts the discipline(s) of IR ... despite its banishment to the margins' (ibid.: 303). That we are as aware as we are of patriarchal power and chauvinism, subjugation and control through social conditioning, brainwashing, violent gender retribution, including the threat of eternal damnation for various 'sins', structural power and gender ordinations, is due in significant part to female intellectual interventions. It has rendered comprehensible the meaning and consequences in terms of wider security of male domination of the international order. Its has challenged the main security discipline's ontologies, epistemologies and priorities, which have contributed little in the way of security for the millions of infant girls and boys, pregnant women and intimate partners who die unnecessarily every year.

Feminist interventions are essential counterweights to realism. They are essential because without such a gendered lens, it is hard to understand why IR cannot see its own power, composition and priorities (which it determines itself by indirect and direct exclusion of women, among others) as part of the cause of mass human insecurity. This irony, and the consequential danger of this narrow, reactionary monologue in IR, led Sylvester to invoke the language of guerrilla warfare. She wrote that the situation required critical feminism to: 'Stalk the shadows of the [IR] field and subvert and enliven, destabilize, disorder, disenchant, insecure, and homestead a field whose internal differences are so tied up with the voices of mainstream and dissident "men" that they smack of debates within the hierarchy of one church' (1994a: 9).

Blanchard also identified and commented on this gender bias, noting that realism is 'dominated by elite, white, male practitioners' (2003: 1292). Sheehan also addressed sex bias in the discipline, describing the security element of IR as 'the most thoroughly gender-biased of the various sub disciplines of International Relations' (2005: 123), while R. B. J. Walker commented that IR was 'one of the most gender-blind and crudely patriarchal of all institutionalized forms of contemporary social and political analysis' (Steans 1998: 36). Grant also conferred similar status on the discipline (1991). For Sheehan, the consequences of a mono-gendered approach cause security to be 'understood not in terms of celebrating and sustaining life, but as safety and separateness from others, and possession of the ability to harm others' (2005: 123). This is a distinctly limiting approach to the understanding of what may constitute security and what security priorities may be. Gender blindness means that IR cannot perceive of current international security institutions in terms other than gender neutrality, rather than interpreting them as the masculine- and female-exclusive bodies they tend to be (Steans 1998: 39; Enloe 1990). Such gender blindness refers not just to male-dominated security studies being unseeing of the security requirements of females and vulnerable children; it also refers to the impact of their own gender's domination and exclusion of critical female voices. This approach ignores the needs and contribution of half the world's population, as well as all the males that die because their security is not part of the privileged hierarchy of interests. We should not forget that of the approximately ten million under-fives that die every year, roughly half will be boys, denied their manhood by other men.

These problems prompted Enloe famously to ask: where were women? Realists might claim that the discipline is a reflection of the world: women are indeed on the global periphery. But male roles in creating this situation are missing from the conceptual thinking of most IR security scholars. Smith and Owens note that posing Enloe's question 'would draw attention to women's presence and importance to world politics, as well as the ways in which their exclusion from world politics was presumed a "natural" consequence of their biological or natural [sic] roles' (2005: 281). But this is not simply a question of voluntary female participation. As they are national-level politics, many women may be disinclined to enter international relations because its (male-governed) priorities may not reflect many women's own priorities. IR has a tendency to draw on liberal feminisms that do not attempt to undo it, while rejecting on sometimes spurious grounds critical feminisms' assaults on IR's very founding assumptions and prerogatives. These are important arguments when trying to establish why such enormous human insecurity can exist globally, and not form a proportionate part of mainstream security debates. The gender dimension to this question of exclusion, or marginalization, of human insecurity reveals the dysfunctionalism of male-dominated security institutions and debates: their gender and the values they prioritize do not allow them to perceive of human security as 'their' security. In overly simplistic terms, for the field of international relations, if the victims are not dominated by men dying from military causes, it is outside their core remit (Jackson and Sorensen 2007: 42). Human security is not a security as IR has constructed or determined security to be, and it is assumed therefore to lie beyond the ambit of the discipline (Tickner 1992: 73). This essential problem, of limited comprehension of security owing to the discipline's composition from only a limited number of the sexes, is well illustrated in Jones's critique of feminist IR, in which he rebuts the degree of male privilege claimed by critical feminists. He asked:

> If masculine privilege is so all-pervasive and absolute, we must ask ... why it is that men live substantially shorter lives than women, kill themselves at rates vastly higher than women, absorb close to 100 per cent of the fatal casualties of society's productive labour, and direct the majority of their violence against their own ranks. (Jones 1996: 423)

This is gender blindness. IR is unwilling, or unable, to consider that much of the violence that men and women face globally is a product of men's formulations, men's institutions and male-dominated ideational structures and the gender blindness associated with this mono-sex predominance. Men kill themselves more than women perhaps because they have created an environment based on hierarchies of competition that lead to conflict, stress and depression. They may suffer more deaths from failures in health and safety protection because they dominate the most physical and dangerous work environments and exclude women from many traditionally dangerous jobs that women are just as capable of completing as men. Furthermore, women are often too busy rearing children in the home – 'society's *unpaid* productive labour' – where tradition prefers them; or they may be working for less than their male counterparts on low part-time rates in service sectors. And the wars in which men kill so many of their own sex were mostly begun by men, their values and their approaches to international relationships; few women have begun international wars. Furthermore, violent conflict is now directed at both sexes, rather than just men, and civilian females and the children of men and women now form a substantial proportion of the casualties of violence. This sex-imposed isolation is important; it reflects and is a reflection of attitudes, values and beliefs that can be rebalanced to be inclusive and representative of both sexes and all securities. In short, realist security studies are dominated by men; the agenda is dominated by 'hard' security; the agenda and its priorities are a result of the exclusion of females; and critical feminism is not treated seriously enough because it represents such a profound challenge to male thinking in security. Enloe's question remains only partly answered.

Male superiority, female inferiority? Some origins of gender inequality

Sylvester reminds us that a serious debate 'on gender and IR has simply not occupied any centre stage of the field' (1994a: 316). Why is IR dominated by males generally suspicious and/or dismissive of critical feminisms, and what is the relationship of this formula to the proportion of human insecurity victims who are female and young boys? To begin with, the gender bias of IR is not at odds with wider gender biases. The organization and leadership of global public society are dominated by males whose institutional make-up, or construction, has also excluded females for millennia. The broad security sector, too, is dominated by men. In other words, the exclusivity of international relations is only part of a wider sex segregation and divide that perpetuates a gender hierarchy that excludes females from proportionate representation. To understand how this status quo has been arrived at, along with its implications for human insecurity, we need to consider some of its origins. In short, we are considering how male perceptions of female inferiority have led to institutionalized and structured female relegation broadly; how this shapes the hierarchies of the security bodies, both academic and armed; and specifically, how this ensures that human insecurity is relegated to a peripheral issue.

Structurally, history appears not to have been very kind to females. Historically, according to Leacock, broadly implemented male control and domination of women have long been reflected through practices including 'women's marriage, male inheritance of land, virilocal residence, [and] male brutality' (1983: 268; Windsor 1988), as well as through the other forms of political and economic domination. Rowland-Serdar and Schwartz-Shea similarly identify 'systemic subordination of women in public and domestic spheres' as historically continuous (1991: 605; Mies 1998: 74–7); while Stets and Pirog-Good remind us that 'traditionally men have been given the right to control women through physical force' (1987: 241; Janssen-Jurreit 1982). Sanday argues, however, that 'male dominance is not an inherent quality of human sex-role plans', adding that man's role in taming nature to accommodate his early needs and those of his family reinforced a sex-role divide that varied across cultures (1981: 3–4).

According to Ortner, that control of nature was extended to control of women by association (1974: 83–4; Ruether 1983: 72). Later, as resource accumulation bifurcated to provide both subsistence and wealth, control of female sexuality became 'important for the inheritance of status and property', two issues that were legalized in favour of men in both the Church and civil society (Leacock 1983: 269). This elevated humans above nature in a process by which 'nature [came] to be ... devalued and inferior to the human' (Ruether 1983: 72–3). But equally importantly for Sanday, although relative control of nature at different stages of human development may explain male or female dominance of each other, 'whether or not men and women mingle or are largely separated in everyday affairs plays a crucial role in the rise of male dominance. Men and women must be physically separated in order for men to dominate women' (1981: 7). For Ruether, that separation is transmitted and amplified during male puberty, 'which uproots the male from the female context of early socialization and forcibly identifies the pubescent male with the male community and its roles and function', a process common in male- or female-led social systems (1983: 73). In other words, social domination is a consequence of separation reinforcing biological difference, perpetuated through adult institutions such as the law or the Church.

Ruether offers a compelling explanation for the evolution of separation and domination, reflected in Sanday's later work. According to this view, nature and women define reproduction; nature was controlled by men, and women's subjugation followed in part because both were associated with a 'lessness' related to the need for physical strength (Sanday 1981). Ruether argued that, after this differentiation in creative capacity, men found different expression of their own creativity through war and protection, while birthing located women in the private home. According to Ruether, '[the] male's ability to define women's realm as inferior depend[ed] on the success of male hunting and warfare [their creative expression] in becoming the link for the domestic units of society. Males then became the lawmakers, ritualists and cultural definers of society' (1983: 73; 1975: 7). Males are associationally acclimatized to male domination through puberty (although social conditioning begins from the earliest days) and through the association of males with the cultural tools they have developed in linking societies and rules, from which women are excluded and 'lessness' is amplified and sustained. The spheres of influence are defined in the private and the public through further association with the external male role and the internal (home) role of the female in which the female is 'burdened' with 'most of the tedious, day-to-day tasks of economic production' and childcare (Ruether 1983: 74). Thus for Ruether are the spheres, sexes and roles defined and separated. The origins of female inferiority, then, are to be found in an early sex-labour divide of necessity, while the external environment was hostile. Once these conditions had been tamed, males associated female reproductivity with nature, while human institutions such as the interpretation of religion associated women with negative forces, and concentrated on female sexuality as dangerous to male strength. Civil law evolved in a mirror image and the social functioning of the sexes was to be institutionally controlled, while the role of women as childbearers was restricted to the private home sphere, with other roles precluded by historical example, evolving custom and institutionalized practice. Much of the last century's social relations have been influenced by females challenging this asymmetry of opportunity and experience and males resisting pressure for sex equality that some fear might undermine their advantages and privileges, as some males see them.

The continuing asymmetry of gender and its meaning for human security

This separation in contemporary day-to-day routines can be seen in the private and public domains of the post-industrial world; such contemporary bipolarity is difficult to distinguish conceptually from the 'primitive' societies studied by the likes of Mead, Sanday and Ruether. Globally, women *mainly* stay at home, service their families and child-rear (often while doing a second, poorly paid job), while for the most part men *mainly* compete in the capitalist labour exchange system; are paid more for their work (in almost all professions except modelling and pornography) than a female counterpart; and tend to dominate higher echelons (UNDP 2005).

For Leacock, this is because 'alienation develops in tandem with the development of exchange systems, as individuals use lineage and extended family units to compete for ranking positions in relation to control over the production and distribution of valued goods' (1983: 269). The sex difference is replicated through the gendered division of labour, and this model of organization is also expressed and projected contemporaneously through globalization and historically through imperialism and colonization (Leacock 1983: 263, 269; Mies 1998). Male domination appears as an ongoing social experience with long historical roots (Leacock 1983: 270). This constructed persistent sex domination is in all likelihood why contemporary public spheres such as security and governance, traditionally male strongholds, are unrepresentative of females, unreceptive to female arguments that are 'illegitimate' because of their sexual identity ('a man's world'), and why lethal female insecurity in the millions is not considered a ranking security issue by the intellectual organization most concerned with violence. IR scholars' security experiences are rarely the experiences of the majority of the world's population, or of those most susceptible to human insecurity.

Young posits 'theoretical connections between male domination and militarism, between masculine gender and the propensity to settle conflicts with violence' (2003: 1). Furthermore, reflecting this, men tend to experience direct violence from boyhood onwards and therefore conceive of violence in terms of direct actions, institutions and ideas. In contrast, women tend to experience more often the consequences of indirect violence, such as inadequate political representation (exclusion/rejection) and (these two are related to one another) inadequate healthcare and nutritional supplies for them and children they assume responsibility for. It is in this sense unsurprising that the males who dominate policy choices in terms of security reflect the adult versions of their earlier conceptions of violence and prioritize weapons of war. This is especially important when we consider the consequences of gender misrepresentation in states' composition.

If we think about sex representation today in powerful institutions such as governments, international financial bodies and all mainstream religions, it is hard to deny that females remain disproportionately represented. Institutional gender relegation persists in the division of labour, especially in very poor countries; in governments, which prioritize state resources; in key global international public organizations, which determine wealth, health and human security; in security academia, which relegates the lives of millions of females; in religion, which excludes females from elite ordination or, in some denominations, from institutional participation per se. This last element deserves some attention, because it provides a link from the past to the present, and because security, government and IFIs have already received substantial treatment. It does not suggest that gender domination begins and ends with religion.

Given that some 95 per cent of the world's population claims to adhere to some form of religion; given that all the mainstream beliefs are male dominated; given religion's influence in constructing, sanctifying and projecting sex-roles differentiation; and given that all states relate to religions to varying degrees, some treatment of this powerful instrument of sex-role creation and endorsement is essential. Religion itself is an abstract construction. Religiosity, however – the interpretation and application by humans of social behavioural codes from constructed and imagined deities – exercises enormous social influence in terms of gender relegation. Equally importantly, its sexist behaviour demonstrates historical continuity, with only slight changes to its sex preference and sex-role reinforcement.

One of the most important themes in religion as far as human development is concerned is the very obvious sex divide. Churches of most denominations are masculine and reflect, for the most part, male deities. Clergy are often exclusively male and many churches, including the Vatican, are keen to maintain traditional gender roles. The *Stanford Dictionary of Philosophy* summarizes eloquently much critical feminist consideration of the sexual identity of God and the related subjugation of women thus:

> The signifier 'God' remains ... subliminally envisioned as a male person-age. Whether taken as real or unreal, inferred validly or invalidly, said to be experienced directly or only projected illusorily, the divine identity ... is unmistakably male. This supreme, ruling, judging, and loving male God is ... named Father ... This construct tends in turn to justify various social and political structures of patriarchy which exalt ... patriarchs at the head of pyramids of power ... Theis[m] legitimates social and intel-lectual structures that ... relegate women, children, and other men to marginalized and subordinated areas ... The divine as male [has created] ideologies which devalue all that is not male; they have formed a consti-tutive element in the oppression of women and other 'Others'.

While many feminists have considered that the male representation of God is broadly responsible for creating and/or perpetuating female relega-tion and concomitant inequality and negative experiences, they are far from the only critics who assert that the use of religion in general is a dangerous form of brainwashing, oppression and control. The literature is replete with examples of dogmatic religious policy that disfavours females and some males. These include Christian-conservative attitudes regard-ing female abortion rights in the USA and bigotry towards homosexuals in the USA and UK; Vatican influence in the non-secular Republic of Ireland through denial of abortion rights to women; the Vatican's view that women's primary role should be in the home; and the brutality of Islamic punishments for women in Asia, Africa and the Middle East.

Sanday argues that this is in part a broader problem: 'no matter how it is produced, sexual separation (for whatever reason) creates two worlds – one male, one female, each consisting of a system of meanings and a program for behaviour' (1981: 7). Sanday maintains that 'there is a connection between religious thought and male and female power ... The relative power between the sexes will change as our culture changes. Change the cultural plot and sex roles are conceived differently. Change sex roles and the plot will change'. (ibid.: 12). In other words, the social construction of religion is male. Gods are socially constructed edifices and are normally males and, while there are varying interpretations of the power of certain female figures in religious history (again demon-strating their social, human construction), males are dominant. Male gods dominate religion; males dominate secular and non-secular states; males dominate policy-making in the neoliberal global economy; males dominate security debates. The underlying theme, then, is structural andrarchy; and, while males and their implicit and explicit values determine security priorities, human insecurity will remain marginal. It is neither ironic, nor a coincidence, that it is mostly females who have pointed this out.

Social constructivism as a critique of realism

Critical feminism denounces realism for being male dominated, unrepresentative of females, and limited in what it can understand security to mean. According to such argument, this explains why human security is marginalized or rejected as inauthentic; it is not a reflection of realism's (male) agendas and priorities. In addition, the evidence of human activity in the causation of human insecurity supports the notion of social constructivism. This in turn is a powerful critique of realist arguments maintaining immutability in international structures and neutrality in international institutions. I provide now a brief reminder of the essence of realist interpretation of international structure, and then demonstrate how the social construction of human insecurity offers a critique of these assumptions.

Realist perceptions of structure were influenced greatly by the work of Hedley Bull (1977) and, while various adjustments have been made to this model, Bull's landmark work underscores realist attitudes to international structure. Bull saw the system in which states operated as one of anarchy, in which states interacted randomly and often violently. Since, unlike in the national state, there was no legitimate absolute law that could be effectively enforced, outcomes were violent as often as not and this violence characterized the anarchic system of states. The international system Bull described mirrored the state: both were composed of a largely biologically fixed and harsh state of human nature characterized by violence as a natural and irreducible characteristic. There was little, if any, independent human creation in the international system.

Thus, three key assumptions of realism, on which security priorities are often based, take form. First, states are reflections of human nature and contain institutions to manage inevitable inter-human violence. Second, the international system mirrors this, but is devoid of a matching overarching institution to manage interstate violence, which is similarly based on a fixed and violent natural state. Accordingly, international institutions are neutral forces for good to manage violence wherever possible. Third, women are biologically sex-divided from men and have reflectively different roles in which women primarily raise children while men provide security; men therefore rightly dominate power institutions in which power is defined according to the dominant sex.

This book's approach to explaining human insecurity offers a substantial challenge to these assumptions. First, the critical feminist element demonstrates that states most probably are reflections of nature, but not human nature. Since men form them and dominate them, is it not reasonable that states will normally be reflections of male nature? Critical feminism and anthropology such as Sanday's work would possibly agree to some extent with the biological element, but might qualify the realist assumption by adding to their formula that human outputs are mainly a product of millennia of social conditioning based on early assumptions and necessities of sex-divisions of labour before humans brought nature under their control, first by defending themselves from its extremities, and second by harnessing and then exploiting it for wealth and profit. These adaptations demonstrate social transformations.

Second, the international structure that states inhabit is a socially engineered extension of a sustained sex-based division of labour based on outdated necessities from much harsher times in earlier human evolution which have taken root in the structure of the state. By extension, the international structure states inhabit is a human-engineered social construction that mirrors sex segregation at the state level. It does indeed reflect various human outputs, which explains human insecurity, but these are male outputs. Females have almost no input into security determinism at state or structure level, with one or two notable exceptions that Eisenstein rightly considers decoys. When women do have this input, they use male institutions and work within the limits of male conceptions of security and power. Inevitably, then, they therefore can only extend and continue male approaches and methods. The findings of this book demonstrate, however, that this is not a permanent arrangement; it changes over time and its reliance on males limits the rate at which it can change further. The global 'order' is therefore not a fixed entity except for as long as males dominate it; furthermore, males have created this system. It is a social construction susceptible by definition to change, in the same way that human behaviour is not fixed but socially constituted and adaptive.

Furthermore, the international institutions that states deploy to manage instability are not neutral but instead reflect the power advantages of those who formally constitute them. They maintain the strict asymmetrical power relationships responsible for the maintenance of poverty and gross human insecurity. This in itself is evidence of the extent of social construction and therefore may be changed. Power relationships of inequality happen because they are built that way by human determinism of security and what is required to maintain security, in the numerous ways this can be defined. If security is defined by economic prowess and military power, then achieving dominance in those areas requires competition in the neoliberal structure and dominance in its andrarchal counterpart. To ensure that these are achieved by those seeking hegemony, the playing field is 'fixed' by 'crooked' institutions. The same processes are to be found in competitive games, business and in the schoolyard.

Third, while females and males have clearly distinct preset evolutionary biological roles, neither men nor women are restricted to those roles solely. Women's successful challenges to such institutionally and ideationally perpetuated male beliefs demonstrate their capacity to take on most roles normally associated with males, while males are also becoming increasingly aware of their capacity to stretch their potential towards the roles realism maintains are the primary domain of females. The essence of the differences in the two perspectives lies in the difference between realism's adherence to fatalistic determinism and social constructivists' belief that humans are responsible for the institutions and structures that surround them and can therefore change them. The primary obstruction to transformation is the persistent belief that the structure is fixed and that male domination is only a reflection of a fixed reality and therefore is meant to be.

We may make a number of observations from this. First, human insecurity, as I discuss it here, is a product of human actions, either directly, institutionally or ideationally. It comes from human thinking and human actions and to argue otherwise is illogical. Second, this process challenges core underlying assumptions and arguments of the realist security school, which is also responsible for arguing that broad human security as discussed here should not be the subject matter of 'serious' security studies. Third, human insecurity affirms the principal arguments of the school of social constructivism: that the global system and human insecurity are not products of immutable biology but of human and, more specifically, male beliefs/fears, priorities, perspectives and approaches. Perhaps it is this kind of an approach to understanding the role of political institutions in security complexes which Rengger and Thirkell-White refer to (2007: 17).

The idea of 'social constructivism' challenges the realist view that the international system is wholly or solely self-deterministic, largely immutable and a product of often random 'anarchic forces' beyond the restraint of man and his 'nature'. It holds instead that realists are quite right in their view that the current international system is a structurally determined violent disorder; but their critical qualification and argument are that this order is a constructed outcome produced by human agency and processes based on ideas and material ownership (Wendt 1999; Onuf 1989). Copeland maintains that social constructivism builds on three important notions. First, it maintains that the events that make up international politics are determined by shared ideas passing between individuals. That is, its overarching framework is made of communicated, human-constructed 'ideas, norms and values [which are] held by actors' (2000: 3). It is these ideas which determine outcomes and, because they are shared between and within humans, they can be described as social in nature. Inherent in this proposition is the assumption that ideas and influence can therefore change, wax or wane. They are not immutable and derive from millions of different people with different views developed over broad intervals of time.

Second, these ideas, values and norms determine human outputs, or actions. These actions, which result in consequences, direct humans from numerous variable perspectives. They are subjective and derive from value systems that direct ideas and beliefs which in turn become policies that determine outcomes and the consequences of outcomes. They make humans responsible as interpreters and translators of beliefs into consequences. Third, this is a reciprocal, evolving and persistent relationship. While structures shape human activity, in a rational and responsive framework, human activities and their consequences shape and reform the ideas that direct them in a progressive learning loop (this is not to suggest they always learn the best lessons). Each feeds the other and refines the process in accordance with ideas and their relationship to the human agency they determine.

Distinguishing this approach from realism, Copeland maintains that 'structures are not reified objects that actors can do nothing about ... Rather, structures exist only through the reciprocal interaction of actors' (ibid.: 3). They are able, writes Copeland eloquently, to 'emancipate themselves from dysfunctional situations that are in turn replicating conflictual practices' (ibid.: 3; Tickner 1992: 128). The essence of social construction lies in the possibility of transformation as an antidote to a darkly fixed and pessimistic interpretation of immutable world events. Its essence also presents humans with the opportunity to realize their capabilities as thinking and responsible actors who, when the misguided templates of 'human nature' and Hobbesianism restricting their potential are revealed as demonstrably flawed and in large part responsible for the insecurity faced by millions of vulnerable people globally, are empowered to move beyond this predatory paradigm.

At its broadest, then, social constructivism is concerned with how humans direct the outcomes of international security or, as Ruggie succinctly put it, it is 'about human consciousness and its role in international life' (1998: 856). Similarly for Barnett, social constructivism is based on the notion that 'ideas define and can transform the organization of world politics, shape the identity and interests of states, and determine what counts as legitimate action' (2005: 251). Its inherently subjective predisposition is thus directly oppositional to realist assumptions regarding the desirability and ineluctability of objectivity and, with this, rationality (Cox 1984). Thus, rather than an abstract entity called the 'international system' being a free-standing, remote body acting according to no fixed agenda and characterized by uncertainty, it is humans who have created a violent global system and who prioritize groups of humans, ideas and resources for securitization – rendering them (before others) safe from threats and violence, direct or indirect. It is humans who determine who, and what, remains safe from the insecurities they prioritize and, given the gender domination of the IR discipline, it is inevitably females and children who are lower in the ranks of security 'tables'. The statistics gathered in the preceding chapters affirm this.

Social constructivism allows us to reinterpret all manner of human insecurity. The architectures that are rendered visible through a social constructivist lens mean that the phenomena experienced in the daily existence of billions of people do not derive from random self-perpetuating acts and fixed behaviours but are instead products of human interventions and omissions. They are made, daily, as a result of human beliefs and priorities. International relations (IR) and international security are thus not to be argued away as consequences of a global system comparable to balls colliding on a billiard table. They are made by human mental activity and converted into institutions by which we order our existence, one core priority of which is our security. Social constructivism varies in type and school, as all social science disciplines do, but it presents an ideational approach to understanding the world. That is, it argues that human ideas shape the environment we inhabit; the habitat is thus a construct of human thinking; and it cannot therefore be fixed and unchangeable. In the words of Rengger and Thirkell-White (2007: 12), this approach can be seen as something which 'liberates us from the flat and sterile materialism of conventional IR theory ... [and allows us to see] possibilities for change and reconstruction'.

While these intellectual departures offer real opportunities for alternative security constructions, social constructivism has lacked concrete expression of connections between structures and agency. At this point, we may consider a more developed version of social constructivism based on this work's identification of causal chains in terminal human insecurity. As we saw in Chapter 6, the various avoidable mortalities, in their millions, are the undeniable consequences of human acts and agency: choices of policy, impacts of implementation, deliberate murder of women and children, unintentional consequences of dangerous international socio-financial policies causing lethal impoverishment, and so on. We also may identify the ideational beliefs involved, namely andrarchy and neoliberalism. But what connects the two ends of this model?

Earlier chapters identified institutions through which acts that cause human insecurity are directed. One might think of them as 'conductors', in the same sense that lightning is conducted through metal and may kill humans and animals on contact. They were the international institutions of male domination and public international finance. These connected, or facilitated the expression of, beliefs and values – ideas – to outcomes, or consequences. These constructed institutions (as distinct from abstract notions) appear absent from Wendt's model of social construction but, again, are evident when causation is associated with human activity rather than 'act of God' or 'fate' or 'interminable structure'. This is a model of social construction that moves beyond actor-agency types to include institutional connectivity between ideation and act.

The empirical critique of IR and human insecurity, conducted in IR's own tradition of positivism, has yet greater import in a deeper and wider debate. The indisputable evidence of human construction of death and insecurity, as opposed to ineluctable determinism, demonstrates the ontological inadequacy of IR to take responsibility for informing policy and policy-makers of the workings of the world. This work adds to the broad body of critical social theory that has concerned itself with IR's inelasticity in facing up to very powerful and reasonable critiques of the way the discipline sees both itself and the wide world.

We have seen above that the ideas of objectivity, rationality and the adoption of scientific methods used reliably to explain the social, human world are profoundly challenged in alternative schools of IR, such as critical feminism and critical security studies. But further still, these foundational issues of knowledge and understanding are challenged and contested from without the discipline. Much critical theory and postmodernism has taken issue with IR's unstinting, seemingly dogmatic tendency and ability to cling to ideas and methods of understanding knowledge about the 'real' world rooted in the Enlightenment of four centuries past. It generalizes about human nature while all the while excluding women from its consideration. It maintains that males are rational and females irrational, another generalization that any human being would immediately be able to tell you, from personal experience and with no need to conduct major research programmes, is nonsense. It makes claims about objectivity which are equally intellectually defunct, and about the objectivity and value neutrality of 'facts', when the very diversity of interpretations of political incidents demonstrates subjective interpretation.

Indeed, the very concept of 'revisionism' is evidence that opinions change over time and 'facts' then cannot be impartial and neutral, or 'value free', in the vernacular. And the discipline is, as R. B. J. Walker has commented (above), a profoundly gender-inadequate and obviously patriarchal and patronizing discipline in many ways (although not all in this intellectual college are so crudely simplistic or exclusionary). Finally, its efforts to generalize from the specific, in the tradition of the natural sciences from which its methodologies are adapted, and to find a universal explanation for such a massively complex and shifting global system of people, processes and systems, is an attempt to engineer a simple world-view that can readily be understood and translated into policy. It has never come close to achieving this, even when the world appeared (but was not) more simple in the cold war. But its dominance of international relations and of international policy excludes or marginalizes critics of its most basic understanding of knowledge and interpretation, with the result that its crude reductionism, dualisms and gender exclusion contribute to policies in 'the real world' that are sometimes narrow, often ineffective and may lead directly or indirectly to mass fatalities of civilians and of soldiery as well. It is its composition and beliefs which create the violence it seeks to engage with, as Galtung made clear and as Vasquez was later to argue as well (1993).

Critical theory outside the IR 'box' makes clear that the foundations upon which IR analysis, arguments and policy rest are in fact not just misplaced but have dangerous outcomes, as I have demonstrated throughout this work. George maintains that because of these problems and dangers, a discursive perspective on International Relations has never been more necessary ... because it ... illustrates the power and (largely unrecognized) dangers of the unsaid, the unreflected and the unwritten in a world that every day and in so many ways defies the simplistic, grad-theorized invocations of its 'reality' ... It is crucial that we go beyond the simple ritualized representation of Traditional theory and practice to seriously question that which for so long has evoked certain irreducible images of reality for the policy and intellectual communities in International Relations. (1994: xi, 3)

The crude reductionism of the world to an anarchical system about which we can do little except regulate institutionally against the periodic excesses of an unchanging human nature as they relate to male priorities of security that leave millions of male and female children dead every year, despite our full awareness of this, is most obviously challenged in the work of this book.

But further to this, these conclusions themselves speak volumes about the failures of IR throughout its history to prevent routinely occurring disasters or to predict seismic political shifts such as the end of the cold war. But they also pose the question of 'why' IR fails again and again to predict or prevent wars of all kinds, and why, in seeming contradistinction to this record, it remains predominant in interpreting the world and forming global policy. The answers are to be found in its outdated, dysfunctional and ill-appropriated understanding of the world and its subjective, shifting human interactions; in its gender composition; in its essentially conservative view of social sciences and knowledge; and in its ability to limit the boundaries of international discourse while maintaining its status within, and ability to define and legitimize, what constitutes 'mainstream' literature. In short, and returning to the eloquence of George, realism, 'even in its most sophisticated form [is] an anachronistic residue of the European Enlightenment ... which continues the futile quest for a grand (non) theory ... in the face of ... widespread recognition that it is seemingly incapable of moving beyond its primitive intellectual agenda' (ibid.: 12). The search for a universal 'truth' through adaptation of natural scientific methods and simplistic and dualistic ontologies based on an imagined objectivity and an ownership of objectivity exiles half the world's population at the stroke of a man's pen to the margins of thought and action. This approach can never find a universal and therefore simple explanation of the world, and resources and time are abjectly wasted in efforts to do so. The dilemma of avoidable but reinforced and repeated global human insecurity tells us this is so, but the social construction it reveals also tells us this is impermanent and changeable. It therefore allows intellectual resources to be directed to formulate variegated policies for which I believe ordinary electorates globally would want to take responsibility, if they were given the knowledge and opportunity, instead of being richly deceived into believing that this is 'the way the world is', when clearly it is not.

Conclusion

The approach of this work has been to conjoin the approaches of critical feminism and social constructivism as a means of understanding and explaining the human insecurity discussed in previous chapters. It has also argued that realist assumptions undermine human security through their limited, gendered field of vision and choices of priorities; this helps determine and create human insecurity. Various elements of feminism have challenged 'malestream' security thinking and argued that its composition explains both the nature of international politics and security, and the exclusion of women from sufficient positions of effective influence. They have also challenged fundamental realist assumptions regarding what is objective; what can be construed as rational; and the extent to which this is reliable or useful.

Social constructivism intersects with such feminist analysis and develops much further the central epistemological critique of objectivity and rationality claimed through the 'masculine' where the converse is associated with the 'feminine', but also argues that as well as the fundamental tenets of realism and neo-realism being subjective, they are constructed concepts that produce subjective and prioritised interpretations of the world and of security. This subjective process in turn has imagined false structures: subjective interpretation of security and human nature, coupled with a masculine composition and focus, has failed to identify the essential structures of global violence that explain and manufacture the situations of the vulnerable women and children described and discussed here. Combining the two intellectual approaches of critical feminist thinking and social constructivism presents a very different image of structure, institution and agency.

On the basis of these understandings, we may draw four conclusions. First, realism is inadequate for understanding the structural and institutional determinism of terminal human insecurity because it is gender blind owing to its overwhelming masculine composition and attendant priorities. Second, the critical feminist insights and analyses that identify and demonstrate the gendered conceptualization, prioritization and marginalization of human security needs in realist thinking conjoin with social constructivism to propose the flexibility and mutability of masculinity itself. It, like the ideas it prioritizes and identifies as structural, can develop in response to empirical evidence and positivist argument to evolve into a higher form of social guidance and identity construction. Third, constructivist epistemology and approaches demonstrate the mentally conceived and socially created nature of the structures and institutions directly and indirectly responsible for human insecurity. Fourth, combining critical feminism with mental and social constructivism explains the relationship between structures, institutions and human agency in causing terminal human insecurity in the fields identified and discussed in this work.

A comment from an unexpected source revealed the extent to which some of these ideas are understood. US Secretary of State for Defence Donald Rumsfeld, not well known for compromise, or sympathy for vulnerable groups, and broadly influenced by traditional security schools, challenged in 2007 the notion that the world could still reasonably be construed as an objectively perceived reality, by claiming that this was 'not the way the world works anymore ... when we act, we create our own reality' (*Guardian*, 14 April 2007: 29). The qualification of social constructivism advanced here does not claim to be the Grand Theory sought by Behnke and many others (2005: 48), but it does act as a powerful critique of some of the most important bodies of thought in international relations and its subset, international security, when the latter is more thoughtfully reconsidered to embrace a maximalist perspective of human security.

It also demonstrates the extent of human causation in terminal human insecurity, from the beliefs that sustain gender domination and kill millions of females and the ideas that dictate social policy that impoverishes and kills boys and girls on a similar scale. Perhaps its most important contribution is that it lays bare responsibility and demonstrates lucidly accountability: not to impersonal and invisible structures, but to interpersonal acts, human-constructed physical and visible institutions and the man-made ideas and beliefs from which they derive. While we cannot 'disinvent' the 'bomb' of human insecurity, the corollary of its existence is that other systems can also derive from ideation and be projected and conducted through institutions to create positive, constructive human agency which rejuvenates our consciences and undermines our most dangerous insecurities.

TEN | Conclusion

This book is concerned with the fundamental problem of the human insecurity of millions of people who die when they do not have to, at the hands of human decision-making, institutional routine and structural determinism. Asking why this massive security problem has not been considered as security by the most important and most influential security literature, and why it barely registers in states' international foreign policies, leads us to identify particularly powerful structures that influence the priorities of states and institutions that have in common male leadership. The subjects of human security are antithetical to masculine identity: they are boys and girls, and women.

The degree of social construction involved is impossible to ignore when it is exposed. Critical feminism has been wise and judicious to persist with the notion of sex and gender causation in violence, and courageous to maintain its arguments relating the (male) gender of power to the problems of domination and control. Masculinism in IR has a potentially huge input to make if it can overcome its gender-centric indolence and cease to refer to broad human insecurity as 'sentimental, feminine, Utopian, and therefore incapable of transfer to the international arena for rigorous analysis' (McSweeney 1999: 15). One might reasonably conclude that the area in which rigour is lacking is IR itself, rather than human security, if the discipline is prepared to dispel avoidable deaths by the millions. One might also ask how 'sentimental' 10 million dead children's lives might have been to their fathers and mothers. A common mistake, then, is for human security to be solely gendered to females; not that this should in any way detract from its import. To advance such a non sequitur would be quite obvious sexism. It is not solely female. Every year, of those 10 million children who die before they reach the age of five, roughly half will be boys. Part of the cause of those deaths is the dominance of masculine beliefs, prioritized and acclimatized over millennia and enjoying hegemony in unsecuritizing human insecurity. Gender approaches have been, and remain, invaluable tools for interpreting human security and critiquing masculine dominion. But they are not the only influences (Hoogensen and Stuvoy 2006: 210; Hoogensen and Rottem 2004).

Critical feminists have also joined with social constructivists and anthropologists in demonstrating that gender is socially constructed. We may at this point reasonably assume that the merging of these intellectual currents in the study of human insecurity manifestly confirms the social construction of power and inequality that underscores the concept and the reasons why it remains 'below the radar' of 'malestream' security studies. In identifying institutions and the idea of structure as both causative of global insecurity and simultaneously transformable, this book opens several doors. Perhaps the most important is the one that, when opened, allows us to fully challenge the notion that our future is fixed like our past. While the past was harsh, neither the present nor the future need be so. Realism's assumptions regarding system immutability and the state of nature and man, already tenuous, are dated by thought, not by evidence.

But this critique is not undertaken with the intention of excluding realism from this debate. It would be profoundly unwise to seek to marginalize the potential in realist positivist methodologies and institutional experience. It would also be reckless to forget their global influence. Other methodologies are as yet insufficiently established in realist global security architectures and thinking. Rather, it would seem intellectually healthy to expand cooperation across disciplines and methodological boundaries and to consider the roles of representation and rights more broadly in human security determinism. In identifying human insecurity creation within the dominant paradigm's assumptions and beliefs itself, we can no longer claim ignorance, or allow our ego defences to bypass our intellectual potential and human responsibilities. To the contrary, this work proposes the possibility of interdisciplinary alliances to reprioritize human security on the mainstream IR security agenda in order that we may accept and confront the institutional and structural roots of such enormous, avoidable human catastrophes as this work outlines. It has not been impossible to draw together different methodologies and epistemologies in a common security cause. Indeed, the basis of the quantitative data involved here reflects the positivist tradition.

Already, at least one attempt has been made to broaden intellectual comprehension of wider security and its relevance to realism and IR in general. The notion of the 'security-development nexus' was expected by some to connect development issues to security debates. This relationship between economic impoverishment and international instability and insecurity has, however, proved difficult to establish and harder to sustain. The limited evidence presented in this book has affirmed relationships between economic impoverishment from international institutional edict, on the one hand, and low-intensity political instabilities at the domestic state level, on the other. But it has not demonstrated long-term damage to states' legitimacy or, on its own, led states to fail. Furthermore, no evidence assessed here indicates terrorist opportunism or interstate 'contagion', whereby one state's problems are transmitted to a neighbouring state, as in a latter-day 'domino theory'. Research is still in its early days, but there is little to sustain the role of the security-development nexus in state destabilization on its own; other factors are normally at work, such as resource finds, corruption, pre-existing ethnic tensions, greed and grievance, and so on (see also Cooper 2006; Duffield 2001). Legitimizing human security through sometimes spurious connections has not yet demonstrably helped undermine human insecurity.

Retaining the development angle, however, and coupling it to legal institutions, might be a route worth considering. Although there is, as realists would rightly confirm, no overarching legal institution capable of reliably and regularly maintaining the rule of law in a state system that has no supra-governmental body, the range and capacity of cooperative international law have enjoyed some welcome successes in areas considered out of range until very recently. Nor would a new architecture of law need to be established; emerging current practice has produced some heartening results for justice. For example, there have been trials at The Hague of dictators and despots; General Pinochet was questioned by police in London and legally harassed by Spanish judge Baltasar Garzon. Dr Henry Kissinger must consider with caution his international movements, a scenario unimaginable only recently. It is not beyond consideration that a similar, robust approach to enforcing the basic right to life enshrined in the UN and other constitutions could be refined, with executive decision-makers in IFIs and state legislatures becoming subject to legal scrutiny for failing to prevent avoidable deaths in the domains this book identifies. Hayden, for one, maintains that 'feasible alternative decisions and actions can be taken; alternative institutional schemes can be implemented which do not produce pervasive, persistent and radical inequality' (2007: 289). Given that the right to life is a basic right, should it not be protected as other essential laws are? And, given that life is being taken in the millions (since so many of these deaths are clearly avoidable), would it not be reasonable to link development to human rights and have that relationship formalized, enshrined and protected? Making moral arguments about human security has so far not made a sufficient difference to the daily casualties; and conceptualizing a potential realist nexus has been problematic. But if human rights were linked to development levels at which lethal human insecurity ceased, and these were taken seriously and enforced, levels of development would presumably have to rise, or those charged with achieving economic development and failing would presumably be held responsible.

There is also evidence that human security itself has emerged as successful governmental policy, on the one hand, and that it has also mobilized global civil society. There is further potential, where governments can be convinced of the 'unassailable integrity' of a human security issue and mindful of the positive benefits to such governments as well, to extend aspects of this approach to the issues outlined in this work. It is said that 'the master's tools will never dismantle the master's house' (Audre Lord). But there are various approaches to challenging the 'deeply sedimented' structures involved; there are processes of institutionalization that may be replicated with different outcomes; and human agency is not solely negative for human insecurity. The current system is composed of ideational structure (andrarchy and neoliberalism) transmitting human agency (resulting in human insecurity) through international institutions. Already in existence are two counterparts for the reduction of human insecurity which also are recognized in the IR and social constructivism literature. Positive human agency exists in the form of the millions of people who are acting already to challenge the poverty that kills millions; in the form of the millions who confront global neoliberalism; in the form of the hundreds of millions of socially aware and responsible human beings who donate to human security and environmental causes (the two are obviously interwoven in some areas); or in the form of activists who lobby individually or in groups about what they perceive as human and social injustice.

Simultaneously, this human agency forms and acts both independently of and in partnership with already extant international institutions. These may be state international bodies such as the UN or private charities like Oxfam, Medicins Sans Frontières, and thousands of other bodies, large and small. In other words, two countervailing elements of global organization for human security are running functionally and with great effect. Where they are lacking is in ideational hegemony: the ability to uproot Waever's 'solidly sedimented' structures (2002: 32). It is regrettable, but this will not happen overnight. We should not, however, rule out the capacity of regimes to form additional international norms and arrangements. We are apprised already of their social construction rather than their magical appearance; it is not unreasonable to expect that the Ottawa Convention outcome that resulted in the banning of landmine use and export by a vast majority of states can be replicated. This outcome relied on a combination of global civil society campaigning; survivor activism, where, for example, Cambodian amputees travelled the Western world and described the physical conditions they experienced and the personal, social and economic ramifications of their experiences; celebrity support; media interventions; and it has also benefited from the high-profile intervention of British royalty (this list is not exhaustive). Many states involved in supporting the campaign were in part influenced by their own publics' increasing consciousness of this single issue of unchallengeable importance and moral value (other than a politician who described landmine clearance as 'politically correct'). According to Keohane, where states' governing politicians share a common interest of serving their citizens and maintaining office over non-zero-sum issues, they have shown a propensity to embark on cooperative action through institutions (1984; Murphy 2000: 798). An issue with such gravitas that might be identified as a single issue, but with a multidimensional background, such as the under-five mortality rate, is one of a number that would engage global public concern through institutional mobilization and heightened public consciousness from the ground up, without having to eliminate or otherwise transform the ideational superstructure that directly and indirectly causes such huge human insecurity in this area. While this approach does little to undo the structural determinism of the U5MR, it does much to instigate international state and civil society mobilization, coordination and human security impact. If the ideational structure's hegemony of status and discourse cannot immediately be deconstructed (in the mechanistic sense), challenging its consequences from the ground upwards can not only have an impact like the Ottawa Convention (which is not without flaws), but can also expose gradually the institutional derivation from neoliberal domination of the human insecurity problem in the first instance. This is not a model for the elimination of global human insecurity, but it is a challenge to those who deny relationships between gender and security; between human agency (social construction) and lethal outcome; and between elite masculine determinism of security and the relative weakness of the boys, girls and women who experience the consequences of the hegemony of the masculine approach to securitization.

Most life philosophies point to the need for balance in the human environment; its most common representation is 'yin' and 'yang', light and dark, the sky and earth. In debate, we seek balanced arguments that take into consideration two sides of a dispute. In modern European law, there is a defence and a prosecution. In loving relationships, there is mutuality. We may try to balance our budgets and our consciences with our consumerist desires; we may try to balance our desire to travel with our carbon footprint. We try to balance our work–life routines. We balance safety against risk. We try to balance the rule of law against intrusive government, or the rights of minorities and majorities. We seek fairness most of the time. But something is out of kilter.

How may we reconcile the imbalances in, for instance, the attention paid to terrorism, which kills a few people periodically, and which receives the highest priorities within many Western polities, with the attention paid to global impoverishment, which kills millions of people, every year, but which is rejected as a significant security concern? Or the billions spent on weapons that are rarely ever used with the paucity that goes to aid and development, which is absorbed immediately? How may we render congruent the differences between military expenditures for potential military catastrophes and health expenditure for potential health catastrophes? How may we synthesize the representation of women in government with the number of women globally? Is it not perplexing to equate the amount spent on perfume in Europe in one year with the amount needed but not provided for clean water access for 2.5 billion people? Why is it so hard to reconcile the failure of IFIs to change with the torrent of criticism of their policies? How is it possible to reconcile the rhetoric of neoliberalism with the reality of 2 billion people existing on less than 2 dollars per day?

In the introduction, it was noted that an essential undercurrent of this book is power and inequality. The propensity of imbalances points towards a fundamental disequilibrium of power. In the subject matter of this book, those that predominate in power and discourse render insecure those that are unable to change the discourse or have their security concerns prioritized. As Newman notes, 'attitudes and institutions that privilege "high politics" above disease, hunger, or illiteracy are embedded in international relations and foreign policy decision-making' (2001: 240). It would appear that power has accrued asymmetrically in part because no independent external regulator (a global court, for example) has been able to present the interests of the most vulnerable millions to an impartial, informed jury that might adjudicate to lessen the obvious biases that belong to the most powerful ideas and institutions. No moderation of excess has been available, and accordingly, power has continued to accrue to andrarchy, neoliberalism and the discourses they dominate and which sustain them. In this case, a critical disequilibrium of power that has been institutionalized since 1944 (but the origins of which long predate that era) has unsurprisingly overcome the technical opposition of communism and adopted a fundamentalist tack which has provided great chattels and treats for a minority of the world while trammelling legitimate opposition and silencing internal dissent. The elite-legitimized disequilibrium that this dualistic discourse has maintained has been largely immune from prosecution; the dead child's eyes staring out from her partial burial place at Bhopal in 1984 remind us of such inequities of justice, while Union Carbide, the offending agent, sets the debate by commandeering first place in Internet searches and presenting a distorted and partial representation of events. But reconnecting basic rights to emphatic prosecution may be an essential pillar in not just the management of previously inviolable international institutions and their dogmatic credos, but also a meaningful response to the power and inequality that underpin global human insecurity.

Bibliography

Associated Press of Pakistan, 20 February 2007, <www.app.com. pk/en/index.php?option=com_ content&task=view&id=4273&Ite mid=2>, accessed 23 May 2007.

BBC News 24, <http://news. bbc.co.uk/1/hi/england/ london/4741098.stm>, accessed 23 May 2007; 9 October 2006.

Cambodia Daily, 20 July 2006.

The Economist, 10 November 1990.

Financial Times, 1 May 2007.

Forbes.com., <www.forbes.com/ business/2007/02/02/leadership- dell-jobs-lead-manage-cx_hc_ 0205ceobounce.html>, accessed 23 May 2007.

Global Issues That Affect Everyone, <www.globalissues.org/Trade- Related/Poverty.asp>, accessed 27 February 2006.

Guardian, 27 May 2006; 27 March 2006; 18 June 2005; 10 November 2006; 15 November 2006; 21 May 2005; 2 September 2003; 30 November 2006; 1 August 2005; 31 July 2004; 6 January 2007; 8 January 2007; 12 January 2007; 8 September 2005; 7 February 2007; 1 March 2007; 8 March 2007; 12 March 2007; 16 April 2007; 17 April 2007.

The Hindu, 24 June 2001; 21 April 2007.

Independent, 17 January 2007; 30 April 2007; 7 September 2005; 21 February 2007; 15 November 2006.

Intercontinental Press, August 1984.

Mumbai Mirror, 23 April 2007.

New Internationalist, 322, April 2000; 312, May 1999, <www.economicexpert.com/a/ Andrarchy.htm>.

New York Daily News, 30 November 2005.

Observer, 2 October 2005.

Sunday Times, 26 November 2006; 1 November 2006.

Telegraph, 19 January 2007; 29 January 2007; 6 September 2005; 2 May 2007.

The Telegraph, Calcutta, 22 February 2005.

The Times, 27 March 2006; 18 December 2006; 4 January 2007; 1 November 2006; 28 February 2007; 13 March 2007; 18 March 2007; 31 March 2007.

Toronto Star, 28 February 1994, <www.globalhealthfacts.org>.

Washington Post, 16 January 2007.

World Alliance of YMCAs, 'Stop Violence against Women', <www. ymca.int/index.php?id=636>.

Adams, P. (1991) *Odious Debts: Loose Lending, Corruption and the Third World's Environmental Legacy*, London: Earthscan.

Agathangelou, A. M. and L. H. M. Ling (2004) 'Power, borders, security, wealth: lessons of violence and desire from September 11', *International Studies Quarterly*, 48.

Ahmed-Ghosh, H. (2004) 'Chattels of society: domestic violence in India', *Violence against Women*, 10(1): 94–118.

Alkire, S. (2004) 'A vital core that must be treated with the same gravitas as traditional security threats', *Security Dialogue*, 35(3): 359–60.

Allahbadia, G. N. (2002) 'The 50 million missing women', *Journal of Assisted Reproduction and Genetics*, 19(9): 411–16.

Amnesty International (2001) *Broken Bodies, Shattered Minds: Torture and Ill-Treatment of Women*, Oxford: Alden Press.

— (2004) *Stop Violence against Women*, <www.amnesty.org/ailib/intcam/femgen/fgm1.htm>.

Anglin, M. K. (1998) 'Feminist perspectives on structural violence', *Identities*, 5(2): 145–51.

Annan, K. (2000) *We the Peoples: The Role of the United Nations in the 21st Century*, New York: United Nations Department of Information.

Arendt, H. (1964) *Eichmann in Jerusalem: A report on the banality of evil*, New York: Viking.

— (1978) 'Eichmann in Jerusalem: an exchange of letters between Gerschom Scholem and Hanna Arendt', in R. Feldman (ed.), *The Jew as Pariah: Jewish Identity and Politics in the Modern Age*, New York: Grove Press.

Armstrong, D., L. Lloyd and J. Redmond (2004) *International Organisation in World Politics*, London: Palgrave.

Arnold, F., S. Kishor and T. K. Roy (2002) 'Sex-selective abortions in India', *Population and Development Review*, 28(4): 759–85.

Bajpai, K. (2004) 'An expression of threats versus capabilities across time and space', *Security Dialogue*, 35(3): 360–61.

Balaam, D. N. and M. Veseth (1996) *Readings in International Political Economy*, New Jersey: Prentice-Hall.

Banda, F. (2005) *Women, Law and Human Rights: An African Perspective*, Oxford: Hart Publishing.

Banerjee, P. (2003) *Burning Women: Widows, Witches, and Early Modern European Travellers in India*, London: Palgrave Macmillan.

Barnett, M. (2005) 'Social constructivism', in J. Baylis and S. Smith (eds), *The Globalization of World Politics: An Introduction to international relations*, Oxford: Oxford University Press.

Barratt Brown, M. (1993) *Fair Trade: Reform and Realities in the International Trading System*, London: Zed Books.

Barratt Brown, M. and P. Tiffen (1992) *Short Changed: Africa and World Trade*, London: Pluto.

Bayart, J.-F. (2005) *The Illusion of Cultural Identity*, London: Hurst and Co.

Baylis, J. and S. Smith (2001) *The Globalization of World Politics: An Introduction to International Relations*, Oxford: Oxford University Press.

Baylis, J. and J. Wirtz (2006) 'Introduction', in J. Baylis, J. Wirtz, C. Gray and E. Cohen (eds), *Strategy in the Contemporary World*, Oxford: Oxford University Press.

BBC News (2007) <www.bbc.co.uk/1/ hi/world/middle_east/1874471. stm>, accessed 5 January.

Behnke, A. (2005) 'Grand theory in the age of its impossibility: contemplations on Alexander Wendt', in S. Guzzini and A. Leander (eds), *Constructivism and International Relations. Alexander Wendt and His Critics*, London: Routledge.

Bellamy, A. J. and M. McDonald (2002) '"The utility of human security": which humans? What security? A reply to Thomas and Tow', *Security Dialogue*, 33(3): 373–7.

Blanchard, E. (2003) 'Gender, international relations, and the development of feminist security theory', *Signs: Journal of Women in Culture and Society*, 28(4): 1289–1312.

Blum, W. (1998) *Killing Hope: US military and CIA interventions since World War II*, London: Black Rose.

Booth, K. (ed.) (2005) *Critical Security Studies and World Politics*, Boulder, CO: Lynne Rienner.

Borhek, J. T. and R. F. Curtis (1975), *A Sociology of Belief*, New York: Wiley-Interscience.

Bull, H. (1977) *The Anarchical Society: A Study of Order in World Politics*, London: Macmillan.

Buzan, B. (1991) *People, States and Fear: An Agenda for International Security Studies in the Post Cold War Era*, Harlow: Pearson.

Buzan, B., O. Waever and J. de Wilde (1998) *Security: A New Framework for Analysis*, Boulder, CO: Lynne Rienner.

Carmen, R. (1996) *Autonomous Development: Humanizing the Landscape – an Excursion into Radical Thinking and Practice*, London: Zed Books.

Caulfield, C. (1996) *Masters of Illusion: The World Bank and the Poverty of Nations*, London: Macmillan.

Chomsky, N. (1994) *World Orders, Old and New*, London: Pluto.

Clamp, A. (2005) *Evolutionary Psychology*, London: Hodder & Stoughton.

Clarke, I. (1980) *Reform and Resistance in the International Order*, Cambridge: Cambridge University Press.

Clemens, W. C. (1998) *Dynamics of International Relations: Conflict and Mutual Gain in an Era of Global Interdependence*, Boston, MA: Rowman & Littlefield.

Cochrane, A. and J. Anderson (1986) 'States and systems of states', in J. Anderson (ed.), *The Rise of the Modern State*, Brighton: Wheatsheaf.

Cohen, G. A. (2001) 'Why not socialism?', in E. Broadbent (ed.), *Democratic Equality: What Went Wrong*, Toronto: University of Toronto Press.

Colgan, A.-L. (2002) 'Hazardous to Health: The World Bank and IMF in Africa', Action Position Paper, April, <www.africaaction.org/ action/sap0204.htm>, accessed 29 May 2007.

Connell, R. W. (1987) *Gender and Power*, Cambridge: Polity.

— (2000) *The Men and the Boys*, Cambridge: Polity.

— (2005) *Masculinities*, Cambridge: Polity.

Coomaraswamy, R. and D. Fonseka (2004) *Peace Work: Women, Armed Conflict and Negotiation*, New Delhi: Women Unlimited.

Cooper, N. (2006) 'Chimeric governance and the extension of resource regulation', *Conflict, Security and Development*, 6(3): 315–36.

Copeland, D. (2000) 'The constructivist challenge to structural realism: a review essay', *International Security*, 25(2): 187–212.

Cox, R. W. (1981) 'Social forces, states and world orders: beyond international relations theory', *Millennium: Journal of International Studies*, 10(2): 126–55.

— (1984) 'Social forces, states, and world orders: beyond international relations theory', in R. B. J. Walker (ed.), *Culture, Ideology and World Order*, London: Westview.

— (1996) *Approaches to World Order*, Cambridge: Cambridge University Press.

Daly, M. (1985) *Beyond God the Father: Toward a Philosophy of Women's Liberation*, Boston, MA: Beacon.

Davies, M. (ed.) (2004) *Women and Violence: Realities and Responses Worldwide*, London: Zed Books.

De Beauvoir, S (1988) *Second Sex*, London : Pan Books.

Deacon, B. (2000) *Globalisation and Social Policy: The Threat to Equitable Welfare*, Geneva: UNRISD.

— (2005) 'From "safety nets" back to "universal social provision"', *Global Social Policy*, 5(1): 19–28.

Deacon, B., M. Hulse and P. Stubbs (1997) *Global Social Policy: International organizations and the future of welfare*, London: Sage.

Deraniyagala, S. (2005) 'Neoliberalism in international trade: sound economics or a question of faith?', in A. Saad-Filho and D. Johnston (eds), *Neoliberalism: A Critical Reader*, London: Pluto.

Dessler, D. (1989) 'What's at stake in the agency–structure debate?', *International Organization*, 43(3): 441–73.

Duffield, M. (2001) 'Governing the borderlands: decoding the power of aid', *Disasters*, 25(4): 308–20.

Duffield, M. and N. Wadell (2006) 'Securing humans in a dangerous world', *International Politics*, 43(1): 1–23.

Eade, D. (1997) 'Preface', in *Development in Practice Reader*, Oxford: Oxford University Press.

Eisenstein, Z. (2007) *Sexual Decoys: Gender, race and war in imperial democracy*, London: Zed Books.

El-Dawla, A.-S. (1999) 'The political and legal struggle over female genital mutilation in Egypt: five years since the ICPD', *Reproductive Health Matters*, 7(13): 128–36.

Enloe, C. (1990) *Bananas, Beaches and Bases: Making Feminist Sense of International Relations*, London: Pandora.

Fadia, F. (2001) 'Intrafamily femicide in defence of honour: the case of Jordan', *Third World Quarterly*, 22(1): 65–82.

Faludi, S. (1999) *Stiffed: The Betrayal of Modern Man*, London: Chatto and Windus.

Farmer, P. (2002) 'Structural violence and the assault on human rights', *Society for Medical Anthropology*, January, pp. 1–2.

Feit, E. (1973) *The Armed Bureaucrats*, Boston, MA: Houghton Mifflin.

Feminist.com (2006) <www.feminist.com/violence/spot/honor.html>, accessed 1 March.

Ferraro, V. and A. E. Chenier (1994) 'Development, debt and global poverty', in M. T. Klare (ed.), *Peace and World Security Studies: A Curriculum Guide*, Boulder, CO: Lynne Rienner.

Fierke, K. M. (2007) *Critical Approaches to International Security*, Cambridge: Polity.

Francis, D. (2004) *Rethinking War and Peace*, London: Pluto.

Freedman, L. (1998) 'International security: changing targets', *Foreign Policy*, Spring, pp. 48–64.

Frynas, J. G. (1998) 'Political instability and business: focus on Shell in Nigeria', *Third World Quarterly*, 19(3): 457–78.

Gaag, N. V. (2004) 'The other side of silence', *New Internationalist*, 373, November.

Galeano, E. (2005) 'The upside-down world', in J. Pilger (ed.), *Tell Me No Lies*, London: Vintage.

Galtung, J. (1969) 'Violence, peace and peace research', *Journal of Peace Research*, 3, pp. 167–91.

— (1985) 'Twenty-five years of peace research: ten challenges and some responses', *Journal of Peace Research*, 22(2): 141–58.

Gelinas, J .B. (1998) *Freedom from Debt: The reappropriation of development through financial self-reliance*, London: Zed Books.

— (2003) *Juggernaut Politics: Understanding Predatory Globalization*, London: Zed Books.

Gendercide Watch (2006) <www.gendercide.org/case_honour.html>, accessed 3 March.

George, J. (1994) *Discourses of Global Politics: A Critical (Re)Introduction to International Relations*, Boulder, CO: Lynne Rienner.

George, S. (1976) *How the Other Half Dies: The Real Reasons for World Hunger*, London: Penguin.

— (1989) *A Fate Worse than Debt*, London: Penguin.

— (1992) *The Debt Boomerang: How Third World Debt Harms Us All*, London: Pluto.

George, S. and F. Sabelli (1994) *Faith and Credit: The World Bank's Secular Empire*, London: Penguin.

Giddens, A. (2002) *Runaway World: How globalization is reshaping our lives*, London: Profile.

Giroux, H. (2004) *The Terror of Neoliberalism*, London: Pluto.

Glasier, A., A. Gülmezoglu, G. Schmid, C. Moreno and P. Van Look (2006) 'Sexual and reproductive health: a matter of life and death', *The Lancet*, 368(9547): 1595–607.

Global Health Watch (2005) *Global Health Watch 2005–2006: An Alternative World Health Report*, London: Zed Books.

Goldstein, J. (2001) *War and Gender*, Cambridge: Cambridge University Press.

— (2002) *International Relations*, New York: Longman.

— (2006) *International Relations*, New York: Longman.

Goldstein, J. S. (1994) *International Relations*, New York: HarperCollins.

Goldstein, M. A. (2002) 'The biological roots of heat-of-passion crimes and honour killings', *Politics and Life Sciences*, 21(2): 28–37.

Goodhand, J. (2001) 'Violent conflict, poverty and chronic poverty', *Chronic Poverty Research Centre*, Working Paper 6, Manchester: University of Manchester Press.

Gould, H. (1998) 'What *is* at stake in the agent-structure debate?', in V. Kubalkova, N. Onuf and P. Kowert (eds), *International Relations in a Constructed World*, London: M. E. Sharpe.

Grant, R. (1991) 'The sources of gender bias in international relations theory', in R. Grant and K. Newland (eds), *Gender and International Relations*, Milton Keynes: Open University Press.

Grant, R. and K. Newland (1991) 'Introduction', in R. Grant and K. Newland (eds), *Gender and International Relations*, Milton Keynes: Open University Press.

Greig, A., D. Hulme and M. Turner (2007) *Challenging Global Inequality: Development Theory and Practice in the 21st Century*, London: Palgrave Macmillan.

Griffin, P. (2007) 'Sexing the economy in a neo-liberal world order: neo-liberal discourse and the (re)production of heteronormative heterosexuality', *British Journal of Politics and International Relations*, 9(2): 220–38.

Griffiths, M. (1992) *Realism, Idealism and International Politics: A Reinterpretation*, London: Routledge.

Grimes, D., J. Benson, S. Singh, M. Romero, B. Ganatra, F. Okonofua and I. Shah (2006) 'Unsafe abortion: the preventable pandemic', *The Lancet*, 368(9550): 1908–19.

Hall, A. and J. Midgley (2004) *Social Policy for Development*, London: Sage.

Hampson, F. H. (2004) 'A concept in need of a global policy response', *Security Dialogue*, 35(3): 349–50.

Hancock, G. (1989) *Lords of Poverty: The freewheeling lifestyles, power, prestige and corruption of the international aid business*, London: Macmillan.

Hanmer, J. and M. Maynard (eds) (1987) *Women, Violence and Social Control*, London: Macmillan.

Harlan, L. and P. B. Courtright (1995) *From the Margins of Hindu Marriage: Essays on Gender, Religion, and Culture*, Oxford: Oxford University Press.

Harris, S. (2002) *Globalisation in the Asia-Pacific Context*, Research Paper 7, <www.aph.gov.au/LIBRARY/pubs/rp/2001-02/02RP07.htm>, accessed 12 April 2006.

Harvey, D. (2007) 'Neoliberalism as creative destruction', *Annals of the American Academy of Political and Social Science*, 610(21): 21–44.

Hatty, S. E. (2000) *Masculinities, Violence and Culture*, London: Sage.

Hayden, P. (2007) 'Superfluous humanity: an Arendtian perspective on the political evil of global poverty', *Millennium: Journal of International Studies*, 35(2): 279–300.

Hilditch, T. (1995) 'A holocaust of little girls', *World Press Review*.

Hoogensen, G. and S. V. Rottem (2004) 'Gender identity and the subject of security', *Security Dialogue*, 35(2): 155–71.

Hoogensen, G. and K. Stuvoy (2006) 'Gender, resistance and human security', *Security Dialogue*, 37(2): 207–28.

Hooper, C. (2006) 'Masculinities, IR and the "gender variable"', in R. Little and M. Smith (eds), *Perspectives on World Politics*, London: Routledge.

— (2001) *Manly States: Masculinities, International Relations and Gender Politics*, Columbia: Columbia University Press.

Howland, C. (ed.) (2001) *Religious Fundamentalisms and the Human Rights of Women*, London: Palgrave.

HRW (Human Rights Watch) (1994) *A Matter of Power: State Control of Women's Virginity in Turkey*, New York: Human Rights Watch.

— (2004) 'Honoring the killers: justice denied for "honour" crimes in Jordan', *Human Rights Watch*, 16(1) (E).

ICFTU (International Conference of Free Trade Unions) (2006) *Fighting for Alternatives: Cases of Successful Trade Union Resistance to the Policies of the IMF and World Bank*, April, <www.icftu. org/displaydocument.asp?Inde x=991223717&Language=EN>, accessed 1 May.

Indira, J. (1995) 'Violence against women: the Indian perspective',

in J. Peters and A. Wolper (eds), *Women's Rights, Human Rights*, New York: Routledge.

International People's Tribunal to Judge the G-7 (1994) *The People vs. Global Capital*, New York: Apex.

Isbister, J. (2003) *Promises Not Kept: Poverty and the Betrayal of Third World Development*, Basingstoke: Palgrave Macmillan.

Jackson, R. and C. Rosberg (1984) 'Personal rule in Africa: theory and practice', *Comparative Politics*, 16(4): 421–42.

Jackson, R. and G. Sorensen (2007) *Introduction to International Relations: Theories and Approaches*, Oxford: Oxford University Press.

Jaquette, J. (2003) 'Feminism and the challenges of the "post-cold war" world', *International Feminist Journal of Politics*, 5(3): 331–54.

Janssen-Jurreit, M. (1982) *Sexism: The Male Monopoly on History and Thought*, New York: Farrar, Strauss and Giroux.

Jeong, H.-W. (2000) *Peace and Conflict Studies: An Introduction*, Hampshire: Ashgate.

Johansson, S. and O. Nygren (1991) 'The missing girls of China: a new demographic account', *Population and Development Review*, 17(1): 40–41.

Johnston, D. (2005) 'Poverty and distribution: back on the neoliberal agenda?', in A. Saad-Filho and D. Johnston (eds), *Neoliberalism: A Critical Reader*, London: Pluto.

Jones, A. (1996) 'Does "gender" make the world go round? Feminist critiques of international relations', *Review of International Studies*, 22(4): 405–29.

Kaiser Foundation (2007) *The Uninsured: A Primer*, <www.kff.org>, accessed 25 May.

Kamrava, M. (1993) *Politics and Society in the Third World*, London: Routledge.

Kardam, F. (2005) *The Dynamics of Honour Killing in Turkey: Prospects for Action*, New York: United Nations Population Fund.

Karkal, M. (1996) 'Patriarchal demography: tracing India's history', *Political Environments*, 4, Autumn.

Keen, D. (2003) 'Greedy elites, dwindling resources, alienated youths: the anatomy of protracted violence in Sierra Leone', *Internationale Politik Und Gesellschaft*, accessed 6 June 2006 at: <http://fesportal.fes.de/pls/portal30/docs/FOLDER/IPG/IPG2_2003/ARTKEEN.HTM>.

Kelly, E., J. Lovett and L. Regan (2005) 'A gap or a chasm? Attrition in reported rape cases', Home Office Research Study 293, London: Home Office Research, Development and Statistics Directorate.

Kelly, L. (1987) 'The continuum of sexual violence', in J. Hanmer and M. Maynard (eds), *Women, Violence and Social Control*, Basingstoke: Macmillan.

Kennedy, H. (1993) *Eve Was Framed*, London: Vintage.

Keohane, R. O. (1984) *After Hegemony: Cooperation and discord in the world economy*, New Jersey: Princeton University Press.

Kim, J. Y., J. V. Millen, A. Irwin and

J. Gershman (2000) *Dying for Growth: Global Inequality and the Health of the Poor*, London: Common Courage Press.

King, G. and C. J. L. Murray (2001) 'Rethinking human security', *Political Science Quarterly*, 116(4): 585–610.

Klasen, S. (1994) '"Missing women" reconsidered', *World Development*, 22(7): 1061–71.

Kohler, G. and N. Alcock (1976) 'An empirical table of structural violence', *Journal of Peace Research*, XIII(4): 343–56.

Koo, K. L. (2007) 'Confronting a disciplinary blindness: women, war and rape in the international politics of security', *Australian Journal of Political Science*, 37(3): 525–36.

Kordvani, A. H. (2002) 'Hegemonic masculinity, domination and violence against women, understanding the complexities of violence against women', Conference paper, University of Sydney, 18–22 February.

Kothari, R. (1993) *Poverty: Human Consciousness and the Amnesia of Development*, London: Zed Books.

Krause, K. (2004) 'The key to a powerful agenda, if properly delimited', *Security Dialogue*, 35(3): 367–8.

Kundera, M. (1996) *The Book of Laughter and Forgetting*, London: Faber and Faber.

Kunzel, R. G. (1993) *Fallen Women, Problem Girls: Unmarried Mothers and the Professionalization of Social Work 1890–1945*, New Haven, CT: Yale University Press.

Lamb, S. (1999) 'Aging, gender and widowhood: perspectives from rural West Bengal', *Contributions to Indian Sociology*, 33(3): 541–70.

Lang, T. and C. Hines (1993) *The New Protectionism: Protecting the Future against Free Trade*, London: Earthscan.

Leacock, E. (1983) 'Interpreting the origins of gender inequality: conceptual and historical problems', *Dialectical Anthropology*, 7(4): 263–84.

LeRoy, M. (2003) *A Look at Structural Violence*, <www.rmpjc.org/19/95/pjsv.html>, accessed 22 October.

Levy, T. M. and M. Orlans (1998) *Attachment, Trauma, and Healing: Understanding and Treating Attachment Disorder in Children and Families*, Maryland: Child Welfare League of America.

Liotta, P. H. (2005) 'Through the looking glass: creeping vulnerabilities and the reordering of security', *Security Dialogue*, 36(1): 49–70.

Lipson, D. J. (2006) 'Implications of the General Agreement on Trade in Services for Reproductive Health Services', in C. Grown, E. Braunstein and A. Malhotra (eds), *Trading Women's Health & Rights? Trade Liberalization and Reproductive Health in Developing Economies*, London: Zed Books.

Mack, A. (ed.) (2005) *The Human Security Report 2005: War and Peace in the 21st Century*, Oxford: Oxford University Press.

MacKinnon, C. (2006) *Are Women Human? And Other International Dialogues*, Cambridge, MA: Harvard University Press.

Mangan, J. (2006) 'Sport and war: combative societies and combative sports', *Soka Gakkai International Quarterly: A Buddhist Forum for Peace, Culture and Education*, 45, July, pp. 2–4.

Massey, D. (2006) 'London inside out', *Soundings: A Journal of Politics and Culture*, 32, March, pp. 62–71.

Mathews, J. T. (1989) 'Redefining security', *Foreign Affairs*, 68(2): 162–77.

Mazurana, D. and S. McKay (2001) 'Women, girls and structural violence', in D. J. Christie, R. Wagner and D. D. Winter (eds), *Peace, Conflict and Violence: Peace Psychology for the 21st Century*, New Jersey: Prentice-Hall.

McSweeney, B. (1999) *Security, Identity and Interests: A Sociology of International Relations*, Cambridge: Cambridge University Press.

Mead, M. (1977) *Male and Female*, Westport: Greenwood Press.

Mearsheimer, J. (2007) 'Structural realism', in T. Dunne, M. Kurki and S. Smith, *International Relations Theories: Discipline and Diversity*, Oxford: Oxford University Press.

Messner, M. (1992) *Power at Play: Sports and the problem of masculinity*, Boston, MA: Beacon Press.

Mies, M. (1998) *Patriarchy and Accumulation on a World Scale*, London: Zed Books.

Mihevc, J. (1992) 'The changing debate on Structural Adjustment Policies in sub-Saharan Africa: churches, social movements and the World Bank', PhD dissertation, University of St Michael's College, Toronto.

— (1995) *The Market Tells Them So: The World Bank and economic fundamentalism in Africa*, London: Zed Books.

Mishra, S. (2006) 'Suicide of farmers in Maharashtra', Mumbai: Indira Gandhi Institute of Development Research, 26 January, <http://mdmu.maharashtra.gov.in/pdf/ExecutiveSummary_SFM_IG-IDR_26Jan06.pdf>, accessed 23 May 2007.

Moore, L. (1995) *A Look at Structural Violence*, <www.rmpjc.org/19/95/pjsv.html>, accessed 14 March 2000.

Mueller, J. (2006) 'Is there still a terrorist threat? The myth of the omnipresent enemy', *Foreign Affairs*, September/October.

Murphy, C. (2000) 'Global governance: poorly done and poorly understood', *International Affairs*, 76(4): 789–803.

Nafziger, E. W. (2002) 'Economic development, inequality, war and state violence', *World Development*, 30(2): 153–63.

Nandy, A. (2002) 'The beautiful, expanding future of poverty: popular economics as a psychological defence', *International Relations and the New Inequality*, 4(2): 107–21.

Narasimhan, S. (1994) 'India: from sati to sex determination tests', in M. Davies (ed.), *Women and Violence: Realities and Responses Worldwide*, London: Pluto.

Nathan, L. (2000) 'The Four Horsemen of the Apocalypse: the structural causes of crisis and violence in Africa', *Peace and Change*, 25(2): 188–207.

Newman, E. (2001) 'Human security and constructivism', *International Studies Perspectives*, 2: 239–51.

— (2004) 'A normatively attractive but analytically weak concept', *Security Dialogue*, 35(3): 358–9.

Nobelprize.org (2006) <http://nobelprize.org/medicine/educational/malaria/readmore/global.html>, accessed 1 March.

O'Brien, R., A. M. Goertz, J. A. Scholte and M. Williams (2000) *Contesting Global Governance: Multilateral Economic Institutions and Global Social Movements*, Cambridge: Cambridge University Press.

Onuf, N. (1989) *World of Our Making: Rules and Rule in Social Theory and International Relations*, Columbia: University of South Carolina Press.

Ortner, S. B. (1974) 'Is female to male as nature is to culture?', in M. Z. Rosaldo and L. Lamphere, *Woman, Culture and Society*, Stanford, CT: Stanford University Press.

Owen, T. (2004) 'Human security – conflict, critique and consensus: colloquium remarks and a proposal for a threshold-based definition', *Security Dialogue*, 35(3): 373–87.

Palmer, B. (2006) *Breaking the Political Glass Ceiling*, London: Routledge.

Paris, R. (2001) 'Human security: paradigm shift or hot air?', *International Security*, 26(2): 87–102.

Pasha, M. K. and C. N. Murphy

(2002) 'Knowledge/power/ inequality', *International Relations and the New Inequality*, 4(2): 1–6.

Patomaki, H. (2002) *Democratising Globalisation: The Leverage of the Tobin Tax*, London: Zed Books.

Payne, A. (2005) *The Global Politics of Unequal Development*, London: Palgrave Macmillan.

Peet, R. (2007) *Unholy Trinity: The IMF, the World Bank and WTO*, London: Zed Books.

Penn, M. L. and R. Nardos (2003) *Overcoming Violence against Women and Girls*, Oxford: Rowman and Littlefield.

Pettman, J. J. (1996) *Worlding Women: A Feminist International Politics*, London: Routledge.

Picciotto, R. and R. Weaving (eds) (2006) *Security and Development: Investing in Peace and Prosperity*, London: Routledge.

Pierce, F. (1991) 'Acts of God, acts of man?', *New Scientist*, 18 May.

Pilisuk, M. (2001) 'Globalism and structural violence', in D. J. Christie et al. (eds), *Peace, Conflict and Violence: Peace Psychology for the 21st Century*, New Jersey: Prentice-Hall.

Pogge, T. (2002) *World Poverty and Human Rights*, Cambridge, Polity.

Prontzos, P. (2004) 'Collateral damage: the human cost of structural violence', in A. Jones, *Genocide, War Crimes and the West*, London: Zed Books.

Radford, J. and D. H. Russell (1992) *Femicide: The Politics of Woman Killing*, Buckingham: Open University Press.

Rapley, J. (2004) *Globalization and Inequality: Neoliberalism's Downward Spiral*, London: Lynne Rienner.

Ratinoff, L. (1999) 'Social policy issues at the end of the 20th century', in D. Morales-Gómez (ed.), *Transnational Social Policies: The new development challenges of globalization*, London: Earthscan.

Reardon, B. A. (1996) 'Women or weapons?', *Peace Review*, 8(3): 315–21.

Rengger, N. and B. Thirkell-White (2007) 'Still critical after all these years? The past, present and future of Critical Theory in International Relations', *Review of International Studies*, 33, Special Issue, pp. 3–24.

Rich, B. (1994a) *Mortgaging the Earth: The World Bank, Environmental Impoverishment and the Crisis of Development*, London: Earthscan.

— (1994b) 'The cuckoo in the nest: fifty years of political meddling by the World Bank', *Ecologist*, 24(1): 8–13.

Riley, S. P. (1991) *The Democratic Transitons in Africa: The end of the one-party state?*, Research Institute for the Study of Conflict and Terrorism.

Rist, G. (1997) *The History of Development: From Western Origins to Global Faith*, London: Zed Books.

RMPJC (Rocky Mountain Peace and Justice Centre) (2003) <www.rmpjc.org/19/95/pjsv.html>, accessed 4 February 2007.

Roberts, D. (2005) 'Empowering the human security debate: making it coherent and meaningful',

International Journal on World Peace, XXII(3): 3-16.

— (2006) 'Human security or human insecurity? Moving the debate forward', Security Dialogue, 37(2): 237-49.

Robinson, F. (1999) Globalizing Care: Ethics, Feminist Theory, and International Relations, London: Westview.

Rowbotham, S. (1977) Hidden from History: 300 Years of Women's Oppression and the Fight against It, London: Pluto.

Rowland-Serdar, B. and P. Schwartz-Shea (1991) 'Empowering women: self, autonomy and responsibility', Western Political Quarterly, 44(3): 605-24.

Ruether, R. R. (1975) New Woman, New Earth: Sexist Ideologies and Human Liberation, New York: Seabury Press.

— (1983) Sexism and God-Talk: Towards a Feminist Theology, London: SCM Press.

Ruggie, J. (1998) Constructing the World Polity: Essays on International Institutionalization, London: Routledge.

Rummel, R. J. (1994) Death by Government: Genocide and Mass Murder since 1900, New Jersey: US Transaction Publishers.

Runyan, A. S. and V. Spike Peterson (1991) 'The radical future of realism: feminist subversions of IR theory', Alternatives, 16: 67-106.

Russell, D. E. H. and R. A. Harmes (2001) Femicide in Global Perspective, New York: Teachers College Press.

Rustow, D. (1970) 'Transitions to democracy: toward a dynamic model', Comparative Politics, 2(3): 337-63.

Sanday, P. R. (1981) Female Power and Male Dominance: On the origins of sexual inequality, Cambridge: Cambridge University Press.

Sandbrook, R. and D. Romano (2004) 'Globalization, extremism and violence in poor countries', Third World Quarterly, 25(6): 1007-30.

Sassoon, I. S. D. (2005) 'The tears of the oppressed: an examination of the Agunah problem', Judaism, 54(1/2): 116-24

Sawer, M., M. Tremblay and L. Trimble (2006) Representing Women in Parliament: A Comparative Study, London: Routledge.

Schwab, P. (2001) Africa: A Continent Self-Destructs, London: Palgrave.

Seabrook, J. (1992) 'Still in the missionary position', New Statesman and Society, 5 June.

— (2004) The No Nonsense Guide to World Poverty, London: Verso.

Seager, J. (2003) The Atlas of Women, London: Women's Press.

Sen, A. (1981) Poverty and Famines: An essay on entitlement and deprivation, Oxford: Clarendon.

— (1993) 'The economics of life and death', Scientific American, May, pp. 40-47.

— (1999) Development as Freedom, Oxford: Oxford University Press.

— (2003) 'Missing women: revisited', British Medical Journal, 327: 1297-8; 304(6827): 577-8.

Sen, G. (2005) 'Neolibs, neocons and gender justice: lessons from global negotiations', Occasional Paper 9, Geneva: UNRISD.

Sev'er, Y. (2001) 'Honour killings in rural Turkey', *Violence against Women*, 7(9): 964–98.

Shah, E. A. (2004) 'Age patterns of unsafe abortion in developing country regions', *Reproductive Health Matters*, 12(24): 9–17.

Sheehan, M. (2005) *International Security: An Analytical Survey*, Boulder, CO: Lynne Rienner.

Siyachitema, R. (2003) 'Threats and physical abuse against women in southern Africa', Stop Violence Against Women, World Alliance of YMCAs, <www.ymca.int/uploads/media/Violence_women.pdf>.

Smith, D. (1997) *The State of War and Peace Atlas*, London: Penguin.

Smith, S. (2000) 'The increasing insecurity of security studies: conceptualising security in the last twenty years', in S. Croft and T. Terriff (eds), *Critical Reflections on Security and Change*, London: Frank Cass.

Smith, S. and P. Owens (2005) 'Alternative approaches to international theory', in J. Baylis and S. Smith, *The Globalisation of World Politics: An introduction to International Relations*, Oxford: Oxford University Press.

Spike Peterson, V. (1992) *Gendered States: Feminist (Re)Visions of International Relations Theory*, Boulder, CO: Lynne Rienner.

Spike Peterson, V and A. S. Runyan (eds) (1999) *Global Gender Issues*, Boulder, CO: Westview.

Steans, J. (1998) *Gender and International Relations: An Introduction*, Cambridge: Polity.

— (2007) 'Debating women's human rights as a universal feminist project: defending women's human rights as a political tool', *Review of International Studies*, 33(1): 11–29.

Stecher, H. (1999) *Time for a Tobin Tax? Some practical and political arguments*, Oxford: Oxfam.

Stets, J. E. and M. A. Pirog-Good (1987) 'Violence in dating relationships', *Social Psychology Quarterly*, 50(3): 237–46.

Stewart, F. (2004), 'Development and security', *Conflict, Security and Development*, 4(3): 261–88.

Stoett, P. (1999) *Human and Global Security: An Exploration of Terms*, Toronto: University of Toronto Press.

Sudha, S. and S. Irudaya Rajan (1999) 'Female demographic disadvantage in India 1981–1991: sex selective abortions and female infanticide', *Development and Change*, 30, July, pp. 585–618.

Sylvester, C. (1994a) *Feminist Theory and International Relations in a Postmodern Era*, Cambridge: Cambridge University Press.

— (1994b) 'Empathetic cooperation: a feminist method for IR', *Millennium: Journal of International Studies*, 23(2): 315–34.

Tambiah, S. J. (1977) 'The galactic polity: the structure of traditional kingdoms in Southeast Asia', in S. Freed (ed.), 'Anthropology and the climate of opinion', *Annals of the New York Academy of Sciences*, vol. 293.

Thakur, R. (2004) 'A political worldview', *Security Dialogue*, 35(3): 347–8.

— (2005) 'The United Nations and human security: incoherent concept or policy template', Public lecture, Magee College, University of Ulster, N. Ireland, 24 October.

Thomas, C. (2000) *Global Governance, Development and Human Security*, London: Pluto.

— (2004) 'A bridge between the interconnected challenges confronting the world', *Security Dialogue*, 35(3): 353–4.

Thomas, N. and W. T. Tow (2002) 'The utility of human security: sovereignty and humanitarian intervention', *Security Dialogue*, 33(2): 177–92.

Tickner, J. A. (1988) 'Hans Morgenthau's principles of realism: a feminist reformulation', *Millennium: Journal of International Studies*, 17(3): 429–40.

— (1992) *Gender in International Relations*, New York: Columbia University Press.

Tobin, J. (1996) 'A currency transactions tax: why and how?', *Open Economies Review*, 7(1): 493–9.

Turshen, M. (1999) *Privatizing Health Services in Africa*, New Brunswick: Rutgers University Press.

Ullman, R. (1983) 'Redefining security', *International Security*, 8(3): 129–53.

UN (United Nations) (2000) *We the Peoples: The United Nations in the 21st Century*, New York: UNDP.

— (2005) *United Nations Human Development Report 2005: International cooperation at a crossroads – aid, trade and security in an unequal world*, New York: UNDP.

UNDP (United Nations Development Programme) (1994) *Human Development Report: New Dimensions of Security*, New York: UNDP.

— (2003) *Human Development Report 2003. Millennium Development Goals: A compact among nations to end human poverty*, New York: UNDP.

— (2005) *International Cooperation at a Crossroads: Aid, trade and security in an unequal world*, New York: UNDP.

UNFPA (2000) *The State of World Population 2000*, New York: United Nations Fund for Population Activities.

— (2005) *State of World Population: Gender Equity, Reproductive Health and the MDGs*, New York: United Nations Fund for Population Activities.

UNICEF (1996) *The Progress of Nations 1996: Women*, <www.unice3f.org/pon96/womfgm.htm>, accessed 3 March 2006.

— (2004) *Vitamin and Mineral Deficiency: A Global Progress Report*, New York: United Nations International Children's Emergency Fund.

— (2007) 'Child poverty in perspective: an overview of child well-being in rich countries', Innocenti Report Card 7, UNICEF Innocenti Research Centre, Florence.

UNIFEM (2003) *Not a Minute More*, <www.unifem.org/attachments/gender_issues/violence_against_women/FactsFigures.pdf>, accessed 26 August 2005.

Various (1999) 'Ending violence against women, population

reports, issues in world health', Series L, no. 11, XXVII, Population Information Program, Johns Hopkins School of Public Health, December.

— (2006) 'Junk the WTO!', *New Internationalist*, 388, April.

Vasquez, J. (1993) *The Power of Power Politics*, London: Frances Pinter.

Venkatramani, S. H. (1992) 'Female infanticide: born to die', in J. Radford and E. H. Russell (eds), *Femicide: The Politics of Woman Killing*, Buckingham: Open University Press.

Von der Lippe, B. (2006) 'Images of victory, images of masculinity?', *Nordicom Review*, 27(1): 63–79.

Wade, R. H. (2005) 'Globalization, poverty and inequality', in J. Ravenhill (ed.), *Global Political Economy*, Oxford: Oxford University Press.

Waever, O. (2002) 'Identity, communities and foreign policy: discourse analysis as foreign policy theory', in L. Hansen and O. Waever (eds), *European Integration and National Identity*, London: Routledge.

Walker, R. B. J. (1984) *Culture, Ideology and World Order*, London: Westview.

Walton, J. and D. Seddon (eds) (1994) *Free Markets and Food Riots: The Politics of Global Adjustment*, Cambridge, MA: Blackwell.

Waltz, K. (2006) 'Structural realism after the Cold War', in R. Little and M. Smith (eds), *Perspectives on World Politics*, London: Routledge.

Warren, M. A. (1985) *Gendercide: The Implications of Sex Selection*, London: Rowman & Littlefield.

Watts, C. and C. Zimmerman (2002) 'Violence against women: global scope and magnitude', *The Lancet*, 359, April, pp. 1232–7.

WDM (World Development Movement) (2003) *States of Unrest III: Resistance to IMF and World Bank policies in poor countries*, London: World Development Movement.

— (2005) *Denying Democracy: How the IMF and World Bank take power from people*, <www.wdm. org.uk/democracy/protest/index. htm>, accessed 6 April 2006.

Weaver, C. and R. Leiteritz (2002) '"Our Poverty is a world full of dreams": the World Bank's strategic compact', Paper, Annual Meeting of the International Studies Association, New Orleans, 24–27 March, accessed 31 October 2006 at <www.isanet. org/noarchive/WeaverLeiteritzISA.html>.

Webb, K. (1986) 'Structural violence and the definition of conflict', in *World Encyclopaedia of Peace*, vol. 2, Oxford: Pergamon.

Weber, M. (1968) *On Charisma and Institution Building*, Chicago, IL: University of Chicago Press.

Weigert, K. M. (1999) 'Structural violence', in *Encyclopaedia of Violence, Peace and Conflict*, New York: Academy Press.

Weinberger, C. (1999) *Ashes of Immortality: Wife Burning in India*, Chicago, IL: University of Chicago Press.

Welchman, L. and S. Hossain (eds)

(2005) *Honour: Crimes, Paradigms and Violence against Women*, London: Zed Books.

Wendt, A. (1999) *Social Theory of International Politics*, Cambridge: Cambridge University Press.

West, R. (1913) 'Mr Chesterton in hysterics: a study in prejudice,' *The Clarion*, 14 November.

Wheeler, D., R. Rechtman, H. Fabig and Y. Boele (2001) 'Shell, Nigeria and the Ogoni. A study in unsustainable development: iii. Analysis and implications of Royal Dutch/Shell group strategy', *Sustainable Development*, 9(4): 177–96.

Whitehead, S. M. (2002) *Men and Masculinities*, Cambridge: Polity.

WHO (World Health Organization) (2002) *World Report on Violence and Health*, Geneva: WHO.

— (2005) *World Health Report 2005: Make Every Mother and Child Count*, Geneva: WHO.

Wight, M. (1991) *International Theory: The Three Traditions*, London: Leicester University Press.

Wilkin, P. (2002) 'Global poverty and orthodox security', *Third World Quarterly*, 23(4): 633–45.

Willetts, S. (2001) 'Insecurity, conflict and the new global disorder', *IDS Bulletin*, 32(2): 35–47.

Williams, M. (1994) *International Economic Organisations and the Third World*, London: Harvester Wheatsheaf.

Wilson, M. and M. Daly (1992) 'Till death us do part', in J. Radford and E. H. Russell (eds), *Femicide: The Politics of Woman Killing*, Buckingham: Open University Press.

Windsor, P. (1988) 'Women and international relations: what's the problem?', *Millennium: Journal of International Studies*, 17(3): 451–60.

Winter, D. D. N. and D. Leighton (2006) 'Structural violence introduction', <www.psych.ubc.ca/~dleighton/svintro.html>, accessed 24 January.

World Bank (2006) World Development Indicators online, <www.worldbank.org>, accessed 21 May.

Yeates, N. (2001) *Globalization and Social Policy*, London: Sage.

— (2005) *'Globalisation' and Social Policy in a Development Context: Regional Responses*, Geneva: UNRISD.

Yoodee, P. and S. Quezada-Zagada (2003) 'Trafficking and other forms of violence against women', Stop Violence Against Women: World Alliance of YMCAs, <www.ymca.int/uploads/media/Violence_women.pdf>, accessed 14 December.

Young, I. M. (2003) 'The logic of masculinist protection: reflections on the current security state', *Signs: Journal of Women in Culture and Society*, 29(1): 1–25.

Young, O. (1999) *Governance in World Affairs*, Ithaca, NJ: Cornell.

Zalewski, M. (2007) 'Do we understand each other yet? Troubling encounters with(in) international relations', *British Journal of Politics and International Relations*, 9(2): 302–12.

Index